XMPP: The Definitive Guide
Building Real-Time Applications with Jabber Technologies

Peter Saint-Andre, Kevin Smith, and Remko Tronçon

O'REILLY®

Beijing · Cambridge · Farnham · Köln · Sebastopol · Taipei · Tokyo

XMPP: The Definitive Guide

by Peter Saint-Andre, Kevin Smith, and Remko Tronçon

Published by O'Reilly Media, Inc., 1005 Gravenstein Highway North, Sebastopol, CA 95472.

O'Reilly books may be purchased for educational, business, or sales promotional use. Online editions are also available for most titles (*http://safari.oreilly.com*). For more information, contact our corporate/institutional sales department: (800) 998-9938 or *corporate@oreilly.com*.

Editor: Mary E. Treseler

Production Editor: Loranah Dimant

Copyeditor: Genevieve d'Entremont

Proofreader: Loranah Dimant

Indexer: Joe Wizda

Cover Designer: Karen Montgomery

Interior Designer: David Futato

Illustrator: Robert Romano

Printing History:

April 2009:   First Edition.

ISBN: 978-0-596-52126-4

[M]

1239727450

Table of Contents

Part I.   An Overview of XMPP

Part II. The XMPP Toolkit

Part III. Putting It All Together

Preface

Why XMPP?

In 1800, it took one or two years to send a message from London to Calcutta and receive a reply. You needed to find a ship's captain you trusted, who piloted his sailing ship around the Cape of Good Hope and probably stopped in various ports along the way. Then your contact in Calcutta needed to write a reply and send it back to London in a similar fashion. Not exactly instant messaging!

With the invention of the steamship and the opening of the Suez Canal, the time was reduced to a month or two. Air mail reduced the time further to a week or two, and eventually to a few days ("when it absolutely, positively has to be there overnight"). The deployment of commercial email systems introduced us to wait times of only a few minutes (depending on how often you polled your server). And instant messaging (IM) systems such as ICQ® took communication to its logical conclusion: nearly immediate interaction.

As a result of these developments, the useful half-life of information has shrunk significantly, in many cases to mere seconds. For many people, IM trumps email. Blogging trumps newspapers and magazines. Microblogging trumps blogging. Groupchat trumps email discussion lists. Shared editing and whiteboarding trump carefully crafted presentations. Immediate notifications trump once-a-day updates. And the list goes on.

What all these technologies have in common is that the interactions happen in close to real time. To make this possible, we need technologies for real-time communication. Ideally such technologies would be open standards providing the real-time equivalent of HTTP, HTML, and the other building blocks of today's Internet, because over the long term open standards provide stronger security, greater extensibility, and the possibility for more innovation at the edges than do closed technologies.

The Extensible Messaging and Presence Protocol (XMPP) is just such an open technology for real-time interaction. Consider some of its advantages:

- XMPP is *proven*. Over 10 years of development has resulted in a stable, widely deployed, seriously tested, Internet-scale technology, with dozens of interoperable codebases, tens of thousands of deployed services, and millions of end users.

- XMPP is *secure*. It provides built-in support for channel encryption and strong authentication, inherent resistance to many forms of malware, a diverse ecosystem of implementations, a decentralized network without a single point of failure, and significant deployment at some of the most security-conscious financial organizations and government agencies worldwide. Work on more advanced features (such as user-friendly end-to-end encryption) continues so that XMPP will be even more secure.

- XMPP is *decentralized*. Unlike standalone communication silos, XMPP technologies are deployed in a decentralized client-server architecture with an unlimited number of servers. Any person or organization can run their own XMPP server and connect it to the rest of the network using standard Internet infrastructure such as the Domain Name System (DNS), and certificates are freely available through the XMPP Standards Foundation (XSF) to enable secure federation of XMPP traffic.

- XMPP is *extensible*. Because XMPP is at its core a technology for rapidly delivering XML from one place to another, it has been used for a wide range of applications beyond instant messaging, including gaming, social networking, Voice over IP (VoIP), real-time collaboration, alerts and notifications, data syndication, geolocation, intelligent workflows, machine-to-machine communication, and custom applications.

- XMPP is *scalable*. The "push" model of information transfer used in XMPP solves serious scaling problems associated with traditional HTTP-based polling approaches; as a result, it enables you to build applications that were literally impossible until now.

- XMPP is a *standard*. The core aspects of XMPP have undergone rigorous public review within the Internet Engineering Task Force (IETF), and extensions to XMPP are published in an open, developer-oriented standards process run by the XSF. This approach has resulted in strong technologies that can be freely implemented under any licensing terms, from open source to shareware to proprietary code.

- XMPP is a *community*. Open standards, a large number of software products, and a communications network are all good, but the "secret sauce" of XMPP may be its vibrant and friendly community of technologists, developers, open source projects, commercial software companies, service providers, and end users. This community is committed to working together to solve problems and build great new applications.

For these reasons, more and more software developers and service providers are using XMPP to build real-time applications or add real-time interfaces to existing applications. And you can, too, because XMPP provides a simple but powerful set of tools that can help you solve real-world problems. This book will show you how.

Jabber and XMPP

Throughout this book, we use the terms "Jabber" and "XMPP" interchangeably. These technologies were originally developed by Jeremie Miller and the Jabber open source community in 1998–1999. When the community submitted its core protocols to the Internet Engineering Task Force (IETF) in 2002, it chose the name "Extensible Messaging and Presence Protocol" to distinguish the protocol from the broader technology and developer community. You can think of the relationship as "XMPP is to Jabber as HTTP is to the Web." The term Jabber was proactively trademarked by Jabber, Inc. (now part of Cisco Systems, Inc.) in 2000 to protect the open source community, but the XSF sublicenses the term for use in open source projects and other community activities.

Is This Book for You?

This book may be for you if:

- You are a software developer who needs a helpful guide to building a real-time application or extending an existing system, as well as relevant reference materials to use during your project.
- You are a product manager or software architect who is looking for suggestive ideas and case studies regarding real-time systems.
- You are a software architect or developer who needs a brief but thorough overview of XMPP.
- You are a researcher, teacher, or student who is designing a research project.
- You are interested in new technologies and the emergence of the real-time Internet.

Above all, this book provides a practical guide to XMPP. Because XMPP is a well-documented protocol, we regularly refer you to the XMPP specifications for relevant details (these specifications come in two flavors: the core protocols are defined in the Requests for Comments or "RFC" series published by the IETF, and dozens of extensions are defined in the XMPP Extension Protocol or "XEP" series published by the XSF). Because XMPP is widely supported by a large number of servers, clients, and code libraries, both open source and commercial, we refer you to those projects for assistance with real-world implementation. Instead of covering all protocol details and possible implementations, we show how XMPP technologies can be used to solve certain classes of problems by helping you to "think in XMPP" and covering the "gotchas" that can trip up those who are new to XMPP technologies.

Throughout this book, we assume that you are familiar with the very basics of computer networking, common Internet applications (such as email and the World Wide Web), and structured data formats (such as HTML). However, we often treat these technologies as the starting points for our discussion or as "contrast objects" for XMPP, which differs from applications such as the Web in important ways that we'll describe as we go. Finally, we include some examples using the Python programming language, so some familiarity with Python can also help you understand the concepts we describe.

Getting the Most Out of This Book

To get the most out of this book, we do not recommend that you read it cover to cover in one sitting (although you are welcome to do so!). Instead, first explore the sections that interest you or that you need to complete a particular task, perhaps after reading the introductory materials in Part I. You might also consider skimming over the details of each XML example on your first reading so that you get the general idea of each use case and protocol extension.

The book is organized as follows:

- Part I provides an overview of XMPP. The first chapter talks about XMPP at a high level and introduces you to some ways XMPP is being used to build real-time applications. The second chapter describes the basics of XMPP technologies, including architectural issues, addressing, and communication primitives. Read this section first if you'd like a relatively quick orientation to XMPP technologies.

- Part II consists of a series of "developer stories" that illustrate how the tools in the XMPP toolkit can help you solve particular classes of problems. Each chapter in Part II introduces the XMPP concepts and services that you need in a given problem domain, describes how to use those tools, and provides examples showing how specific protocols come into play. Read the chapters here that interest you most. The order doesn't matter, because we recap concepts where needed, and provide cross-references to more detailed treatments in other chapters.

- Part III shows you how to put it all together by walking you through the thought processes and design decisions involved in building an XMPP-based application. Read this part after you have a feel for XMPP from the first two parts, and as you begin to dig into a large project that uses XMPP to construct a business application or real-time service.

- Part IV consists of the appendixes, which help you understand the terminology of XMPP; introduce you to the wealth of XMPP servers, clients, and code libraries; and guide you through the large "stack" of XMPP protocol specifications so you can quickly find what you need. Use these appendixes as reference material on an ongoing basis, or as a quick index to the myriad of XMPP resources available on the Internet.

Conventions Used in This Book

The following typographical conventions are used in this book:

Italic

Indicates new terms, URLs, email addresses, filenames, and file extensions.

`Constant width`

Used for protocol examples and sample code, as well as within paragraphs to refer to protocol aspects such as XML elements, attributes, and namespaces, code features such as variable and function names, databases, data types, environment variables, statements, keywords, etc.

`Constant width bold`

Indicates user input in examples showing an interaction. Also indicates emphasized code elements to which you should pay particular attention.

 This icon signifies a tip, suggestion, or general note.

 This icon indicates a warning or caution

About the Examples

In Parts I and II, we include a large number of protocol examples (but not nearly as many as you will find in the XMPP specifications, which are extremely thorough). Each example contains a snippet of XML that would be sent over the wire to communicate a message, share presence information, retrieve data, initiate a command sequence, return an error, and the like. These chunks of XML are essentially copied directly from the XMPP specifications with additional notes to highlight their most important and relevant aspects. However, sometimes our examples are incomplete or shortened for readability, so be sure to check the official XMPP specifications for the most accurate examples and protocol descriptions!

Most of the examples in this book use Lewis Carroll's *Alice's Adventures in Wonderland* as the backdrop (Alice and her friends are much more interesting than "User A" and "User B"!). The domain names in these examples are things like `wonderland.lit`, which clearly don't work on today's Internet, because the .lit top-level domain has not yet been assigned. This is intentional (we don't want to bother anyone who owns a real domain name like `wonderland.com`).

In Part III, we intersperse protocol examples with software code showing one possible implementation of several protocol interactions. This software code is written in the Python programming language, a popular, easy-to-read language for scripting and application development.

Using Code Examples

This book is here to help you get your job done. In general, you may use the code in this book in your programs and documentation. You do not need to contact us for permission unless you're reproducing a significant portion of the code. For example, writing a program that uses several chunks of code from this book does not require permission. Selling or distributing a CD-ROM of examples from O'Reilly books does require permission. Answering a question by citing this book and quoting example code does not require permission. Incorporating a significant amount of example code from this book into your product's documentation does require permission.

We appreciate, but do not require, attribution. An attribution usually includes the title, author, publisher, and ISBN. For example: "*XMPP: The Definitive Guide*, by Peter Saint-Andre, Kevin Smith, and Remko Tronçon. Copyright 2009 Peter Saint-Andre, Kevin Smith, and Remko Tronçon, 978-0-596-52126-4."

If you feel your use of code examples falls outside fair use or the permission given above, feel free to contact us at *permissions@oreilly.com*.

Safari® Books Online

When you see a Safari® Books Online icon on the cover of your favorite technology book, that means the book is available online through the O'Reilly Network Safari Bookshelf.

Safari offers a solution that's better than e-books. It's a virtual library that lets you easily search thousands of top tech books, cut and paste code samples, download chapters, and find quick answers when you need the most accurate, current information. Try it for free at *http://my.safaribooksonline.com*.

How to Contact Us

Please address comments and questions concerning this book to the publisher:

O'Reilly Media, Inc.
1005 Gravenstein Highway North
Sebastopol, CA 95472
800-998-9938 (in the United States or Canada)
707-829-0515 (international or local)
707-829-0104 (fax)

We have a web page for this book, where we list errata, examples, and any additional information. You can access this page at:

http://www.oreilly.com/catalog/9780596521264/

To comment or ask technical questions about this book, send email to:

bookquestions@oreilly.com

For more information about our books, conferences, Resource Centers, and the O'Reilly Network, see our website at:

http://www.oreilly.com

Finally, the authors of this book can usually be found on the XMPP network in the jdev@conference.jabber.org chat room.

Acknowledgments

We would like to thank Mary Treseler for her editorial guidance throughout this project, and her patience with an enthusiastic but not entirely disciplined group of authors. We'd also like to thank our technical reviewers for their thorough comments on, and insight into, the contents of this book; it was greatly improved by their input. Thank you Dave Cridland, Brian Dainton, Kellan Elliott-McCrea, Michelle Fisher, Nathan Fritz, and Jack Moffitt.

Peter Saint-Andre

Thanks are due to the many developers who helped me understand these technologies as they were being designed in the early days of the Jabber open source community. I would like to especially recognize the help of my friend Peter Millard, who patiently answered my never-ending questions about Jabber technologies from 1999 until his death in 2006. I dedicate my work on this book to his memory.

I would not have been able to contribute to XMPP all these years without the generous support of my employer, Jabber, Inc. (now part of Cisco Systems, Inc.).

Most fundamentally, my wife, Elisa, has always cheerfully tolerated my obsession with XMPP despite countless hours working on specs, posting to discussion lists, writing blog entries, traveling to conferences, and all the rest.

Kevin Smith

Many of the members of the XMPP community have been supportive over the last seven or so years since my first involvement, and I'd like to acknowledge particularly those people I've worked with in the Psi and Sleek projects, and those I've worked with on the XMPP Council in expanding my knowledge of XMPP and software development. Thanks to Peter and Remko especially, for all the fun we've had with this book.

My wife, Cath, has my unending gratitude for her support in my numerous XMPP-related and other free-time-swallowing commitments.

Remko Tronçon

My first words of gratitude go to my coauthors, Peter and Kevin. Not only did they make the writing of this book an incredibly fun experience, but they are also the reason why I got into XMPP in the first place. Thanks to Kevin, the other Psi developers, and the whole Psi userbase, I got the chance to take my first steps into the XMPP world. Thanks to the support of "patron saint" Peter and the rest of the XMPP community, I was able to take this involvement one step further, and joined the conversation to define the XMPP standards. The XMPP community is without a doubt one of the most pleasant and accessible groups of people out there on the interwebs. Thanks to everyone out there who ever talked to me!

My most important source of inspiration, however, comes from outside the digital world. Kim has always unconditionally supported me in all my time-consuming activities, and has continuously pushed me to work harder, even in times when she hardly received any of the attention she deserved.

PART I

An Overview of XMPP

CHAPTER 1

Introduction

What Can You Do with XMPP?

The *Extensible Messaging and Presence Protocol* (XMPP) is an open technology for real-time communication, using the *Extensible Markup Language* (XML) as the base format for exchanging information. In essence, XMPP provides a way to send small pieces of XML from one entity to another in close to real time.

XMPP is used in a wide range of applications, and it may be right for your application, too. To envision the possibilities, it's helpful to break the XMPP universe down at a high level into *services* and *applications*. The services are defined in two primary specifications published by the Internet Engineering Task Force (IETF) at *http://ietf.org/* (the "RFC" series), and in dozens of extension specifications published by the XMPP Standards Foundation at *http://xmpp.org/* (the "XEP" series); the applications are software programs and deployment scenarios that are of common interest to individuals and organizations, although the core services enable you to build many other application types as well.

RFC Revisions

As of this writing, [RFC 3920] and [RFC 3921] are under active revision to incorporate errata, clarify ambiguities, improve their readability, define additional error codes, etc. These documents, called [rfc3920bis] and [rfc3921bis] in the terminology of the IETF, provide the most accurate definition of XMPP and might have been published as replacement RFCs (with new numbers) once you read this book. For the latest versions of the revised specifications, visit *http://xmpp.org*.

Services

In this context, a *service* is a feature or function that can be used by any given application. XMPP implementations typically provide the following core services:

Channel encryption

This service, defined in [RFC 3920] and explained in Chapter 12 of this book, provides encryption of the connection between a client and a server, or between two servers. Although channel encryption is not necessarily exciting, it is an important building block for constructing secure applications.

Authentication

This service, also defined in [RFC 3920] and explained in Chapter 12 of this book, is another part of the foundation for secure application development. In this case, the authentication service ensures that entities attempting to communicate over the network are first authenticated by a server, which acts as a kind of gatekeeper for network access.

Presence

This service, defined in [RFC 3921] and explained in Chapter 3 of this book, enables you to find out about the network availability of other entities. At the most basic level, a presence service answers the question, "Is the entity online and available for communication, or offline and not available?" Presence data can also include more detailed information (such as whether a person is in a meeting). Typically, the sharing of presence information is based on an explicit presence subscription between two entities in order to protect the privacy of user information.

Contact lists

This service, also defined in [RFC 3921] and explained in Chapter 3 of this book, enables you to store a contact list, or *roster*, on an XMPP server. The most common use for this service is an instant messaging "friend list," but any entity that has an account on a server can use the service to maintain a list of known or trusted entities (e.g., it can be used by bots).

One-to-one messaging

This service, defined in [RFC 3920] and explained in Chapter 4 of this book, enables you to send messages to another entity. The classic use of one-to-one messaging is personal IM, but messages can be arbitrary XML, and any two entities on a network can exchange messages—they could be bots, servers, components, devices, XMPP-enabled web services, or any other XMPP entity.

Multi-party messaging

This service, defined in [XEP-0045] and explained in Chapter 7 of this book, enables you to join a virtual chat room for the exchange of messages between multiple participants, similar to Internet Relay Chat (IRC). The messages can be plain text, or can contain XML extensions for more advanced functionality, such as room configuration, in-room voting, and various session control messages.

Notifications

This service, defined in [XEP-0060] and explained in Chapter 8 of this book, enables you to generate a notification and have it delivered to multiple subscribers.

This service is similar to multi-party messaging, but it is optimized for one-to-many delivery with explicit subscriptions to specific channels or topics (called "nodes").

Service discovery

This service, defined in [XEP-0030] and explained in Chapter 5 of this book, enables you to find out which features are supported by another entity, as well as any additional entities that are associated with it (e.g., rooms hosted at a chat room service).

Capabilities advertisement

This service, defined in [XEP-0115] and explained in Chapter 5 of this book, is an extension to the presence service that provides a shorthand notation for service discovery data so that you can easily cache the features that are supported by other entities on the network.

Structured data forms

This service, defined in [XEP-0004] and explained in Chapter 6 of this book, enables you to exchange structured but flexible forms with other entities, similar to HTML forms. It is often used for configuration and other tasks where you need to gather ad-hoc information from other entities.

Workflow management

This service, defined in [XEP-0050] and explained in Chapter 11 of this book, enables you to engage in a structured workflow interaction with another entity, with support for typical workflow actions, such as moving to the next stage of a business process or executing a command. It is often used in conjunction with data forms.

Peer-to-peer media sessions

This service, defined in [XEP-0166] and explained in Chapter 9 of this book, enables you to negotiate and manage a media session with another entity. Such a session can be used for the purpose of voice chat, video chat, file transfer, and other real-time interactions.

These are some of the core services available to you (or your application) as a participant in an XMPP network. The XMPP developer community has defined additional features in various XMPP extensions, but here we focus on the services that we think you will find most useful in building real-time applications.

Applications

Given that you have a dozen core services at your disposal, what can you build? Here are a few possibilities:

Instant messaging

The classic instant messaging systems that most people are familiar with combine three of the core services: presence, contact lists, and one-to-one messaging. Such systems can and often do include more services and features, but if you have these three services, you can build a bare-bones IM application.

Groupchat

The multi-party messaging service enables you to build groupchat systems similar to IRC. Often, groupchat systems are used for more specific applications, such as real-time trading systems in the financial industry, situation rooms for first responders and military personnel, and virtual classrooms.

Gaming

Combined with custom extensions, both one-to-one messaging and multi-party messaging enable you to build simple gaming systems. For example, the Chesspark service (*http://www.chesspark.com/*) is built entirely using XMPP. Other game developers are using XMPP to add presence and contact list features to existing multi-party games.

Systems control

The combination of one-to-one messaging and data forms makes it possible to deploy lightweight systems for control of and interaction with remote systems. Deployed applications in this domain include network management, scientific telemetry, and robotic control.

Geolocation

The XMPP notification service is payload-agnostic. One defined payload format is geolocation, which enables you to build fascinating location-based applications, such as vehicle tracking.

Middleware and cloud computing

A number of companies and research groups are actively working on XMPP-based systems for computation services, lightweight middleware, and management of cloud computing infrastructures. While the use of XMPP may be surprising here because such applications have traditionally relied on heavyweight messaging technologies, we have seen XMPP begin to nibble away at the lower end of this market. It appears that companies that already have an XMPP infrastructure in place figure they might as well use it for non-IM use cases. These systems often use the workflow extensions we explore in Chapters 6 and 11 for structured message exchange. Specific applications include bioinformatics.

Data syndication

Popular social networking applications are increasingly using the XMPP notification service to solve a particular problem they have: constant polling for updated information. Existing HTTP-based deployments have been found not to scale, because quite often a particular feed has not changed since the last time it was polled. By contrast, the XMPP notification service sends out an update only when a feed has changed, saving a significant amount of bandwidth and server resources that otherwise would be wasted on polling.

Voice over IP (VoIP)

The Google Talk application that launched in August 2005 first popularized the use of XMPP for voice chat. Since then, the XMPP extensions for media session services (called Jingle) have been formalized through the XSF, and have been implemented and deployed by the likes of Nokia and the One Laptop Per Child project. The same extensions can also be used to negotiate a wide range of media session types, including video, file transfer, whiteboarding, and collaborative editing.

Identity services

Given the existence of stable identifiers (JabberIDs) and a robust authentication service, it is possible to use XMPP in building identity and authorization services such as OpenID and OAuth.

Other application examples include data transfer, live chat integrated into websites, mobile device communications, and presence-enabled directories. We will mention relevant applications throughout this book to illustrate the most popular and interesting uses of XMPP.

Although we highlight many applications of XMPP, unfortunately we can't cover all of them. Not only do we lack the space and time, but the list keeps growing every day. Moreover, the most cutting-edge uses of XMPP are not standardized yet, which makes them too much of a moving target to describe in a book. Examples of ongoing work at the time of this writing include collaborative document editing, whiteboarding, calendar integration, file sharing, and personal media networks. If you want to learn more about these topics, we suggest that you get involved with the XMPP community (see Chapter 13) as we define new ways of using XMPP.

What does the future hold for XMPP technologies? Although we don't know for sure, the trends seem clear: deployment of XMPP systems at more organizations and service providers, XMPP interfaces to more web applications, use of XMPP features to solve more business problems, and continued growth in the XMPP developer community. It's an exciting time to be working on XMPP technologies, and we invite you to join the conversation!

Brief History

Jabber/XMPP technologies were invented by Jeremie Miller in 1998. Jeremie was tired of running four different clients for the closed IM services of the day, so in true open source fashion, he decided to scratch an itch, releasing an open source server called *jabberd* on January 4, 1999. Before long, a community of developers jumped in to help, writing open source clients for Linux, Macintosh, and Windows; add-on components that worked with the server; and code libraries for languages such as Perl and Java. During 1999 and early 2000, the community collaboratively worked out the details of the wire protocols we now call XMPP, culminating in the release of *jabberd 1.0* in May 2000.

As the community grew larger and various companies became interested in building their own Jabber-compatible (but not necessarily open source) software, the loose collaboration evident in 1999 and 2000 became unsustainable. As a result, the community (spearheaded by a company called Jabber, Inc., acquired by Cisco in late 2008) formed the Jabber Software Foundation in August 2001. Ever since, this nonprofit membership organization, renamed the XMPP Standards Foundation in early 2007, has openly documented the protocols used in the developer community, and has defined a large number of extensions to the core protocols.

After several years of implementation and deployment experience, members of the developer community decided to seek a wider review of the core protocols by formalizing them within the IETF, which has standardized most of the core technologies for the Internet (including TCP/IP, HTTP, SMTP, POP, IMAP, and SSL/TLS). Given that most good protocols seem to be three- or four-letter acronyms ending with the letter "P," the relevant IETF working group labeled its topic the Extensible Messaging and Presence Protocol (XMPP). After less than two years of intensive work (mostly focused on tightening communications security), the IETF published the core XMPP specifications in its Request for Comments (RFC) series as [RFC 3920] and [RFC 3921] in October 2004.

Publication of these RFCs has resulted in widespread adoption of XMPP technologies. In August 2005, the Google Talk IM and Voice over Internet Protocol (VoIP) service was launched on a basis of XMPP. Thousands more services have followed. Prominent and emerging software companies use XMPP in their products, including the likes of Apple, Cisco, IBM, Nokia, and Sun. Countless businesses, universities, and government agencies have deployed XMPP-based instant messaging systems for their users. Many game developers and social networking applications are building XMPP into their services, and a number of organizations have used XMPP as the "secret sauce" behind some of their most innovative features.

Open Source and Open Standards

Although XMPP was originally developed in the Jabber open source community, the protocol itself is not an open source project like Apache, but rather an open standard like HTTP. As a result, XMPP is an open technology that is not tied to any single software project or company. The XMPP specifications define open protocols that are used for communication among network entities. Much as HTTP and HTML define the protocols and data formats that power the World Wide Web, XMPP defines the protocols and data formats that power real-time interactions over the Internet. The protocols are as free as the air, which means they can be implemented in code that is licensed as free software, open source software, shareware, freeware, commercial products, or in any other way. This open standards model is different from the open source or free-software model for software code, wherein the code is often licensed so that modifications must be contributed back to the developers.

That said, XMPP emerged from an open source developer community, specifically the community that formed around the open source *jabberd* server that Jeremie Miller released. Thus there are many open source implementations of XMPP, which can be downloaded for free by end users, system administrators, and developers alike. Much of this software is focused on instant messaging, as befits a technology that started as an open alternative to closed IM silos that did not interoperate. There are open source clients for just about every operating system and device; as a result, millions of end users communicate using XMPP-based services. There are open source servers that can be deployed at companies, schools, and service providers; as a result, tens of thousands of XMPP services inter-connect every day. There are open source libraries for all the major programming languages, which can be used to write bots, components, and other real-time applications; as a result, there are thousands of active developers in the XMPP community. Much of this software is linked to from *http://xmpp.org/*, and we provide an overview of some of the most popular codebases in Appendix C.

Extensibility

The original Jabber developers were focused on building an instant messaging system. However, the extensible nature of XML has made XMPP attractive to application developers who need a reliable infrastructure for rapidly exchanging structured data, not just IM features. As a result, XMPP has been used to build a wide range of applications, including content syndication, alerts and notifications, lightweight middleware and web services, whiteboarding, multimedia session negotiation, intelligent workflows, geolocation, online gaming, social networking, and more.

Over the years, the developer community defined a large number of extensions to the core protocols. These extensions are developed through an open, collaborative standards process and published in the XSF's XMPP Extension Protocol (XEP) series at *http://xmpp.org/*. As you'll discover, the core protocols and various extensions provide a long "runway" for just about any feature you might need in developing real-time applications. But if you find that a feature is missing from the XMPP protocol stack, it is easy enough to extend the protocol for your own purpose, and (optionally) work with the community in standardizing these new features, as we discuss in Chapter 13.

Summary

In this chapter, we looked at the core services XMPP provides and sampled the kinds of applications you can build with those services. Next, you'll get acquainted with the basic workings of XMPP, after which we'll dive into each of the core XMPP services in detail.

CHAPTER 2

Basics of XMPP

This chapter outlines the fundamental features used by all XMPP-based applications. We first describe the generic architecture of XMPP systems and then the addressing scheme for XMPP communications, the three communication "primitives," the model for sharing information about availability on the network (called *presence*), and the processes for session establishment.

Architecture

All good Internet technologies have an "architecture"—a way that various entities fit together, link up, and communicate. For example, the World Wide Web consists of millions of web servers running software like Apache, and many more millions of web clients (browsers) running software like Firefox, all using standard protocols and data formats like HTTP and HTML. As another example, the email infrastructure consists of millions of email servers running software like Postfix, and many more millions of email clients running software like Thunderbird, all using standard protocols like SMTP, POP, and IMAP.

Similarly, the Internet's infrastructure for instant messaging, presence, and other forms of real-time communication increasingly consists of hundreds of thousands of Jabber servers running software like ejabberd and Openfire, and millions of Jabber clients running software like Adium, Gajim, Pidgin, and Psi, all using the standard protocol we call XMPP.

XMPP technologies use a decentralized client-server architecture similar to the architectures used for the World Wide Web and the email network. The diagram in Figure 2-1 is a simplified representation showing three servers, each with three clients.

The beauty of using a decentralized client-server architecture is that it enables an intelligent separation of concerns (client developers can focus on user experience, and server developers can focus on reliability and scalability), it is much easier for organizations to manage than a purely peer-to-peer technology, it is quite robust because the full system does not have a single point of failure (anyone can run their own XMPP

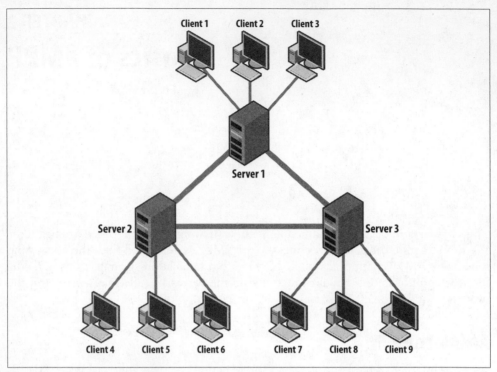

Figure 2-1. XMPP uses a client-server architecture similar to email and the World Wide Web

server and thereby join the network), and the servers can enforce important security policies such as user authentication, channel encryption, and prevention of address spoofing. Finally, the XMPP community has always worked to keep clients simple and to push as much complexity as possible onto the servers, further enabling widespread adoption of the technology. (We discuss the core XMPP design principles more fully in Chapter 13.)

However, there are some important architectural differences between the Web, email, and Jabber.

When you visit a website, your browser connects to a web server, but web servers typically do not connect to each other in order to complete a transaction (see Figure 2-2). Instead, the HTML of the web page may refer to other web servers (e.g., to load images or scripts), and your browser opens sessions with those web servers to load the full page. Thus, the Web typically does not involve inter-domain connections (often called *federation*, and shown in Figure 2-1 by the double line).

When you send an email to one of your contacts at a different domain, your email client connects to your "home" email server, which then seeks to route the message to your contact. Thus, unlike the Web, the email system consists of a federated *network* of servers. However, your message might be routed through multiple intermediate email

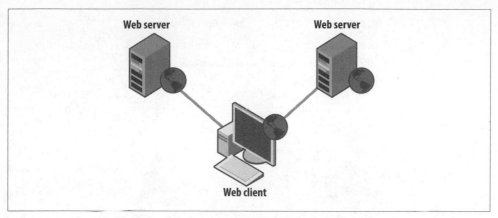

Figure 2-2. The World Wide Web has many servers and clients, but very few server-to-server connections

servers before it reaches its final destination (see Figure 2-3). Thus, the email network uses multiple *hops* between servers to deliver messages.

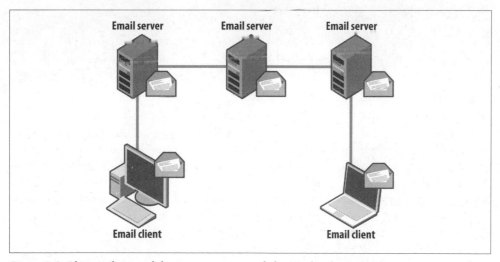

Figure 2-3. The email network has many servers and clients, plus the servers are interconnected in a multi-hop network

Like email, but unlike the Web, XMPP systems involve a great deal of inter-domain connections. However, when you send an XMPP message to one of your contacts at a different domain, your client connects to your "home" server, which then connects directly to your contact's server without intermediate hops (see Figure 2-4). This *direct federation* model has important differences from the *indirect federation* model used in email (in particular, it helps to prevent address spoofing and certain forms of spam).

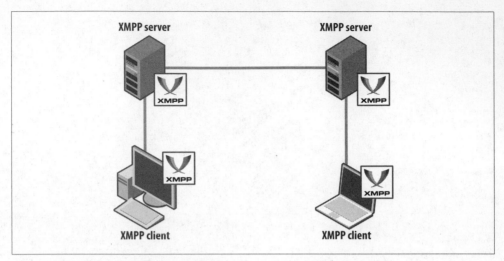

Figure 2-4. The XMPP network has many servers and clients, plus the servers are interconnected in a single-hop network

Table 2-1 summarizes these differences.

Table 2-1. Client-server architectures

Feature	Web	Email	Jabber
Interdomain Connections	No	Yes	Yes
Multiple Hops	N/A	Yes	No

Although clients and servers are the fundamental entities on an XMPP network, other entities play a part, too. Automated clients called *bots* provide a wide range of communication services, including assistance in chat rooms and human-friendly interfaces to non-XMPP services such as social networking applications. Furthermore, most XMPP servers are written in a modular way that enables administrators to add specialized services or server *components*, such as multi-user chat rooms, publish-subscribe topics, gaming arbiters, and the like. We discuss bots and components later in this book, especially in Part III.

Addresses

Because XMPP communications happen on a network, every XMPP entity needs an address, called a *JabberID* (JID). XMPP typically relies on the *Domain Name System* (DNS) to provide the underlying structure for addressing, instead of using raw *Internet Protocol* (IP) addresses. After all, it's much easier to remember that there is an XMPP service running at jabber.org than to remember 208.68.163.220. Similarly, JabberIDs for users look like email addresses (e.g., stpeter@jabber.org) because the format `user@domain.tld` is already familiar to people; furthermore, this format uses the complete DNS infrastructure as its address space, unlike older IM systems that used numbers or names without any domain identifier.

Domains

Every JabberID contains a domain portion, which typically maps to a *fully qualified domain name* (FQDN). When you install your favorite XMPP server software, you choose a domain name for the deployment, such as `jabber.org` or `gmail.com`. Using DNS service label records, your domain name maps to one or more particular machines, such as `hermes.jabber.org` or `talk1.l.google.com`. Those machine names in turn map to particular IP addresses, such as 208.68.163.220 or 72.14.253.125. (We discuss deployment scenarios further in the appendixes.) However, for the purposes of addressing on the network, all we need to care about is the domain name itself (e.g., `jabber.org` or `gmail.com`), rather than the lower-level machine names and IP addresses. Finally, for ASCII characters, the domain portion of a JID is case-insensitive (so that `JABBER.ORG` is the same as `jabber.org`); as we explain later, the rules for non-ASCII characters are a bit more complex.

Users

When you create an account at an XMPP service such as `jabber.org`, you choose a JabberID that functions as your virtual identity on the network. Alternatively, your JabberID might be assigned to you automatically. Your JabberID looks much like an email address (e.g., `stpeter@jabber.org`). Depending on deployment policies, it might even be the same as your email address at a service or company (e.g., your Google Talk address on the XMPP network looks the same as your Gmail address on the email network). As for the domain portion of the JabberID, the username portion of a JID is case-insensitive for ASCII characters (so that `StPeter@jabber.org` is the same as `stpeter@jabber.org`). XMPP developers usually call an address of the form `user@domain.tld` a *bare JID*.

Resources

When you connect your client to an XMPP server, you choose (or the server assigns to you) a *resource identifier* for that particular connection. This resource is used for routing traffic to that connection instead of any other connections you might have open at the moment. The resource is added to the end of your account address, such as `stpeter@jabber.org/roundabout` or `remko@el-tramo.be/home`. This enables someone to query or exchange messages with a particular device that is associated with your account; it also means that each device is a separate "point of presence," with different availability states, capabilities, etc. The resource is often the name of your computer, your location, or the client software you are using, but can be any string (including spaces and other special characters). Contrary to the other parts of a JID, the resource portion *is* case-sensitive (e.g., `remko@el-tramo.be/home` is different from `remko@el-tramo.be/Home`). XMPP developers usually call an address of the form `user@domain.tld/resource` a *full JID*.

Internationalization

A major difference between JabberIDs and email addresses is that XMPP is fully internationalized. This means that XMPP domain names and user names are not limited to the boring old ASCII character range, but can include virtually any Unicode character. If you live in the Czech Republic, you could run a Jabber server at a domain such as `čechy.cz`, and you could have an address such as `jiři@čechy.cz`. Or, if you enjoy mathematics and happen to own the domain `math.it`, your JabberID could be something fun like `∞@math.it` (try *that* with email!). For non-ASCII characters (i.e., most of the characters in the world), we don't talk about case-sensitivity, but instead about *case-folding*. Although some rather complicated rules for character comparison and decomposition can come into play when using Unicode characters, these case-folding rules (defined by a technology called *stringprep*, as specified in [RFC 3454]) are typically enforced by a lower-level library, and so most developers don't need to deal with this directly.

XMPP URIs

On the XMPP network itself, JabberIDs are provided as raw addresses without a *Uniform Resource Identifier* (URI) scheme. This is similar to the convention of telling someone to visit `www.oreilly.com` (instead of `http://www.oreilly.com/`), or sending an email to the `standards@xmpp.org` list (instead of `mailto:standards@xmpp.org`). However, there is an XMPP URI scheme that can be used to identify JabberIDs as URIs, such as `xmpp:jabber.org` or `xmpp:stpeter@jabber.org` (note the lack of a "//"—think mailto, not http). This URI scheme is defined in [RFC 5122]. The XMPP community has also defined ways to include various "commands" in XMPP URIs, such as `xmpp:user@domain.tld?message` to send a message (see [XEP-0147] for details).

Streaming XML

XMPP is, in essence, a technology for streaming XML. When you want to start a session with an XMPP server, you open a long-lived TCP connection and then negotiate an XML stream to the server (the server also opens a stream in return, i.e., there is one stream in each direction). We discuss the details of XML streams in Chapter 12, but for now you can think of a stream as an XML document that is built up incrementally over time between your client and your server.

Once you have negotiated an XML stream with your server, you and your server can exchange three special XML snippets over the stream: `<message/>`, `<presence/>`, and

`<iq/>`. These snippets, called *XML stanzas*, are the basic units of meaning in XMPP, and once you have negotiated an XML stream you can send an unlimited number of stanzas over the stream. Example 2-1 illustrates a simplified XMPP session, including the interaction between streams and stanzas, as well as the outbound stanzas sent from the client (prefaced with "C:") and the inbound stanzas delivered from the server (prefaced with "S:").

Example 2-1. In an XMPP session, the stream element acts as a wrapper for an unlimited number of outbound and inbound XML stanzas; outbound stanzas sent from the client are prefaced with C:, and inbound stanzas delivered from the server are prefaced with S:

```
C: <stream:stream>

C:    <presence/>

C:    <iq type="get">
        <query xmlns="jabber:iq:roster"/>
      </iq>

S:    <iq type="result">
        <query xmlns="jabber:iq:roster">
          <item jid="alice@wonderland.lit"/>
          <item jid="madhatter@wonderland.lit"/>
          <item jid="whiterabbit@wonderland.lit"/>
        </query>
      </iq>

C:    <message from="queen@wonderland.lit"
               to="madhatter@wonderland.lit">
        <body>Off with his head!</body>
      </message>

S:    <message from="king@wonderland.lit"
               to="party@conference.wonderland.lit">
        <body>You are all pardoned.</body>
      </message>

C:    <presence type="unavailable"/>

C: </stream:stream>
```

The XMPP approach of opening a long-lived TCP connection and then asynchronously exchanging an unlimited number of XML snippets differs radically from the traditional approach used in web and email technologies, where you open a TCP connection, complete a transaction (say, retrieving a web page or downloading some email), then close the connection again. These transactional connections do not lend themselves to real-time communication, because the server does not have an "always-on" channel available to push information down to the client. As a result, constant polling for new information is the order of the day (this is true even in recent HTTP techniques such as Ajax and Comet, although the polling has gotten smarter over time). By contrast, in XMPP, the client can send out multiple requests without "blocking" while it waits for replies, and the server will return those replies dynamically as soon as they are answered. These design decisions have important implications for the XMPP user experience and for the kinds of applications you can build with XMPP. But they also introduce new challenges for developers, who are not necessarily accustomed to thinking in terms of asynchronous information flows and streaming XML snippets. As you explore XMPP, remember that you may need new tools and a new mindset to see the possibilities.

The Layered Look

Although XMPP is defined in a number of exhaustive (not to say boring!) specifications, in most cases, you won't need to worry about lower levels, such as XML streams. Instead, existing code libraries typically abstract away from the raw XML layer so that you can focus on adding real-time features to your application.

Communication Primitives

These XML "stanzas" sound rather poetic, but what do they mean in practice? In XMPP, a stanza can be thought of as the basic unit of communication, similar to a packet or message in other network protocols (the term was suggested by Lisa Dusseault, who cochaired the IETF's XMPP Working Group along with Pete Resnick).

Several factors determine the meaning of a stanza:

- The stanza element name, which is `message`, `presence`, or `iq`. Each kind of stanza is routed differently by servers and handled differently by clients.
- The value of the `type` attribute, which varies depending on the kind of stanza in question. This value further differentiates how each kind of stanza is processed by the recipient.
- The child element(s), which define the payload of the stanza. The payload might be presented to a user or processed in some automated fashion as determined by the specification that defines the namespace of the payload.

The following sections provide a brief introduction to these factors, and we will explore them throughout this book as we unfold the meaning of various stanza kinds, `type` attribute values, and payload definitions.

Message

The XMPP `<message/>` stanza is the basic "push" method for getting information from one place to another. Because messages are typically not acknowledged, they are a kind of "fire-and-forget" mechanism for quickly getting information from one place to another. Messages are used for IM, groupchat, alerts and notifications, and other such applications.

Message stanzas come in five flavors, differentiated by the `type` attribute:

normal
> Messages of type `normal` are most similar to email messages, since they are single messages to which a response may or may not be forthcoming.

chat
> Messages of type `chat` are exchanged in a real-time "session" between two entities, such as an instant messaging chat between two friends.

groupchat
> Messages of type `groupchat` are exchanged in a multi-user chat room, similar to Internet Relay Chat (we discuss groupchat messages in Chapter 7).

headline
> Messages of type `headline` are used to send alerts and notifications, and a response is not expected at all (a client that receives a headline should not enable a user to reply).

error
> If an error occurs in relation to a previously sent message, the entity that detects the problem will return a message of type `error`.

In addition to the `type` attribute, message stanzas contain a `to` and `from` address, and can contain an `id` attribute for tracking purposes (we discuss IDs in more detail in relation to IQ stanzas, where they are used more widely). Naturally enough, the `to` address is the JabberID of the intended recipient, and the `from` address is the JabberID of the sender. The `from` address is not provided by the sending client, but instead is stamped by the sender's server to avoid address spoofing.

Messages also contain payload elements. The core XMPP specifications define some very basic payloads, such as `<body/>` and `<subject/>`, which are used for person-to-person chat messages. For example, a simple message could look like this:

```
<message from="madhatter@wonderland.lit/foo"
         to="alice@wonderland.lit"
         type="chat">❶
  <body>Who are you?</body>
  <subject>Query</subject>
</message>
```

❶ The order of attributes is insignificant (we usually show the attributes in alphabetical order, but they can appear in any order).

Messages (and other kinds of stanzas) can also contain payloads that are not defined in the core XMPP specifications, as we explore throughout this book.

Presence

One of the distinctive features of real-time communication systems is presence, which we discuss in Chapter 3. Presence advertises the network availability of other entities, and thus enables you to know whether other entities are online and available for communication. Many people liken presence to a "dial tone" for the real-time Internet. But this analogy implies that, by itself, presence is fairly boring: who picks up the phone to listen to the dial tone? The exciting thing about presence is that it is a catalyst for communication and collaboration over the Internet, because people are more likely to interact with you if they know you are online.

But don't worry: people can't see that you're online unless you authorize them. This authorization is called a *presence subscription*. In order for someone to see your presence, that person needs to send you a subscription request, which you need to approve. Once you have approved the subscription, that user will automatically receive regular notifications about your network availability. This subscription model implies that the XMPP <presence/> stanza is in essence a simple, specialized *publish-subscribe* method, wherein people who subscribe to your presence receive updated presence information when you come online, change your status to "in a meeting" or "at lunch," and then go offline.

At its most basic, presence is an on-off indication that an entity is either online or offline. However, core XMPP presence is often extended by some common states such as "away" and "do not disturb." These states can be personalized using status messages such as "on a train" or "I'm writing, don't bother me right now" (a state we have used quite a bit recently). For example:

```
<presence from="alice@wonderland.lit/pda">
  <show>xa</show>
  <status>down the rabbit hole!</status>
</presence>
```

In IM applications of XMPP, presence is typically displayed in your *roster*, which is a kind of presence-enabled contact list. Your roster contains a list of JabberIDs and the state of your presence subscriptions with those entities. When you come online, you announce your presence to your server and it handles the rest—both notifying your contacts that you are online and fetching their current presence for display in your client interface. We delve into these details in Chapter 3.

IQ

The *Info/Query* (or IQ) stanza provides a structure for request-response interactions and simple workflows, similar to the GET, POST, and PUT methods that you may be familiar with from HTTP. Unlike the <message/> stanza, an IQ stanza can include only one payload, which defines the request to be processed or action to be taken by the recipient. In addition, the entity that sends an IQ stanza must always receive a reply (usually generated by the intended recipient or the recipient's server). Requests and responses are tracked using the id attribute, which is generated by the requesting entity and then included by the responding entity. Finally, the type attribute has special values for IQ stanzas:

get
> The requesting entity asks for information, such as requirements for registering an account (similar to HTTP GET).

set
> The requesting entity provides some information or makes a request (similar to HTTP POST or PUT).

result
> The responding entity returns the result of a **get** operation (such as the information that an entity must provide to register an account), or acknowledges a **set** request (similar to an HTTP 200 status code).

error
> The responding entity or an intermediate entity, such as an XMPP server, notifies the requesting entity that it was unable to process the **get** or **set** request (e.g., item because the request is malformed, the requesting entity does not have permission to perform the operation, etc.). The early use of HTTP-style numeric error codes has been superseded by XML elements for extensible error conditions.

IQ or Message?

XMPP message stanzas provide a "fire-and-forget" transport that is best used for human-readable text, alerts, notifications, and whenever you don't need assurance that the content was truly delivered. IQ stanzas provide a more reliable transport that is optimized for a structured exchange of data, typically non-human-readable data. (Although the Advanced Message Processing extension defined in [XEP-0079] provides mechanisms that can make message stanzas a more reliable transport, it is not yet widely implemented or deployed.)

Using the values of the IQ stanza's **type**, we can generate a fairly structured IQ interaction between two entities, as shown in Figure 2-5. To illustrate this kind of interaction in more detail, consider the process for getting your roster and then updating it:

```
<iq from="alice@wonderland.lit/pda"
    id="rr82a1z7"
    to="alice@wonderland.lit"
    type="get">
  <query xmlns="jabber:iq:roster"/>
</iq>
```

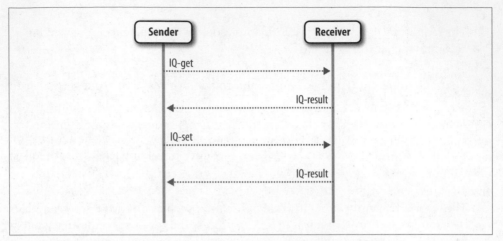

Figure 2-5. The IQ stanza provides structured interactions between entities

Here Alice has asked her server (`wonderland.lit`) to give her the contact list she stores on the server by sending an IQ-get containing an empty payload qualified by the `jabber:iq:roster` namespace. The server then replies with a non-empty payload qualified by that namespace, in this case, containing a single `<item/>` element for each contact in her roster. (The client knows that this roster result relates to its initial request because the server includes an `id` attribute with a value of `rr82a1z7`.)

```
<iq from="alice@wonderland.lit"
    id="rr82a1z7"
    to="alice@wonderland.lit/pda"
    type="result">
  <query xmlns="jabber:iq:roster">
    <item jid="whiterabbit@wonderland.lit"/>
    <item jid="lory@wonderland.lit"/>
    <item jid="mouse@wonderland.lit"/>
    <item jid="sister@realworld.lit"/>
  </query>
</iq>
```

Alice can also use an IQ-set to add a new contact to her roster:

```
<iq from="alice@wonderland.lit/pda"
    id="ru761vd7"
    to="alice@wonderland.lit"
    type="set">
  <query xmlns="jabber:iq:roster">
    <item jid="madhatter@wonderland.lit"/>
  </query>
</iq>
```

Her server then simply acknowledges the roster update by returning an empty IQ-result:

```
<iq from="alice@wonderland.lit"
    id="ru761vd7"
    to="alice@wonderland.lit/pda"
    type="result"/>
```

As you can see from these roster examples, the payload of an IQ-get or IQ-set is always defined by its own format qualified by a particular XML namespace, as specified in one of the many XMPP protocol documents. You can think of each payload format as a command to be processed by the recipient. An IQ-get requests a particular kind of information, such as a registration form, configuration data, service discovery information, or a contact list. An IQ-set creates, updates, or deletes a particular kind of information, such as a completed form, updated configuration data, or an addition to a contact list. Throughout the following chapters, we explore these IQ interactions in great detail as we describe how particular XMPP protocol extensions work.

Extensibility

An XML stanza can contain any number of other child elements, including XHTML-formatted message bodies, pointers to URLs, RSS or Atom notifications, forms to be filled out (or submitted forms), XML-RPC or SOAP data for web services, geographical locations, and a wide range of other payloads. (The "X" in XML and XMPP stands for "extensible," so payload types are limited only by your imagination!)

Because XMPP is a pure XML technology, it makes extensive use of XML namespaces as a way to "scope" stanza payloads. You can think of these namespaces as the XML equivalent of packages and namespaces in programming. So far, the XMPP developer community has defined dozens of extensions to the core XMPP stanza layer. Most often these extensions are published by the XMPP Standards Foundation at *http://xmpp.org/*, but you can also define your own private extensions for custom features.

Extensions are matched on both the element name and the namespace. In the early days of the Jabber open source projects, developers used an `<x/>` element for extensions that would be placed in message or presence stanzas and a `<query/>` element for extensions that would be placed in IQ stanzas. You will see examples of these early extensions in this book (e.g., `<query xmlns="jabber:iq:roster"/>`), but it is important to realize that this usage was merely conventional; extensions developed later do not follow the same practice.

What's in a Name?

You'll notice many different types of XML namespaces. In general, the earliest namespaces were things like `jabber:iq:roster`, namespaces defined from 2001 to 2005 were like `http://jabber.org/protocol/muc`, and more recent namespaces are things like `urn:xmpp:jingle`. Don't worry about the differences; they are all just namespace names.

Asynchronicity

In XMPP, you exchange stanzas asynchronously with other entities on the network. This model is different from HTTP, where your client sends a request to a server and then waits for a reply before it makes another request. By contrast, in XMPP your client can "pipeline" requests to your server or to other entities and then receive replies as they come back. Certain events can also trigger information that is pushed to your client (e.g., when one of your devices adds an item to your roster, the item is pushed out to all of your devices so that they stay in sync). This rapid-fire, event-driven approach can be confusing at first to developers who are more accustomed to traditional web development, but it has a number of advantages, such as real-time notifications and the ability to work around the need to continually poll for updated information.

Error Handling

Unlike some communication technologies, XMPP does not acknowledge every packet or message that is sent over the wire. Typically, you assume that a message or presence stanza has been delivered if you don't receive an error. IQ stanzas are more structured: you must always receive either an IQ-result or an IQ-error in response to an IQ-get or an IQ-set. Errors are reported by setting the stanza's `type` attribute to a value of `error`, along with an `<error/>` child element that is qualified by the `urn:ietf:params:xml:ns:xmpp-stanzas` namespace. Here is an example:

```
<message from="sister@realworld.lit"
         to="alice@wonderland.lit"
         type="error">
  <error type="cancel">
    <service-unavailable xmlns="urn:ietf:params:xml:ns:xmpp-stanzas"/>
  </error>
</message>
```

The `type` attribute of the `<error/>` element is one of `auth`, `cancel`, `continue`, `modify`, or `wait` (the values hint at how to handle the error). However, the primary meaning of the error is specified by the native child element, for example, `<item-not-found/>` or `<forbidden/>`. XMPP error conditions generally follow the model of errors from HTTP and SMTP, except that they are structured not as numeric codes, such as 404, but as (you guessed it!) XML elements. A full list of stanza error conditions can be found in [RFC 3920].

Know the Code

In the early days of the Jabber community, errors were specified with HTTP-style error codes, such as 404 and 501. When the Jabber protocols were standardized at the IETF, the error syntax was expanded to provide a more flexible data format. However, you may still see the HTTP-style error codes on the wire. For a full mapping between the older codes and newer conditions, refer to [XEP-0086].

The `<error/>` element can also include application-specific child elements that specify further details about the error condition. For example, the following error stanza indicates that a pubsub subscription request (which we discuss in Chapter 8) has failed because the pubsub node is closed to new subscriptions:

```
<iq from="notify.wonderland.lit"
    id="t2w4qax3"
    to="alice@wonderland.lit/rabbithole"
    type="error">
  <error type="cancel">
    <not-allowed xmlns="urn:ietf:params:xml:ns:xmpp-stanzas"/>
    <closed-node xmlns="http://jabber.org/protocol/pubsub#errors"/>
  </error>
</iq>
```

In addition to the stanza error conditions described here, [RFC 3920] also defines stream error conditions as well as errors related to SASL authentication. The main difference is that stream errors are unrecoverable and result in closing the XML stream, whereas stanza errors are recoverable and therefore are used for reporting problems with particular stanzas (without termination of the underlying stream).

We don't show a lot of error flows in this book, because it would make the text twice as long. If you want all the details about errors that can result in a particular use case, refer to the relevant XMPP specification, which usually will show all the error cases in addition to the "happy path."

Hello Hello World World: Building a Basic XMPP Application

Believe it or not, at this point you have enough technical baggage to go off and start implementing your own XMPP application. In fact, we'll prove it to you: in this section, we will implement a simple XMPP service, using only the basic building blocks of XMPP introduced in this chapter. The task of our service is simple: reply to every incoming message with an identical message. You can see our service in action in Figure 2-6. Our service acts as a regular contact for its users, but automatically echoes back every message that it receives. Unmanned contacts like this service are typically called *bots*.

Figure 2-6. The "echo" service in action; "echo bot" acts as an ordinary IM contact, but automatically echoes back every message you send it

To implement the bot we just described, we chose Python as our implementation language, and delegate the actual XMPP protocol details to SleekXMPP, one of the many available XMPP libraries (a few of which are listed in Appendix B). We now walk through the steps that lead to the implementation of this "echo" service, displayed in Example 2-2.

Example 2-2. Implementation of a basic bot that echoes all incoming messages back to its sender

```
def main() :
  bot = EchoBot("echobot@wonderland.lit/HelloWorld", "mypass")
  bot.run()

class EchoBot :
  def __init__(self, jid, password) :
    self.xmpp = sleekxmpp.ClientXMPP(jid, password)
    self.xmpp.add_event_handler("session_start", self.handleXMPPConnected)
    self.xmpp.add_event_handler("message", self.handleIncomingMessage)

  def run(self) :
    self.xmpp.connect()
    self.xmpp.process(threaded=False)

  def handleXMPPConnected(self, event):
    self.xmpp.sendPresence(pstatus = "Send me a message")

  def handleIncomingMessage(self, message) :
    self.xmpp.sendMessage(message["jid"], message["message"])
```

The first step in the implementation of our service is to make sure that the echo bot is available on the XMPP network. In order to do this, the service connects to an XMPP server under a given username, just like one would connect with an ordinary IM client. Our bot happens to be registered as `echobot` with the `wonderland.lit` server. Since there will be only one instance of our bot running, we pick `HelloWorld` as an arbitrary resource name to identify the instance of the bot. Putting all these pieces together, we get `echobot@wonderland.lit/HelloWorld` as the JID with which our bot connects to the server (and through which our service will be reachable).

Connecting to the server is done by initializing a `ClientXMPP` object from the SleekXMPP library, and calling `connect()` to set up the connection to the server. The subsequent call to `process()` starts the *event loop* of the bot. The event loop is a seemingly infinite loop that waits for XMPP events to occur (incoming messages, notifications about connection errors, etc.); whenever an event occurs, the event loop calls the *event handler* method that is associated with the event. For reasons explained in the following paragraphs, our bot registers event handlers for two types of events: `session_start` and `message`.

Once the bot is connected to the server, it needs to announce that it's available for service. This is why the bot registers with the XMPP library to receive notification of the `session_start` event, which will fire when the bot is connected and the XMPP session has started. Upon the beginning of a session, the bot sends out basic availability presence by calling `sendPresence()`. As a result, every user that is subscribed to the bot's presence will see the bot appear in his roster.

The core functionality of our bot is triggered whenever a message is received. The handler of the `message` event extracts the sender and the body of the incoming message, and sends it back to the originator using `sendMessage()`.

That's all there is to it! With only a handful of lines of code, we created a fully functional XMPP service. We showed that XMPP applications are typically event-driven, implementing their functionality in terms of asynchronous events that occur. Of course, this book wouldn't be over 250 pages long if all you could do with XMPP was read back simple messages to users. That's why we develop a larger XMPP application in Chapter 14, showing more aspects of implementing XMPP applications.

Summary

In this chapter, we outlined the architecture, addressing, underlying data transport, and communication primitives of XMPP. As a result, you might already have some ideas about how to XMPP-enable an existing application (for example, you might send an XMPP `<message/>` stanza when someone checks a file into a source control system, or you might add presence indicators to a website directory).

However, we have only begun to scratch the surface of what XMPP can do. In the remainder of this book, our explorations will proceed in two directions:

- We will move "up the stack" by describing many of the core XMPP extensions that enable more specific functionality, such as the extensions for service discovery (Chapter 5), multi-party messaging (Chapter 7), publish-subscribe (Chapter 8), and multimedia session management (Chapter 9).

- We will move "down the stack" by describing some of the ins and outs of session establishment (including authentication, channel encryption, the HTTP binding, and serverless messaging over a local network). You may not need to know about these details to build your application, because typical XMPP libraries provide a "login" or "connect" function. However, these lower-level options give you additional tools that can prove extremely useful in more advanced XMPP applications, so we discuss them in Chapter 12.

Now let's look at the key tools in the XMPP toolkit.

PART II

The XMPP Toolkit

CHAPTER 3

Presence

Is Anybody Home?

Imagine that you want to contact a friend or colleague. In the old days, you might have sent the person a letter (you know, one of those pieces of paper that is delivered to your home or office), and then waited for a reply. Or you might have phoned the person and hoped she was around (if not, you would have left a message with a person or an automated system, perhaps playing "phone tag" for a few days). Or, more recently, you might have sent an email, perhaps receiving a reply in 10 minutes or so, but perhaps days later.

In XMPP, you can know when a contact of yours is online and available for communication, using a technology called *presence*. So instead of waiting and wondering, or just getting lucky, your Jabber client will show you the network availability of your contacts, usually with an indicator such as a light bulb icon (on the theory that if someone is home, the lights will be on). Figure 3-1 shows an example of such a presence-enabled contact list in an IM client.

However, presence is not limited to pretty little icons; it enables you to get real work done. In this chapter, we delve more deeply into presence, and explore how you can use it to build smarter, more interactive applications.

Authorization Required: The Subscription Handshake

One of the reasons why presence provides a key tool for application development is that it's voluntary. No one is forcing you to share information about your network availability with anyone else. But if you do choose to share that information, you have made a trust decision, which separates someone who can see your presence from everyone else on the network. As we shall see, this distinction provides important benefits to XMPP-based systems.

Figure 3-1. Your roster provides a visual representation of the people you know and trust on the network, including information about their network availability or "presence"

The trust or access decision behind presence happens naturally in IM systems, because people you approve are automatically added to your contact list (called a *roster* in XMPP), which is typically the "home base" for any instant messaging or real-time communications application.

In addition, presence access is usually bidirectional: you allow a contact to see your presence, and your contact allows you to see his presence. This happens through a subscription "handshake," as shown in Figure 3-2. If the handshake is completed successfully, the result is a bidirectional presence subscription between the two parties. (XMPP servers also add the contact to the user's roster and add the user to the contact's roster during this process, plus manage a state machine of subscription states, but we don't need to worry about those details here; refer to [RFC 3921] for a full description.)

Let's see how the subscription handshake works in practice.

To request someone's presence, you send him a subscription request, which is a `<presence/>` stanza of type `subscribe`:

```
<presence from="alice@wonderland.lit" to="sister@realworld.lit" type="subscribe"/>
```

When the intended recipient receives your presence subscription request, he can either approve it (via a `<presence/>` stanza of type `subscribed`) or deny it (via a `<presence/>` stanza of type `unsubscribed`):

```
<presence from="sister@realworld.lit" to="alice@wonderland.lit" type="subscribed"/>
```

As you might imagine, to create a bidirectional presence subscription, the person who approved the original subscription request needs to send a subscription request of his own:

```
<presence from="sister@realworld.lit" to="alice@wonderland.lit" type="subscribe"/>
```

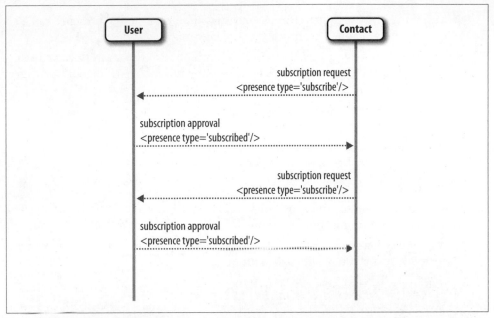

Figure 3-2. A bidirectional subscription handshake; after the contact subscribed to the user's presence, the user in turn subscribes to the contact's presence

Typically, your client will auto-reply at this point, rather than asking you to manually approve the reverse request:

```
<presence from="alice@wonderland.lit" to="sister@realworld.lit" type="subscribed"/>
```

Once you are subscribed to another person's presence, you will automatically be notified when the other party's network or communications availability changes. This presence notification takes the form of a `<presence/>` stanza with no `type` attribute (i.e., implicitly indicating availability):

```
<presence from="alice@wonderland.lit/rabbithole" to="sister@realworld.lit">
  <show>xa</show>
  <status>down the rabbit hole!</status>
</presence>
```

The next section describes how that happens.

How Presence Is Propagated

Now that you and your contact are subscribed to each other, how does presence information flow between the two of you? Here is a brief overview:

1. You negotiate an XML stream with your server (see Chapter 12).
2. You send an initial presence stanza to your server:

```
<presence/>❶
```

❶ Yes, this is the smallest XMPP stanza you will ever see! Initial presence can also include more detailed availability status information, as described next.

3. Your server checks your roster and sends a presence notification to each person who is subscribed to you, making sure to add the full JabberID of your connected resource as the from address:

```
<presence from="alice@wonderland.lit/rabbithole"
          to="sister@realworld.lit"/>

<presence from="alice@wonderland.lit/rabbithole"
          to="madhatter@wonderland.lit"/>

[etc.]
```

4. Now, everyone who is subscribed to your presence knows that you are online and available for communication. But how do *you* know if *they* are online?

Here, your server once again comes to the rescue, because it sends a *presence probe* to everyone you're subscribed to:

```
<presence from="alice@wonderland.lit/rabbithole"
          to="sister@realworld.lit"
          type="probe"/>

<presence from="alice@wonderland.lit/rabbithole"
          to="madhatter@wonderland.lit"
          type="probe"/>

[etc.]
```

5. Once your contacts' servers receive the probes, they check permissions according to their records. If you are allowed to see your contacts' presence, you will receive at least one presence notification from each of your contacts who is online, and often a notification if your contact is offline, including information about when her last presence notification was sent:

```
<presence from="sister@realworld.lit/home"
          to="alice@wonderland.lit/rabbithole"
          type="unavailable">
  <delay xmlns="urn:xmpp:delay"
         stamp="2008-11-26T15:59:09Z"/>❶
</presence>

<presence from="madhatter@wonderland.lit/foo"
          to="alice@wonderland.lit/rabbithole"/>

<presence from="madhatter@wonderland.lit/bar"
          to="alice@wonderland.lit/rabbithole"/>

[etc.]
```

❶ The <delay/> element is added by the contact's server, and the UTC timestamp is the time when the presence stanza was sent by the contact (in this case, when the contact went offline).

Note that you might receive more than one presence stanza, because any given contact might have multiple connected resources. (Look closely at the presence notifications received from the Mad Hatter in the previous example.)

Do You Always Receive Unavailable Presence?

Some server implementations do not return an unavailable presence notification in response to a presence probe; instead, they simply ignore the presence probe, on the theory that if the probing entity does not receive any presence notification, it will assume that the probed entity is *not* online.

Availability Status

So far, our examples of presence notification stanzas have been extremely simple (either available or unavailable). But a presence stanza can contain more information than basic on-off network availability. There are two primary presence elements that express more detailed information: the <show/> element and the <status/> element.

The <show/> element is limited to four predefined values, which provide insights into a human user's availability for and interest in communication (these are not shown directly to end users but are used to provide availability hints in a user interface):

chat
> Announces that you are available for, and actively seeking, conversation (perhaps you're feeling especially sociable).

away
> Indicates that you are gone from your IM client, computer, or device for a short period of time; this state is often triggered without human intervention through a feature known as *auto-away*, commonly found in many IM clients.

xa
> Indicates that you are gone for a longer period of time (xa is shorthand for "eX-tended Away"); your IM client can also automatically generate this state.

dnd
> Announces that you are busy and don't want to be interrupted right now (dnd is shorthand for "do not disturb").

Furthermore, the <status/> element enables a user to specify some free-form, human-readable text that describes the user's availability in more detail. For example, a user might combine a <show/> value of away with a <status/> value of "Having tea with the White Rabbit," or a <show/> value of dnd with a <status/> value of "On a deadline."

The `<show/>` and `<status/>` elements are not limited to human users. They could also be used by automated processes; for example, a particular unit in a computing farm could be dnd if it cannot accept any new jobs at the moment. However, for more sophisticated handling of presence from automated entities, it would probably be preferable to define a custom presence extension rather than overloading existing text values.

Typically, these elements are used to send updated availability information during the life of a user's presence session, as in the following example:

```
<presence>
  <show>away</show>
  <status>Having a spot of tea</status>
</presence>
```

Just as with the initial presence notification, subsequent presence updates are also broadcast by the sender's server to everyone who is subscribed to the user's presence. If the presence subscription is bidirectional, the user's server will often send the subsequent notifications only to contacts who are online. This optimization helps to reduce traffic, since presence uses a great deal of bandwidth in a real-time communications system.

Presence Priorities

The presence stanza can include one more optional element: `<priority/>`. Unlike many other IM systems, XMPP allows you to connect multiple devices or clients to the same account at the same time. This introduces interesting possibilities for inter-device communication (e.g., you could control a set-top box at home from your computer at the office). However, it also introduces the need to differentiate between those devices. For addressing purposes, this is done through the resource portion of a JabberID, such as me@myserver.tld/TV as opposed to me@myserver.tld/office. (XMPP developers usually refer to a JID of the form user@domain.tld as a *bare JID* and a JID of the form user@domain.tld/resource as a *full JID*.) For presence purposes, each connected resource can specify a priority, in the range from −127 to +128. A higher-priority resource is more likely to receive a message sent to the account's bare JID. A resource with a negative priority will never receive such a message (although it will receive a message sent directly to that resource). The latter is useful for network-enabling a device that doesn't intercept human-oriented chat messages.

```
<presence from="me@myserver.tld/office">
  <priority>7</priority>
</presence>

<presence from="me@myserver.tld/TV">
  <priority>-1</priority>
</presence>
```

Directed Presence

The presence notifications we've looked at so far have been *broadcast*—that is, they are sent to everyone in your roster (you indicate that you want a presence notification to be broadcast by leaving off the to address). But what if you want to send presence to someone who is not in your roster? Perhaps you want to chat with someone for a little while but don't want to add that person to your roster and therefore share presence on a permanent basis. In this case, you can send *directed presence* to the other person, i.e., presence that has a to address.

Consider what happens when Alice goes down the rabbit hole and meets the White Rabbit. Because the rabbit isn't in her roster, she sends a message but also sends directed presence:

```
<message from="alice@wonderland.lit/rabbithole"
         to="whiterabbit@wonderland.lit"
         type="chat">
  <body>If you please, sir--</body>
</message>

<presence from="alice@wonderland.lit/rabbithole"
          to="whiterabbit@wonderland.lit"/>
```

The White Rabbit is too frightened to reply, but his IM client at least sends directed presence back to Alice:

```
<presence from="whiterabbit@wonderland.lit/mobile"
          to="alice@wonderland.lit/rabbithole"
          type="unavailable"/>
```

This kind of temporary presence sharing without a long-term subscription is a best practice for brief interactions over the network. And as we'll see in Chapter 4, directed presence is also used to join and leave multi-user chat rooms (another form of temporary interaction).

Going Offline

When you're tired of real-time interactions or just need to disconnect from the network, you can easily go offline by telling your server that you are now unavailable:

```
<presence type="unavailable"/>❶
```

❶ There is no presence type of available, because presence implicitly describes network availability (i.e., if there is no type attribute, then the entity is assumed to be available).

Going offline has several implications:

- Your server broadcasts your unavailable notification to everyone in your roster.

- Your server also broadcasts your unavailable notification to all the entities to which you've sent directed presence (see the earlier example of the White Rabbit).

- If you have no other online resources, when your contacts' servers receive the unavailable notification, they will probably stop sending presence notifications to you.

- If you have no other online resources, your server will stop sending presence subscription requests to you, instead storing them up for delivery the next time you are online.

- If you have no other online resources, your server will stop sending messages to you, instead storing them up for delivery the next time you are online (we describe these "offline messages" more fully in Chapter 4).

Naturally, if you have other online resources, your server will continue to send messages and presence subscription requests to you, but the *presence session* for your newly offline resource is now over.

Rich Presence

The presence stanza provides a convenient and relatively efficient method for publishing information about a user to interested others. In the past, enterprising developers of XMPP clients have used this presence "transport" to push out information about much more than network availability. For example, why not use presence stanzas to advertise what music you're listening to?

```
<presence>
  <status>Pink Floyd - Dogs</status>
</presence>
```

This kind of information is typically called *rich presence* or *extended presence*, and can include a very wide range of transient data: your current mood or activity, the music you listen to, the videos you watch, the chat rooms or web pages you visit, the games you play, your physical location, etc.

There are several problems with putting all these payloads inside presence stanzas:

- It's not very XML-friendly to put all of this information into the `<status/>` element as an unstructured text string.

- Sending all of this information in presence will result in a lot more presence stanzas, and those stanzas will probably be bigger (perhaps *much* bigger) than existing presence stanzas. Given that presence already uses far more bandwidth in XMPP than messaging does, piling on more and bigger presence stanzas could seriously degrade network performance.

- Not everyone in your roster will be interested in things like the music you listen to, so why send them that information?

- You might want to restrict who can know your physical location or other sensitive information to a special sub-group of those who can know your network availability. *Publish-Subscribe* [XEP-0060] and the *Personal Eventing Protocol* [XEP-0163] provide this kind of access control, but basic presence is broadcast to everyone in your roster.

Because of considerations like these, rich presence is typically not sent via the presence transport, but instead uses a specialized publish-subscribe method that we describe in Chapter 8.

Presence and Rosters

Figure 3-1 shows that presence information is usually displayed as one aspect of a user's roster. By retrieving the user's roster when the user logs in, an IM client is able to integrate the presence data it receives into a useful, familiar interface.

Your roster is managed by your client, but it is stored on your "home" server. This enables you to connect from anywhere and still retrieve your contact list, which your client typically does when you start your session by sending an IQ-get to the server:

```
<iq from="alice@wonderland.lit/rabbithole"❶
    id="jh2gs675"
    to="alice@wonderland.lit"❷
    type="get">
  <query xmlns="jabber:iq:roster"/>
</iq>
```

❶ The server ignores the `from` address on the roster request, because it always delivers the roster to the entity that requested it (for security reasons, you can't request someone else's roster).

❷ The `to` address on the roster request is the bare JID of the user. This means that the server handles the request on behalf of the user's account. Equivalently, the sender could include no `to` address at all, since no `to` address is treated the same as a `to` address of the sending user. ([RFC 3921] recommends including no `to` address, and [rfc3921bis] recommends including it, but the result is the same.)

The user's server then retrieves the user's roster from a server-side data storage mechanism and returns it to the resource that made the request:

```
<iq from="alice@wonderland.lit"
    id="jh2gs675"
    to="alice@wonderland.lit/rabbithole"
    type="result">
  <query xmlns="jabber:iq:roster">
    <item jid="whiterabbit@wonderland.lit"/>
    <item jid="lory@wonderland.lit"/>
    <item jid="mouse@wonderland.lit"/>
    <item jid="queen@wonderland.lit"/>
    <item jid="sister@realworld.lit"/>
```

```
            </query>
        </iq>
```

Each item in your roster has a JabberID associated with it, which acts as the "key" to storing and identifying the item. Each item has a particular presence subscription state that reflects the presence authorizations we've already looked at, and can also specify a user-friendly name. Therefore, the data returned by the server will in fact be a little more complete:

```
<iq from="alice@wonderland.lit"
    id="jh2gs675"
    to="alice@wonderland.lit/rabbithole"
    type="result">
  <query xmlns="jabber:iq:roster">
    <item jid="whiterabbit@wonderland.lit"
          name="The White Rabbit"
          subscription="none"/>
    <item jid="lory@wonderland.lit"
          name="The Lory"
          subscription="to"/>
    <item jid="mouse@wonderland.lit"
          name="The Mouse"
          subscription="both"/>
    <item jid="queen@wonderland.lit"
          name="Her Royal Highness"
          subscription="from"/>
    <item jid="sister@realworld.lit"
          name="Sis"
          subscription="both"/>
  </query>
</iq>
```

The roster can be used not only to store a flat list of contacts, but also to *group* into various categories. Because these roster groups are not exclusive (a bot could also be a friend—though that would be rather sad), it's better to think of them as flexible tags instead of exclusive buckets. Roster groups become increasingly important in organizing your contact list as you befriend more and more people on the XMPP network (the average roster size for us is 800 and rising!). Therefore, the data returned by the server will in fact be even more complete:

```
<iq from="alice@wonderland.lit"
    id="jh2gs675"
    to="alice@wonderland.lit/rabbithole"
    type="result">
  <query xmlns="jabber:iq:roster">
    <item jid="whiterabbit@wonderland.lit"
          name="The White Rabbit"
          subscription="none">
      <group>Wonderlanders</group>
    </item>
    <item jid="lory@wonderland.lit"
          name="The Lory"
          subscription="to">
      <group>Wonderlanders</group>
```

```
        </item>
        <item jid="mouse@wonderland.lit"
              name="The Mouse"
              subscription="both">
          <group>Wonderlanders</group>
        </item>
        <item jid="queen@wonderland.lit"
              name="Her Royal Highness"
              subscription="from">
          <group>Nobility</group>
        </item>
        <item jid="sister@realworld.lit"
              name="Sis"
              subscription="both">
          <group>Family</group>
        </item>
      </query>
    </iq>
```

Roster groups can be edited through the roster management protocol, via the
element:

```
    <iq id="u4tsf153" type="set">
      <query xmlns="jabber:iq:roster">
        <item jid="mapbot@wonderland.lit">
          <group>Bots</group>
        </item>
      </query>
    </iq>
```

When one of your connected clients modifies the roster (e.g., by adding a new contact
or changing the group for a particular item), the server then pushes that change to all
of your connected clients by sending an IQ-set containing only that item to each resource. This IQ-set, called a *roster push*, enables all of the resources to remain
synchronized:

```
    <iq from="alice@wonderland.lit"
        id="vzx274k7"
        to="alice@wonderland.lit/rabbithole"
        type="set">
      <query xmlns="jabber:iq:roster">
        <item jid="mapbot@wonderland.lit">
          <group>Bots</group>
        </item>
      </query>
    </iq>
```

Getting Pushy

Because the server always pushes a roster change to a connected client, the client can simply wait for and process roster pushes. This is easier than closely monitoring incoming presence stanzas of type subscribed, unsubscribe, and unsubscribed. It also removes the need to perform a roster set before sending the presence subscription request (if the contact doesn't exist or denies the request, then you would need to remove the roster item, whereas the server will automatically perform this cleanup). Thus the use of roster pushes helps to simplify the task of writing an XMPP client; this is consistent with the early Jabber philosophy of "simple clients, complex servers," as defined in the *Protocol Design Guidelines* [XEP-0134] and described further in Chapter 12.

Finally, in enterprise and school settings, it's not uncommon for parts of your contact list to be centrally managed by appropriate IT staff, in which case, they might be pulled straight out of an LDAP database or other backend storage location (e.g., when Bob in the QA department is fired or when Alice drops the symbolic logic course, they will automatically disappear from the relevant contact list group). However, methods for doing so are not yet part of the standard roster functionality and tend to be specific to particular XMPP server implementations, so talk with the developers of your favorite open source project or commercial product.

Using Presence

In this chapter, we looked at several core features of XMPP: presence subscriptions (which are typically bidirectional); presence notifications, such as available, away, and unavailable; and rosters, including roster groups.

These features provide a few building blocks for XMPP applications, so let's look at how they are used higher up in the XMPP protocol stack, and how you might be able to use them, too.

Presence-Based Routing

Once you know that someone or something is online, and perhaps know the priorities of its resources, you can make some decisions about whether and how to deliver information to that entity.

Some of these decisions are made by the server that handles traffic on behalf of an account. So, to use our example of a set-top box and an office computer, a message sent to me@myserver.tld typically would be delivered to the office resource but not the TV resource (although some XMPP servers can be configured to deliver the message to all resources, or at least to all resources with non-negative priority).

However, the sender can also make messaging decisions based on presence data. Consider a workflow application, in which five different people have authority to approve a given purchase order. If two of them are offline, one of them has only a resource with negative priority, one of them has a resource with positive priority that is dnd, and the last one has a resource with positive priority and no <show/> value, it might make sense to send the approval form to both of the positive resources but not to the others. Such presence-based messaging determinations can expedite decision-making and application processing. (Often such addressing choices will also incorporate information about the capabilities of each resource, as we discuss in Chapter 5.)

Access Control

In our discussion of rich presence, we observed that basic presence is an all-or-nothing affair (either someone receives your presence information or they don't). However, sometimes you want more granular control over who can chat with you or who can receive certain kinds of information (e.g., your geolocation). All of these matters essentially boil down to access control. Although basic presence publishing and roster data do not by themselves provide such access control methods, they can be used to build such methods. In particular, the communications-blocking techniques discussed in Chapter 4 makes use of information about both presence subscriptions and roster groups to make access control decisions. The same is true of the *Personal Eventing Protocol*, or PEP [XEP-0163], which is used to publish rich presence data, as described in Chapter 8.

Presence As a Transport

XMPP developers try to resist the temptation to push out arbitrary information in presence stanzas. As mentioned earlier, even though presence stanzas tend to be small, there are a lot of them, and so presence tends to be the most bandwidth-intensive aspect of XMPP (much more so than messaging). Therefore, it is best to keep presence stanzas small and send them only when the client generates information that is relevant to communication.

Terms like "small" and "relevant" are, unfortunately, vague. Couldn't the tune I'm listening to be relevant to communication (e.g., in an online music service)? Maybe. But XMPP developers tend to be conservative about the payloads they include in a presence stanza.

One exception is capabilities information—data about what XMPP features and extensions a device supports. Because there are a lot of XMPP features and extensions, and because users want to know when, for example, a friend has plugged in a video camera and can now engage in a video chat, it's helpful to dynamically publish capabilities data in presence. We discuss this usage in depth in Chapter 5.

Summary

Presence lies at the core of many uses of XMPP. Indeed, the fact that your XMPP server knows when you are online (and with which devices) is what makes real-time communication possible, whether it is instant messaging, multi-user chat, just-in-time notifications, or voice and video chat. As we've seen, your presence is broadcast only to other people or entities you have *authorized* through subscription requests that you approve. These subscription states are stored on the server in your roster, a presence-enabled contact list that is the central focus of instant messaging applications. This chapter also provided an overview of specific availability states, presence priorities, directed presence, and how presence is propagated on the network. In upcoming chapters, we will see how presence is used to interact with XMPP chat rooms; dynamically advertise device capabilities; and enable advanced personal eventing and "lifestreaming" applications, such as microblogging, location sharing, and social music services.

CHAPTER 4

Instant Messaging

I Think, Therefore IM

The initial goal of the early Jabber project, well before the protocol was named XMPP, was to create an open *Instant Messaging* (IM) platform. Although IM is often thought of as person-to-person chat, at its core it really provides the ability to quickly route messages from one place to another over the network (no matter who or what the intended recipient is). For this reason, XMPP servers are optimized for handling large numbers of relatively small messages with very little latency. When you are exchanging instant messages, you don't want to experience any delivery delays (which can be almost as annoying in IM as they are on the phone).

In XMPP, messages are delivered as fast as possible over the network. Let's say that Alice sends a message from her new account on the wonderland.lit server to her sister on the realworld.lit server. Her client effectively "uploads" the message to wonderland.lit by pushing a message stanza over a client-to-server XML stream. The wonderland.lit server then stamps a from address on the stanza and checks the to address in order to see how the stanza needs to be handled (without performing any deep packet inspection or XML parsing, since that would eat into the delivery time). Seeing that the message stanza is bound for the realworld.lit server, the wonderland.lit server then immediately routes the message to realworld.lit over a server-to-server XML stream (with no intermediate hops). Upon receiving the message stanza, the realworld.lit server checks to see whether Alice's sister is online; if so, the server immediately delivers the message to one or more of her online devices over a server-to-client XML stream (without storing it or otherwise performing much processing on it). As a result, the message is delivered very quickly from Alice to her sister.

These design decisions have important implications. First and foremost, the clients and servers need to be event-driven and ready to take appropriate action whenever they receive an incoming stanza. XMPP servers don't have the luxury of storing a message and waiting for a client to poll for it; instead, they deliver the message as soon as they receive it. Second, all entities (but especially the servers) need to be presence-aware, since it is the concept of being online that makes rapid delivery possible in the crucial "last mile" between the recipient's server and the recipient's device(s). Third, fast and accurate handling of DNS lookups, domain name resolution, long-lived TCP connections, connectivity outages, and network congestion is critical to the success of the overall system.

Several types of XMPP messages exist, fundamentally differentiated by the value of the `type` attribute:

normal
> This message type is delivered immediately or stored offline by the server, and handled by the client as a "standalone" message outside of any chat or groupchat session. This is the default message type.

chat
> Messages of type `chat` are sent within a burst of messages called a "chat session," usually over a relatively short period of time. Instant messaging clients show such messages in a one-to-one conversation interface for the two parties.

groupchat
> XMPP servers usually route messages of type `groupchat` to a specialized component or module that hosts multi-user chat rooms, and this component then generates one outbound message for each of the room occupants. (We discuss groupchat messages in Chapter 7.)

headline
> Headline messages usually are not stored offline, because they are temporal in nature. In addition, XMPP servers often send a message of type `headline` to all of the online devices associated with an account (at least those with non-negative `<priority/>` values).

error
> A message of type `error` is sent in response to a previously sent message, to indicate that a problem occurred in relation to the earlier message (the recipient does not exist, message delivery is not possible at the moment, etc.).

Both chat and normal messages are usually handled by the recipient's server in a particular way: if the message is addressed to the bare JID (`user@domain.tld`) of the account, the server immediately delivers the message to the highest-priority resource currently associated with the account. If there is only one online resource, this decision is easy, but if there are multiple online resources, the recipient's server delivers the message to the resource with the largest value for its presence priority. For example, a resource with a presence priority of 7 will receive messages addressed to the bare JID, but another resource with a presence priority of 3 will not. (Resources with negative priority will never receive a message sent to the bare JID, but all resources will receive a message addressed to the full JID of that resource.)

Finally, although XMPP technologies put a premium on near real-time data delivery, almost all XMPP servers include support for "offline messages" if the intended recipient is not online when the server receives a normal or chat message addressed to that

JabberID. These messages are automatically pushed to the recipient's client when the user next logs in. When the recipient's server pushes out the offline message, it also adds a small extension noting when the message was originally received, using the protocol extension defined in *Delayed Delivery* [XEP-0203]. This enables the recipient's client to properly order the messages it receives in a user interface.

Chat Sessions

When two people "IM" with each other, the conversation usually happens in a burst of messages over a short period of time. This pattern mimics real life, where you might chat with someone for 5 or 10 minutes when you meet them on the street or talk on the phone, but not chat with them again for a week or two. In XMPP, we call this kind of burst a *chat session*, and you can see an example of such a session in Figure 4-1.

Figure 4-1. A chat session consists of a "burst" of messages sent over a short period of time

XMPP chat sessions are not formally negotiated but proceed naturally. The entity that initiates the conversation sends a message to the bare JID of the responder, and this message is stamped by the initiator's server with the full JID of the initiator. When the responder sends a reply, it too is stamped by the recipient's server with the full JID of the responder. At this point, the initiator knows the responder's full JID and the responder knows the initiator's full JID, so the parties have "locked in" to each other's XMPP resource identifiers. Each party now addresses stanzas to the full JID of the other party when sending subsequent messages, until and unless receiving a presence change from the other party (which might trigger resending a message to the bare JID).

The features we discuss in the following sections all relate in one way or another to instant messaging, and to chat sessions in particular: chat state notifications tell you whether your conversation partner is actively engaged; XHTML lets you add a bit of dash and style to your messages; vCards enable you to learn something about the people you chat with; and blocking and filtering help you avoid unpleasant conversations with some of the unsavory characters you might meet online.

Are You There? Chat State Notifications

Consider the following IM conversation between you and your nine-year-old daughter:

> You: Hi honey!
>
> *She: Hi*
>
> You: How was school today?
>
> *She: Great*

This is the moment where she starts typing about all the great and exciting things she learned about. Unfortunately, her typing skills aren't at the 80 words per minute you're hitting. While she's composing her answer, you assume that she's not in the mood to talk about school right now, so you continue the conversation:

> You: Did you visit grandma this afternoon? What did she tell you?

Now you're waiting for an answer. In the meantime, your daughter has been typing away about her day at school. After a while, she decides to pause composing her answer to your first question, and looks up from the keyboard she'd been concentrating on for the past few minutes. She now sees that you have already moved on from the previous question, so she's left with the choice to delete everything she wrote so far, send half of the answer she wanted to send and move on, or just continue typing (thus slowing the conversation down even further). She bites the bullet, deletes everything she wrote so far, and moves on:

> *She: Yes, I did*

Now, you're waiting for the second part of the answer as to what grandma told her. After waiting for two minutes, you wonder whether she's just typing slowly, or she just missed the fact that you asked a second question. So, just to be sure, you repeat the question:

> You: And?

It turns out that she started writing the answer, but suddenly had to go downstairs to answer the phone. So, she comes back, and finishes the answer:

> *She: Everything was fine. I have to go do my homework now.*

Since the answer wasn't coming immediately, you decided to do something else while waiting for it. When switching back, you notice that your daughter wants to finish the conversation, so you'll have to say goodbye. Or, wait, maybe she finished it already, and started doing her homework, in which case you don't really want to distract her.

The problem with this (fairly common) scenario is that neither of you know anything about the other person's activity level with regard to the conversation. The exact same conversation over the phone would have been a lot less awkward: it would have been easy to tell whether the other person was answering your question or not, and the sound of a dial tone would leave no doubt that the conversation was actually finished. In order to avoid the inconvenient situations like the preceding conversation, you need the notion of *chat states* in your IM system, as defined in *Chat State Notifications* [XEP-0085].

Chat states describe your involvement with a conversation, which can be one of the following:

Starting
    Someone started a conversation, but you haven't joined in yet.

Active
    You are actively involved in the conversation. You're currently not composing any message, but you are paying close attention.

Composing
    You are actively composing a message.

Paused
    You started composing a message, but stopped composing for some reason.

Inactive
    You haven't contributed to the conversation for some period of time.

Gone
    Your involvement with the conversation has effectively ended (e.g., you have closed the chat window).

During the conversation, your chat state will most likely change: after composing a message while in the `composing` state, you will become `active` while waiting for a reply to your message. However, it does not always make sense to go from one specific state to another one. For example, from composing a message, you can't really become inactive for a long period without pausing for at least a short time. Figure 4-2 shows the possible transitions between chat states.

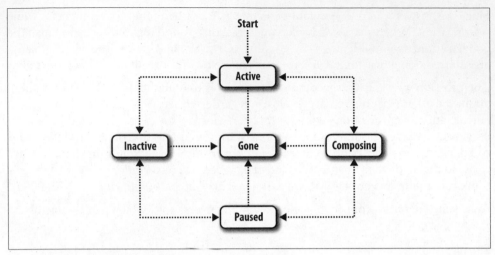

Figure 4-2. The transitions between chat states are well defined

Changing state in a conversation is done by embedding the corresponding chat state element into a message stanza. For example, the mother-daughter conversation would start off like this:

```
<message from="you@yourdomain.tld/work"
         to="daughter@yourdomain.tld"
         type="chat">
  <body>Hi honey!</body>
  <active xmlns="http://jabber.org/protocol/chatstates"/>
</message>
```

By adding the `<active/>` element to your message, you indicate that you are actively engaged with the conversation. Your daughter starts typing her response, so her client sends you a chat state update by adding a `<composing/>` element to an empty message:

```
<message from="daughter@yourdomain.tld/home"
         to="you@yourdomain.tld/work"
         type="chat">
  <composing xmlns="http://jabber.org/protocol/chatstates"/>
</message>
```

Shortly after the notification, the actual message comes in, making her an active participant of the conversation again:

```
<message from="daughter@yourdomain.tld/home"
         to="you@yourdomain.tld/work"
         type="chat">
  <body>Hi</body>
  <active xmlns="http://jabber.org/protocol/chatstates"/>
</message>
```

The conversation goes on for a while, up to the point where you ask her about grandma:

```
<message from="you@yourdomain.tld/work"
         to="daughter@yourdomain.tld/home"
```

```
          type="chat">
  <body>Did you visit grandma this afternoon? What did she tell you?</body>
  <active xmlns="http://jabber.org/protocol/chatstates"/>
</message>

<message from="daughter@yourdomain.tld/home"
         to="you@yourdomain.tld/work"
         type="chat">
  <composing xmlns="http://jabber.org/protocol/chatstates"/>
</message>
```

This is where she suddenly stops typing to go answer the phone, and so after a few seconds, her client notifies you of that fact by sending you a `<paused/>` notification:

```
<message from="daughter@yourdomain.tld/home"
         to="you@yourdomain.tld/work"
         type="chat">
  <paused xmlns="http://jabber.org/protocol/chatstates"/>
</message>
```

After a while, she resumes her answer:

```
<message from="daughter@yourdomain.tld/home"
         to="you@yourdomain.tld/work"
         type="chat">
  <composing xmlns="http://jabber.org/protocol/chatstates"/>
</message>
```

Finally, skipping to the end of the conversation, she sends her goodbye and closes her chat window:

```
<message from="daughter@yourdomain.tld/home"
         to="you@yourdomain.tld/work"
         type="chat">
  <body>Everything was fine. I have to go do my homework now.</body>
  <active xmlns="http://jabber.org/protocol/chatstates"/>
</message>

<message from="daughter@yourdomain.tld/home"
         to="you@yourdomain.tld/work"
         type="chat">
  <gone xmlns="http://jabber.org/protocol/chatstates"/>
</message> s
```

The person you are communicating with may not always be interested in receiving notifications about your chat state. For example, when she is using her mobile phone for IM, she would rather save on the usage of the limited network capacity, at the price of not being able to see when you are typing. In order to discover whether the other party is interested in your chat state, you start the conversation as usual, by adding an `<active/>` element to your message. If the reply comes back without any chat state information, you have to assume that the other person either does not know how to handle chat state updates, or does not want to receive them. From then on, you both continue the conversation, without adding any chat state information to your subsequent messages. (Naturally, if you know that the other party does not support the chat states protocol, you would leave off the notifications entirely. We talk about ways to discover support for various protocol extensions in Chapter 5.)

Another reason why you may not want to send chat state notifications is privacy. You may not want other people to know when you are physically using your IM client (information that chat state notifications would reveal). However, it does not always have to be as drastic as disabling all types of notifications. You could configure your client to send only basic chat state information (i.e., whether you are active or composing), and not send any information about more fine-grained states, such as paused, inactive, or gone. This basic information would only reveal whether you started composing an answer or not, and leave out any hints to whether you physically went away from your IM client, or reconsidered talking and closed the conversation.

So far, we have talked about chat state notifications only in the context of one-to-one conversations. To a certain degree, chat state notifications can be useful inside multiparty chats as well (we talk about groupchat in Chapter 7). However, note that if the number of participants starts growing, the total number of notifications sent will increase drastically as well.

Looks Matter: Formatted Messages

Some folks think plain-text messages are boring. For example, let's say you are really excited about a new movie that you just watched, so you send a message to your friend:

> You: I love this movie I saw last night, it's awesome!

If you said that over the phone or in person, you'd probably emphasize some of the words:

> You: I *love* this movie I saw last night, it's **awesome**!

One way to represent that kind of emphasis is by using some special characters in the plain text:

> You: I /love/ this movie I saw last night, it's *awesome*!

That's a bit of a kludge, though. Thankfully, XMPP enables you to customize the look or presentation of messages, using a subset of HTML as defined in *XHTML-IM* [XEP-0071]:

```
<message from="you@yourdomain.tld/home"
         to="friend@theirdomain.tld"
         type="chat">
  <body>I love this movie I saw last night, it's awesome!</body>
  <html xmlns="http://jabber.org/protocol/xhtml-im">
    <body xmlns="http://www.w3.org/1999/xhtml">
      <p>
        I <em>love</em>, this new movie I saw last night,
        it's <strong>awesome</strong>!
      </p>
    </body>
```

```
    </html>
  </message>
```

As you can see, your client sends the plain-text message body *plus* the marked-up version. That way, if your friend is using a client that doesn't understand XHTML markup, the key content of the message still gets through.

Although we formatted the italics and bold text using the XHTML `<strong/>` and `<em/>` elements, you can also format text using Cascading Style Sheets (CSS). This enables you to include a number of popular stylistic formats, including colors, font families, text sizes, font weights (e.g., bold) and styles (e.g., italic), margins, text alignment (e.g., center), and text decoration (e.g., underline).

The XHTML-IM subset also provides support for some of the core HTML presentation features, including numbered and unordered lists, hypertext links, and images.

Missing from that list are more advanced HTML features such as tables and media objects, as well as anything that normally goes in the `<HEAD>` tag of an HTML document, such as scripts. This is intentional, because some of these features could be used to include malicious code (yes, the designers of XMPP are always thinking hard about security!). Instead, XHTML-IM is focused on a simple subset of HTML features that can be used for lightweight presentation in the context of rapid-fire chat conversations. Even so, XMPP clients should exercise caution about receiving XHTML-formatted messages from unknown entities, since even the inclusion of image references could introduce security vulnerabilities. One such preventive measure is to accept XHTML-IM formatting only from people in your roster.

Who Are You? vCards

Sometimes you want to find out more information about the people you chat with. Perhaps someone has sent you a message out of the blue or asked to subscribe to your presence information. Before you continue the conversation or approve the subscription request, you wonder to yourself: just who *is* this person?

Don't worry, XMPP has you covered. The extension we're interested in here is called *vCard-temp* [XEP-0054], and enables you to publish a kind of electronic business card called a vCard, and to retrieve vCards that other people have published.

The vCard standard (originally published in *vCard MIME Directory Profile* [RFC 2426]) defines many of the basic data fields you might want to advertise, including your name, nickname, address, phone and fax number, company affiliation, email address, birthday, a pointer to your website, a photo of you, and even your PGP key. You don't have to publish any of that information if you don't want to, but doing so enables people to find out more about you, which can grease the wheels of communication.

So let's say that Alice in Wonderland sends an unsolicited message to a poor, hapless mouse:

```
<message from="alice@wonderland.lit/pda"
         to="mouse@wonderland.lit">
  <body>O Mouse, do you know the way out of this pool?</body>
</message>
```

Before replying, the mouse might check Alice's vCard by sending an IQ-get to her JabberID:

```
<iq from="mouse@wonderland.lit/pool"
    id="pw91nf84"
    to="alice@wonderland.lit"
    type="get">
  <vCard xmlns="vcard-temp"/>
</iq>
```

Because the request was sent to Alice's bare JID, Alice's server replies on her behalf:

```
<iq from="alice@wonderland.lit"
    id="pw91nf84"
    to="mouse@wonderland.lit/pool"
    type="result">
  <vCard xmlns="vcard-temp">
    <N>
      <GIVEN>Alice</GIVEN>
    </N>
    <URL>http://wonderland.lit/~alice/</URL>
    <PHOTO>
      <EXTVAL>http://www.cs.cmu.edu/~rgs/alice03a.gif</EXTVAL>
    </PHOTO>
  </vCard>
</iq>
```

As a result, the mouse can at least visit Alice's website and view a picture of her before continuing the chat. Naturally, all of the data in a vCard can be faked, so it pays to take any given vCard result with a grain of salt. But in many situations, it's better than nothing!

To update your vCard, send an IQ-set to your server. Here Alice adds an email address and uploads the entire vCard to her server (no, it's not possible to upload only a "diff," as the vCard-temp specification does not provide for that feature):

```
<iq from="alice@wonderland.lit/pda"
    id="w0s1nd97"
    to="alice@wonderland.lit"
    type="set">
  <vCard xmlns="vcard-temp">
    <N>
      <GIVEN>Alice</GIVEN>
    </N>
    <URL>http://wonderland.lit/~alice/</URL>
    <PHOTO>
      <EXTVAL>http://www.cs.cmu.edu/~rgs/alice03a.gif</EXTVAL>
    </PHOTO>
    <EMAIL><USERID>alice@wonderland.lit</USERID></EMAIL>
  </vCard>
</iq>
```

Is vCard Really "temp"?

The vCard format used by the early Jabber developers was derived from an experimental XML representation of the official vCard format. Recently, the IETF has begun work on a more modern and stable approach to XML vCards, and it is possible that the XMPP community will adopt that standard instead of using vCard-temp (which has been "temp" since 1999!).

Talk to the Hand: Blocking and Filtering Communication

Lots of people use XMPP-based IM services (probably over 50 million of them, although we have no way of knowing, because XMPP is a distributed, decentralized technology). But you might not want to chat with them all. In fact, you might want to actively block a certain person from chatting with you— say, your old boss, a childhood enemy, or that weird guy you met in a chat room last week.

Because the XMPP developers care about privacy, they have defined an extension for communications blocking (defined in *Privacy Lists* [XEP-0016]), as well as a stripped-down interface to privacy lists (defined in *Simple Communications Blocking* [XEP 0191]).

First we'll look at simple communications blocking because it's, well, simple

Blocking: The Simple Approach

Let's say you want to block communications from your old boss at BigCompany.com. It's easy enough to do if your server supports simple communications blocking—just send an appropriate IQ-set:

```
<iq from="you@yourdomain.tld/newjob"
    id="yu4er81v"
    to="you@yourdomain.tld"
    type="set">
  <block xmlns="urn:xmpp:blocking">
    <item jid="boss@bigcompany.com"/>
  </block>
</iq>
```

Now, what does blocking boss@bigcompany.com mean exactly?

First of all, you want to appear offline to your old boss. When you add the block rule for that JabberID, your server sends out an unavailable presence packet, so that your old boss sees you go offline. From then on, whenever you update your presence (e.g., by coming online), the associated presence stanzas will not be sent to boss@bigcompany.com (as far as he is concerned, it's as if you never log in anymore).

Second, your server needs to make sure that your old boss cannot find out that you are online in any other way. This means that your server will respond to every incoming IQ-get or IQ-set with a `<service-unavailable/>` error, ignore any incoming

`<message/>` message (or, again, return a `<service-unavailable/>` error), and drop any incoming `<presence/>` stanza.

Finally, your server needs to prevent you from doing something daft, like sending a message or IQ request to your old boss, so it will reply to any outbound stanza intended for `boss@bigcompany.com` with a `<not-acceptable/>` error.

You can also block entire domains. Let's say that you have started to receive unsolicited messages from a rogue server on the XMPP network (perhaps `spammers.lit`). You can block messages from any JabberID at that domain by setting another block rule:

```
<iq from="you@yourdomain.tld/newjob"
    id="i3s91xc3"
    to="you@yourdomain.tld"
    type="set">
  <block xmlns="urn:xmpp:blocking">
    <item jid="spammers.lit"/>
  </block>
</iq>
```

Now when you retrieve your "block list," you will see two items:

```
<iq from="you@yourdomain.tld/newjob"
    id="92h1nv8f"
    to="you@yourdomain.tld"
    type="get">
  <blocklist xmlns="urn:xmpp:blocking"/>
</iq>
```

```
<iq from="you@yourdomain.tld"
    id="92h1nv8f"
    to="you@yourdomain.tld/newjob"
    type="result">
  <blocklist xmlns="urn:xmpp:blocking">
    <item jid="boss@bigcompany.com"/>
    <item jid="spammers.lit"/>
  </blocklist>
</iq>
```

In simple communications blocking, it is also straightforward to unblock someone. Simply send an IQ-set with the JabberID contained in an `<unblock/>` element instead of a `<block/>` element:

```
<iq from="you@yourdomain.tld/newjob"
    id="ng23h57w"
    to="you@yourdomain.tld"
    type="set">
  <unblock xmlns="urn:xmpp:blocking">
    <item jid="boss@bigcompany.com"/>
  </unblock>
</iq>
```

Advanced Blocking and Filtering

Sometimes you want to have more control over blocking and filtering rules than simple communications blocking will give you. For example, when you are using your mobile phone to log into your IM server, you don't want to receive status updates from your 200 coworkers, as this would clog up your very limited bandwidth. On the other hand, you *do* want to receive the occasional messages they send you. Moreover, you also don't want to block all incoming presence packets, as you want to know which members of your family are online, so you can chat with them before leaving on an overseas trip. Thus you need a finer-grained protocol for controlling your traffic filtering rules.

Here, again, XMPP comes to the rescue. Whereas simple communications blocking used a basic block list, the full-featured privacy protocol uses a more advanced *privacy list*. A privacy list is a list of rules that are matched against all traffic, both incoming and outgoing. If one of the rules matches an outgoing packet, the associated action of the rule is applied on the packet. For example, consider the following privacy list:

```
<list name="mylist">
  <item type="jid" value="boss@bigcompany.com" action="deny" order="1">
    <iq/>
    <message/>
    <presence-out/>
  </item>
  <item type="group" value="Work" action="deny" order="2">
    <presence-in/>
  </item>
  <item action="allow" order="3"/>
</list>
```

Let's see how to parse this into plain English:

- An incoming message from boss@bigcompany.com would match the first rule. Therefore, if your server receives an IQ or message stanza from your old boss, it will discard the stanza or return an error.

- However, if your server receives a presence stanza from your old boss, that stanza is not matched by the first privacy rule, so your server proceeds to the next rule. Since you don't work with your old boss anymore, he is not in the "Work" group of your roster. Therefore, your server proceeds to the next (and, in this case, final rule). Lo and behold, the inbound presence stanza matches the final rule, so your server allows the stanza through. Now you can see when your old boss is online, but he can't communicate with you!

The possible combinations of particular privacy rules provide a powerful tool for allowing and blocking communication, because your privacy list can include an unlimited number of privacy rules in any specified order (each identified by an <item/> element, as shown earlier). The *action* for any given rule is either allow or deny, and the *rule type* processes stanzas based on a specific or wildcard JabberID, on a roster group name, or on a presence subscription state. Finally, stanzas are matched based on whether they are messages, inbound presence notifications (i.e., not including subscription-related presence stanzas), outbound presence notifications, IQs, or all stanzas (including subscription-related stanzas). In practice, these more advanced block and allow methods provide basic filtering instead of just simple blocking (although at the price of greater complexity).

More Messaging Extensions

This chapter provided an overview of various messaging-related extensions in XMPP. But not all of them! Here is a quick look at a few more. Refer to the specifications for all the details, and make sure you check for support in your favorite client, server, or library, because some of these are not yet widely implemented:

- *Extended Stanza Addressing* [XEP-0033] lets you send a single message to multiple recipients at the same time, without using a dedicated chat room.

- *Advanced Message Processing* [XEP-0079] provides a way to control the delivery of a message; examples include message expiration and preventing messages from being stored offline for later delivery.

- *Message Receipts* [XEP-0184] do just what you would expect it to do based on the title: they provide an end-to-end mechanism for determining whether the intended recipient has indeed received a message (by contrast, Advanced Message Processing notifications are generated by servers, not clients).

- *Message Archiving* [XEP-0136] defines a technology for storing messages on your server instead of archiving them to your local machine. There are many scenarios in which this is helpful: perhaps you are using a web client that does not have local storage, the device you are using (e.g., a PDA or mobile phone) has limited storage capacity, or you move between different devices quite a bit and you want all of your message history in one place.

Summary

Instant messaging is not only the most visible application of the ability to quickly route data from one point to another, but it is also the most popular (with over 50 million XMPP users worldwide). IM interactions usually take the form of chat sessions: short bursts of messages exchanged between two parties. The XMPP extension for chat state notifications provides support for chat sessions by communicating up-to-date information about the involvement of one's conversation partner in the discussion. In XMPP, XHTML is used to provide user-friendly formatting, such as bold, italics, and colored text. Furthermore, vCards enable you to find out more about people you might want to chat with, and privacy lists can prevent unwanted communication from other entities. The XMPP developer community continues to work XMPP extensions that will optimize the IM experience.

CHAPTER 5

Discovering the World

Throughout this book, we talk about many varieties of XMPP *entities*: servers, clients, bots, chat rooms, pubsub nodes, etc. On the public XMPP network, all of these entities come in multiple flavors. For instance, there are at least half a dozen popular XMPP server implementations, and many more XMPP clients for just about every device and operating system. Furthermore, there are hundreds of possible features that an XMPP entity can support, including standardized protocols (to which the XMPP Standards Foundation is always adding), user-configurable options, client plug-ins, server modules, and more. And let's not forget that many of these software projects are quite active, frequently releasing updated versions.

This diversity is tremendously powerful, but it raises two important questions:

1. How can you learn what entities are out there on the network?
2. Once you find them, how can you determine which XMPP features they support?

To answer these questions, you need *service discovery* (often called "disco" by XMPP developers).

When might you want to use service discovery? You might be learning a foreign language, so you want to find a chat room where you can practice; you might be interested in using a specific publish-subscribe mechanism, so you want to discover a pubsub service where that mechanism is supported; you might like to figure out whether one of your friends or colleagues has video chat capabilities; you might even want to announce to all your contacts that you're interested in finding out what music they're listening to. All of these tasks (and more) can be completed using the techniques discussed in this chapter.

Items and Info

The XMPP service discovery protocol defined in [XEP-0030] provides two basic discovery methods. The first, known as `disco#items`, enables you to discover entities. The second, known as `disco#info`, enables you to discover which features a given entity supports. Let's look at each of these in turn.

It does you no good to discover features unless you have first discovered some entities. A client always knows about at least one entity: the server it connects to. And since XMPP servers typically host additional entities such as pubsub topics and multi-user chat rooms, clients often need to discover those additional entities. Such discovery happens using the `disco#items` half of the XMPP service discovery protocol by sending an IQ-get to the server. Here, the Mad Hatter queries the `wonderland.lit` server:

```
<iq from="hatter@wonderland.lit/home"
    id="xl391n47"
    to="wonderland.lit"
    type="get">
  <query xmlns="http://jabber.org/protocol/disco#items"/>
</iq>
```

That command means "please send me all the items that are associated with `wonderland.lit`; the server then replies with a list of associated entities, which the client tracks by the value of the `id` attribute:

```
<iq from="wonderland.lit"
    id="xl391n47"
    to="hatter@wonderland.lit/home"
    type="result">
  <query xmlns="http://jabber.org/protocol/disco#items">
    <item jid="conference.wonderland.lit"/>
    <item jid="notify.wonderland.lit"/>
  </query>
</iq>
```

The only two associated entities in this case are `conference.wonderland.lit` and `notify.wonderland.lit`. But what are these entities? What features do they support? To find out, the Mad Hatter needs to query each one individually using the `disco#info` method. Here the Mad Hatter queries the `conference.wonderland.lit` service:

```
<iq from="hatter@wonderland.lit/home"
    id="gq02kb71"
    to="conference.wonderland.lit"
    type="get">
  <query xmlns="http://jabber.org/protocol/disco#info"/>❶
</iq>
```

❶ The XML element for both the items request and the info request is `<query/>`, but the requests are differentiated by the XML namespace: the items request is qualified by the `http://jabber.org/protocol/disco#items` namespace, whereas the info request is qualified by the `http://jabber.org/protocol/disco#info` namespace.

Now, the `conference.wonderland.lit` service returns some information about itself. (Web developers can think of this as similar to the results returned in the HTTP `Accept`, `Accept-Charset`, `Accept-Encoding`, `Accept-Language`, and `Accept-Ranges` response headers, except that the `disco#info` response is more extensible.)

```
<iq from="conference.wonderland.lit"
    id="gq02kb71"
    to="hatter@wonderland.lit/home"
```

```
        type="result">
    <query xmlns="http://jabber.org/protocol/disco#info">
      <identity category="conference" type="text" name="Chatrooms"/>
      <feature var="http://jabber.org/protocol/muc"/>
      <feature var="jabber:iq:register"/>
      <feature var="vcard-temp"/>
    </query>
  </iq>
```

By interpreting the XML in the foregoing example, the Mad Hatter learns that
wonderland.lit hosts a service conference.wonderland.lit, which provides a text con-
ferencing service that supports the Multi-User Chat protocol (the http://jabber.org/
protocol/muc namespace defined in [XEP-0045]), in-band registration of usernames
(the jabber:iq:register namespace defined in [XEP-0077]), and component vCards
(the vcard-temp namespace defined in [XEP-0054]).

What's Your Identity?

In most uses of service discovery, we're mainly interested in the particular *features* that another entity supports. The <identity/> element
provides a more general clue about what *kind* of entity this is. The first
discovery protocol used in the XMPP community, called "Agent Information" (see the historical [XEP-0094]), did not disclose detailed features, but did advertise basic identities, which is why the modern service
discovery protocol includes identities as well. (In fact, an entity can advertise multiple identities at the same time, such as a groupchat service that is simultaneously a native XMPP Multi-User Chat service and a
gateway to Internet Relay Chat.)

Using Service Discovery with Servers and Services

The disco#items and disco#info methods are typically used together to "walk the tree"
of entities. Consider a typical sequence:

1. Send a disco#items query to the wonderland.lit server, discovering (among others)
   the conference.wonderland.lit service.

2. Send a disco#info query to the conference.wonderland.lit room, in order to discover that the conference.wonderland.lit service is a multi-user chat service.

3. Send a disco#items query to the conference.wonderland.lit service, discovering
   (among others) the tea@conference.wonderland.lit room.

4. Send a disco#info query to the tea@conference.wonderland.lit room to find out
   more information about the room (e.g., its name, natural language, and other configuration options).

5. Send a disco#items query to the tea@conference.wonderland.lit service, discovering the tea@conference.wonderland.lit/alice user.

Clearly, quite a bit of back-and-forth is needed to generate a complete picture of an entity hierarchy. In common usage, a client would not walk the entire tree automatically. Instead, it would not go beyond the first few queries unless the user requests detailed information about, say, a particular chat room and its users.

What follows is the full sequence just outlined.

First, query the `wonderland.lit` server for its associated items:

```
<iq from="hatter@wonderland.lit/home"
    id="ris71b37"
    to="wonderland.lit"
    type="get">
  <query xmlns="http://jabber.org/protocol/disco#items"/>
</iq>

<iq from="wonderland.lit"
    id="ris71b37"
    to="hatter@wonderland.lit/home"
    type="result">
  <query xmlns="http://jabber.org/protocol/disco#items">
    <item jid="conference.wonderland.lit"/>
    <item jid="notify.wonderland.lit"/>
  </query>
</iq>
```

Second, query the `conference.wonderland.lit` service to see what kind of entity it is:

```
<iq from="hatter@wonderland.lit/home"
    id="hs82bd67"
    to="conference.wonderland.lit"
    type="get">
  <query xmlns="http://jabber.org/protocol/disco#info"/>
</iq>

<iq from="conference.wonderland.lit"
    id="hs82bd67"
    to="hatter@wonderland.lit/home"
    type="result">
  <query xmlns="http://jabber.org/protocol/disco#info">
    <identity category="conference" type="text" name="Chatrooms"/>
    <feature var="http://jabber.org/protocol/muc"/>
    <feature var="jabber:iq:register"/>
    <feature var="vcard-temp"/>
  </query>
</iq>
```

Third, query the `conference.wonderland.lit` service for its associated items:

```
<iq from="hatter@wonderland.lit/home"
    id="skf81ga8"
    to="conference.wonderland.lit"
    type="get">
  <query xmlns="http://jabber.org/protocol/disco#items"/>
</iq>
```

```
<iq from="conference.wonderland.lit"
    id="skf81ga8"
    to="hatter@wonderland.lit/home"
    type="result">
  <query xmlns="http://jabber.org/protocol/disco#items">
    <item jid="pool@conference.wonderland.lit"/>
    <item jid="tea@conference.wonderland.lit"/>
  </query>
</iq>
```

Fourth, query a particular conference room for its information:

```
<iq from="hatter@wonderland.lit/home"
    id="ow8x71b6"
    to="tea@conference.wonderland.lit"
    type="get">
  <query xmlns="http://jabber.org/protocol/disco#info"/>
</iq>
```

The room then returns a list of its configured features, such as the fact that it is public (anyone can discover it), persistent (it won't go away when the last person leaves), open (anyone can join it), semi-anonymous (only the room admins can find out your real JabberID), unmoderated (new users have voice), and unsecured (no password is required to join). Here, the room also provides additional information about itself by including a data form of the kind we discuss in Chapter 6 (this extension mechanism for service discovery is defined in [XEP-0128]):

```
<iq from="tea@conference.wonderland.lit"
    id="ow8x71b6"
    to="hatter@wonderland.lit/home"
    type="result">
  <query xmlns="http://jabber.org/protocol/disco#info">
    <identity category="conference" type="text" name="The Tea Room"/>
    <feature var="http://jabber.org/protocol/muc"/>
    <feature var="muc_public"/>
    <feature var="muc_persistent"/>
    <feature var="muc_open"/>
    <feature var="muc_semianonymous"/>
    <feature var="muc_unmoderated"/>
    <x xmlns="jabber:x:data" type="result">
      <field type="hidden" var="FORM_TYPE">
        <value>http://jabber.org/protocol/muc#roominfo</value>
      </field>
      <field label="Number of occupants" var="muc#roominfo_occupants">
        <value>4</value>
      </field>
    </x>
  </query>
</iq>
```

Furthermore, querying a conference room with the disco#items namespace may return a list of JIDs in the room, as shown in the following examples:

```
<iq from="hatter@wonderland.lit/home"
    id="ac4cf"
    to="tea@conference.wonderland.lit"
    type="get">
  <query xmlns="http://jabber.org/protocol/disco#items"/>
</iq>

<iq from="tea@conference.wonderland.lit"
    id="ac4cf"
    to="hatter@wonderland.lit/home"
    type="result">
  <query xmlns="http://jabber.org/protocol/disco#items">
    <item name="Alice" jid="tea@conference.wonderland.lit/Alice"/>
    <item name="Hare" jid="tea@conference.wonderland.lit/Hare"/>
    <item name="Hatter" jid="tea@conference.wonderland.lit/Hatter"/>
    <item name="Dormouse" jid="tea@conference.wonderland.lit/Dormouse"/>
  </query>
</iq>
```

Using Service Discovery with Clients

When it comes to discovering the capabilities of other clients on the network, there are two tools at your disposal: explicit service discovery of the kind we've already discussed, and a kind of service discovery shorthand that is advertised in XMPP presence notifications. We'll look at each of these in turn.

Explicit Service Discovery

In the last section, we said that a client always knows about at least one entity: its server. Yet we've also seen that usually a client knows about some other entities: the items in its roster. What can *those* entities do?

Presence plays an important part in helping us find out. As you may recall from Chapter 3, when a client goes online, its server sends presence probes to each of the user's contacts. The server for each contact then returns information about the available resources for that contact. This information is not a service discovery list, but a series of presence stanzas, such as the following presence notifications that Alice's sister receives when she logs in:

```
<presence from="alice@wonderland.lit/rabbithole"
          to="sister@realworld.lit"/>

<presence from="alice@wonderland.lit/party"
          to="sister@realworld.lit"/>

<presence from="friend@school.lit/laptop"
          to="sister@realworld.lit"/>
```

Disco and Presence

Presence helps here because in order to exchange IQ stanzas with another user, you need to know the person's full JID (`user@domain.tld/`
`resource`). Because presence notifications come from the full JID, they
are essentially a kind of push format for the data you would need to poll
for via the `disco#items` namespace for each of your contacts.

Now let's say that Alice's sister wants to find out what each of Alice's devices can do
(this kind of information can be used to populate a drop-down box of possible actions,
such as "send a file" or "start voice chat"). To find out, she sends a `disco#info` request
to each of Alice's resources:

```
<iq from="sister@realworld.lit/home"
    id="p982bs61"
    to="alice@wonderland.lit/rabbithole"
    type="get">
  <query xmlns="http://jabber.org/protocol/disco#info"/>
</iq>

<iq from="sister@realworld.lit/home"
    id="sc374g15"
    to="alice@wonderland.lit/party"
    type="get">
  <query xmlns="http://jabber.org/protocol/disco#info"/>
</iq>
```

For each of Alice's resources, she receives a reply telling her what features are supported:

```
<iq from="alice@wonderland.lit/rabbithole"
    id="p982bs61"
    to="sister@realworld.lit/home"
    type="result">
  <query xmlns="http://jabber.org/protocol/disco#info">
    <identity category="client" name="Exodus 0.9.1" type="pc"/>
    <feature var="http://jabber.org/protocol/caps"/>
    <feature var="http://jabber.org/protocol/disco#info"/>
    <feature var="http://jabber.org/protocol/disco#items"/>
    <feature var="http://jabber.org/protocol/muc"/>
    <feature var="jabber:iq:version"/>
  </query>
</iq>

<iq from="alice@wonderland.lit/party"
    id="sc374g15"
    to="sister@realworld.lit/home"
    type="result">
  <query xmlns="http://jabber.org/protocol/disco#info">
    <identity category="client" name="Psi" type="pc"/>
    <feature var="http://jabber.org/protocol/bytestreams"/>
    <feature var="http://jabber.org/protocol/si"/>
    <feature var="http://jabber.org/protocol/si/profile/file-transfer"/>
    <feature var="http://jabber.org/protocol/disco#info"/>
    <feature var="http://jabber.org/protocol/commands"/>
```

```
        <feature var="http://jabber.org/protocol/rosterx"/>
        <feature var="http://jabber.org/protocol/muc"/>
        <feature var="jabber:x:data"/>
        <feature var="http://jabber.org/protocol/chatstates"/>
        <feature var="http://jabber.org/protocol/mood+notify"/>
        <feature var="http://jabber.org/protocol/tune+notify"/>
        <feature var="http://jabber.org/protocol/physloc+notify"/>
        <feature var="http://jabber.org/protocol/geoloc+notify"/>
        <feature var="http://www.xmpp.org/extensions/xep-0084.html#ns-metadata+notify"/>
        <feature var="http://jabber.org/protocol/xhtml-im"/>
        <feature var="urn:xmpp:tmp:sxe"/>
        <feature var="http://www.w3.org/2000/svg"/>
    </query>
  </iq>
```

That's a lot of namespaces! Imagine if you sent a `disco#info` request to everyone in your roster, and you had 500 or 1,000 or 2,000 contacts. You're probably thinking, "Isn't all that traffic going to get expensive? There must be a better way!" And there is. We discuss it in the next section.

Entity Capabilities: Service Discovery Shorthand

The XMPP community has developed an optimized protocol for discovering supported features, at least when you share presence (which you typically do with people in your roster). This *Entity Capabilities* [XEP-0115] protocol uses presence as the transport for a kind of shorthand service discovery notation. (In fact, just as presence itself is a specialized push version of `disco#items` data, the entity capabilities protocol uses the XMPP presence "transport" to push out a shorthand notation for `disco#info` data.)

Entity Capabilities is based on the observation that many of the entities with which you interact will be running the same software, and that this software changes relatively infrequently (that is, if you see version 0.13 of the Psi client today, there's a good chance you'll see it again tomorrow). Under this scheme, entities advertise the features they support in their presence stanzas. However, it wouldn't save any bandwidth to send along the full list of features. Therefore, the features are concatenated and hashed into a short verification code that uniquely identifies the current feature set. The first time your client sees this code, it sends a standard `disco#info` request to find out which features correspond to the code. The good thing is that whenever your client sees this code in the future, it automatically knows exactly which features the person supports, so no `disco#info` requests are needed, thus saving a lot of bandwidth (especially on login).

How does this work in practice? When Alice logs in, her client concatenates and hashes all of the features it supports and then attaches a `<c/>` child to the presence packet containing the verification code in the `ver` attribute:

```
<presence from="alice@wonderland.lit/rabbithole">
  <c xmlns="http://jabber.org/protocol/caps"
      hash="sha-1"❶
      node="http://code.google.com/p/exodus"❷
```

```
        ver="QgayPKawpkPSDYmwT/WM94uAluO="/>
    </presence>
```

❶ The hash attribute identifies the hashing algorithm used (the default is SHA-1).

❷ The node attribute identifies the software application in use by means of a URI that provides further information about the codebase.

Both Alice's sister and the White Rabbit receive Alice's presence notification. Alice's sister has received this verification code before and her client has remembered the capabilities associated with it, so she doesn't need to send a disco#info request to Alice. However, this is the first time that the White Rabbit's client has seen this verification code, and so it sends a disco#info request to Alice's client for the full capabilities:

```
<iq from="rabbit@wonderland.lit/pool"
    id="v584fak2"
    to="alice@wonderland.lit/rabbithole"
    type="get">
  <query xmlns="http://jabber.org/protocol/disco#info"
         node="http://code.google.com/p/exodus#QgayPKawpkPSDYmwT/WM94uAluO="/>
</iq>
```

This query can be recognized as a standard service discovery query, with an extra node attribute specified, constructed from the node and ver attributes of the <c/> element. The reason for the node specification, rather than using a disco query without the node attribute, is to prevent the possible race condition where the White Rabbit's client "discos" Alice, but Alice's client has changed its capabilities before receiving the disco request, replying with a set of capabilities that do not match the verification code.

Alice replies to the disco#info request in the usual way:

```
<iq from="alice@wonderland.lit/rabbithole"
    id="v584fak2"
    to="rabbit@wonderland.lit/pool"
    type="result">
  <query xmlns="http://jabber.org/protocol/disco#info"
         node="http://code.google.com/p/exodus#QgayPKawpkPSDYmwT/WM94uAluO=">
    <identity category="client" name="Exodus 0.9.1" type="pc"/>
    <feature var="http://jabber.org/protocol/caps"/>
    <feature var="http://jabber.org/protocol/disco#info"/>
    <feature var="http://jabber.org/protocol/disco#items"/>
    <feature var="http://jabber.org/protocol/muc"/>
  </query>
</iq>
```

Upon receiving the response from Alice's client, the White Rabbit's client can cache the result, remembering that future clients seen with the same <c/> element support the features that Alice has advertised. The result: no need to send a flood of service discovery requests when you log in. (The XMPP network thanks you!)

In Chapter 8, we'll see how entity capabilities are used to optimize the processes of discovering and subscribing to real-time information sources over the XMPP network.

Summary

Service discovery is a key building block of XMPP-based services because it is extremely helpful to determine what entities are out there on the network and exactly which XMPP features those entities implement. Using only the ability to find other entities (`disco#items`) and to query their capabilities (`disco#info`), you can discover a wealth of services on the network and discover how those services and the entities in your roster can interact with you in real time.

CHAPTER 6

Data Forms

The World Wide Web started out as a way to publish physics papers, and only later gained transactional capabilities, such as electronic commerce. One of the key building blocks that enabled this transition was the HTML `<FORM>` tag, which made it possible for a website to offer an empty, but structured, form to the user and for the user to submit a completed form to the website.

XMPP includes a very similar technology for lightweight workflows called *Data Forms*, defined in [XEP-0004]. Because Data Forms are used throughout the technologies we'll discuss in the following chapters, we introduce them now. In Chapter 11, we build on these basic concepts to explore more advanced workflows.

Basic Structure

A data form is made up of several pieces, as shown in the following "stub" example:

```
<message from="sender@wonderland.lit/foo" to="receiver@wonderland.lit/bar">
  <x xmlns="jabber:x:data" type="form">
    <title>My Special Form</title>
    <instructions>Please fill in the following form</instructions>
    <field label="Text Input" type="text-single" var="field-1"/>
    <field label="Make a Choice" type="boolean" var="field-2"/>
    <field label="For Your Eyes Only" type="text-private" var="field-3"/>
    <field label="Pick One" type="list-single" var="field-4">
      <option label="First Option"><value>single-1</value></option>
      <option label="Second Option"><value>single-2</value></option>
      <option label="Third Option"><value>single-3</value></option>
    </field>
    <field label="Pick a Few" type="list-multi" var="field-5">
      <option label="First Option"><value>multi-1</value></option>
      <option label="Second Option"><value>multi-2</value></option>
      <option label="Third Option"><value>multi-3</value></option>
      <option label="Fourth Option"><value>multi-4</value></option>
    </field>
  </x>
</message>
```

Let's walk through these pieces one by one.

First, the form is structured as an `<x/>` element qualified by the `jabber:x:data` namespace. (Because of the namespace name, XMPP developers often refer to this technology as "x:data.")

The `<x/>` element includes a `type` attribute that specifies where this `<x/>` element lives in the workflow. The overall flow of a data forms exchange is illustrated in Figure 6-1.

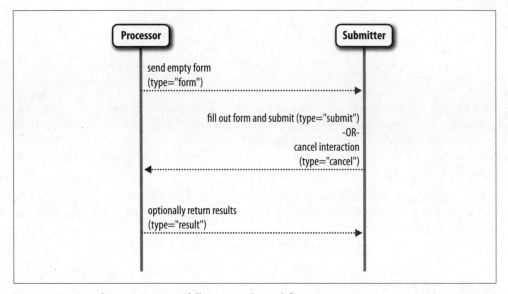

Figure 6-1. Data form interactions follow a simple workflow

The form can include both a human-readable title and human-readable instructions.

The bulk of the form consists of fields for which the user will provide values. As in HTML forms, there are several kinds of fields. In x:data, these are differentiated by the `type` attribute of the `<field/>` element, which can have any of the following values:

`boolean`

> A true/false option, usually presented as a checkbox or a set of two mutually exclusive radio buttons. This is similar to an `<INPUT>` tag of type `checkbox` or `radio` in HTML forms. The lexical representation for a boolean field can be `0` or `false` for the logical value FALSE and `1` or `true` for the logical value TRUE.

`fixed`

> A field that's presented to the user, but isn't editable; these are used for labels and instructions. This is similar to the `<LABEL>` tag in HTML forms.

`hidden`

> Hidden fields aren't presented to the user and aren't usually edited. This is similar to an `<INPUT>` tag of type `hidden` in HTML forms.

jid-multi

> A list of JabberIDs, each provided in a separate `value` element. This is equivalent to a specialized `list-multi` (explained later).

jid-single

> A single valid JabberID. This is equivalent to a specialized `list-single` (explained later).

list-multi

> A field that allows multiple selections from a list. This is similar to the `<SELECT>` tag in HTML forms with the `multiple` attribute set to TRUE.

list-single

> A field allowing a single selection from a list. This is similar to the `<SELECT>` tag in HTML forms with the `multiple` attribute set to FALSE (the default for HTML `<SELECT>` tags).

text-multi

> Multi-line text input. Each line is stored in a separate `value` element. This is similar to the `<TEXTAREA>` tag in HTML forms.

text-private

> Acts like `text-single`, except the input is masked to the user (typically used for entering passwords). This is similar to an `<INPUT>` tag of type `password` in HTML forms.

text-single

> A single line of text input. This is similar to an `<INPUT>` tag of type `text` in HTML forms. The `text-single` type is the default.

The `<field/>` element's `var` attribute specifies the name of the field. This is similar to the `name` attribute in HTML forms.

Both the `<field/>` element and the `<option/>` child element (for fields of type `list-multi` and `list-single`) can also include a human-readable `label` attribute for presentation to an end user.

Finally, the `<value/>` child of the `<field/>` element specifies the initial or "pre-checked" value of a field (in empty forms of type `form`) or the provided value (in completed forms of type `submit`).

Figure 6-2 illustrates how the form could be presented to a user.

Using Data Forms

Usually a data form is wrapped inside an application-specific element that is sent within an IQ or message stanza. For example, let's imagine that poor Alice has been receiving some automated spam messages lately, and she's not happy about it. She therefore installs a new plug-in for her favorite XMPP client, which sends a challenge message to unknown entities that try to send her messages, using the techniques described in

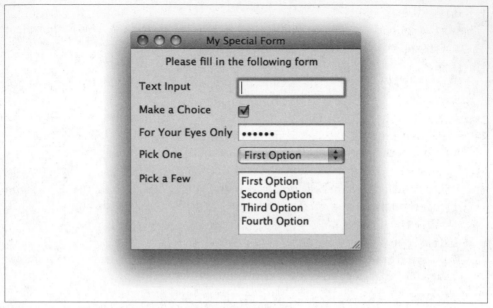

Figure 6-2. Presentation of a data form in a user interface

CAPTCHA Forms [XEP-0158]. A CAPTCHA is a "Completely Automated Public Turing Test to Tell Computers and Humans Apart." Typically it is a little image with squiggly letters that you need to interpret, but it can also be purely textual, such as a simple math question. (Researchers have questioned the effectiveness of these tests, but they continue to be popular with website developers and, increasingly, with XMPP developers.)

Here we assume that Alice has received a message from knave@wonderland.lit/pda, so her client sends a challenge, which is an x:data form of type form, wrapped in a <captcha/> element qualified by the urn:xmpp:captcha namespace:

```
<message from="alice@wonderland.lit/rabbithole"❶
         to="knave@wonderland.lit/pda"
         id="A4C7303D">
  <body>
    You will not be allowed to send messages to me
    until you complete the attached form.
  </body>
  <captcha xmlns="urn:xmpp:captcha">
    <x xmlns="jabber:x:data" type="form">
      <field type="hidden" var="FORM_TYPE">
        <value>urn:xmpp:captcha</value>
      </field>
      <field type="hidden" var="challenge">
        <value>A4C7303D</value>
      </field>
      <field label="What is 5+2?" type="text-single" var="qa">
        <required/>❷
```

```
        </field>
      </x>
    </captcha>
  </message>
```

❶ In real life, Alice's client probably would not send this message, because doing so exposes her full JID (this is called a *presence leak*); instead, her server would probably send it on her behalf as described in [XEP-0158].

❷ The `required` element denotes a field that must be returned in the submitted form.

Now the Knave's client presents the message to him. He completes the puzzle and clicks the Submit button, so his client submits the form to Alice using an x:data form of type `submit`:

```
<message from="knave@wonderland.lit/pda"
         to="alice@wonderland.lit/rabbithole"
         id="A4C7303D">
  <captcha xmlns="urn:xmpp:captcha">
    <x xmlns="jabber:x:data" type="submit">
      <field type="hidden" var="FORM_TYPE">
        <value>urn:xmpp:captcha</value>
      </field>
      <field type="hidden" var="challenge">
        <value>A4C7303D</value>
      </field>
      <field var="qa">
        <value>7</value>
      </field>
    </x>
  </captcha>
</message>
```

If the text value provided by the Knave is correct, Alice's client will then allow an exchange of messages to occur.

Defining Your Terms: Form Types

By nature, data forms are extremely loose. In the same way that HTML forms can contain just about any data fields, so can XMPP data forms. However, XMPP forms can be more tightly defined using the special `FORM_TYPE` field, which is defined in [XEP-0068]. We saw this field in the previous example:

```
<field type="hidden" var="FORM_TYPE">❶
  <value>urn:xmpp:captcha</value>
</field>
```

❶ Because this field is of type `hidden`, it is not shown to the recipient; instead, the recipient's client silently returns it to the form provider when the recipient submits the form.

The FORM_TYPE enables application developers to define the meaning of given fields ahead of time (e.g., to limit the allowable values), or even to register the form fields with the XMPP Registrar. For example, in CAPTCHA forms, the qa field is predefined to be used only for textual question-and-answer challenges. This usage scopes the fields so that clients and other entities can know how to present the information. You can think of it as a little like a schema for a data form.

Including Media in Data Forms

Sometimes, it is helpful to include a small image or other piece of media data in a form. As we mentioned, the CAPTCHAs that most people are familiar with consist of a small image that you must identify. So far, x:data forms have not included images, so in true XML fashion, we need to define an extension to make this possible.

In XMPP, CAPTCHA images are referenced from within a data form using a new field type for data forms: the media field type specified in [XEP-0221]. In fact, because XMPP is extensible, the media field type is a specially "namespaced" child of the standard `<field/>` element. This media element is then used to reference the image of the CAPTCHA.

So let's extend the CAPTCHA example we looked at earlier by including a media element:

```
<message from="alice@wonderland.lit/rabbithole"
         to="knave@wonderland.lit/pda"
         id="A4C7303D">
  <body>
    You will not be allowed to send messages to me
    until you complete the attached form.
  </body>
  <captcha xmlns="urn:xmpp:captcha">
    <x xmlns="jabber:x:data" type="form">
      <field type="hidden" var="FORM_TYPE">
        <value>urn:xmpp:captcha</value>
      </field>
      <field type="hidden" var="challenge">
        <value>A4C7303D</value>
      </field>
      <field label="Enter the text you see" var="ocr">
        <media xmlns="urn:xmpp:media-element"❶
               height="80"
               width="290">
          <uri type="image/jpeg">
            http://www.wonderland.lit/challenges/ocr.jpg?A4C7303D
          </uri>
        </media>
      </field>
      <field label="What is 5+2?" type="text-single" var="qa"/>
    </x>
  </captcha>
</message>
```

❶ The `<media/>` element is qualified by the `urn:xmpp:media-element` namespace, which the receiving application will ignore if it does not understand the namespace.

This form now shows two possible CAPTCHAs: the textual challenge we saw earlier, plus an optical character recognition test. The CAPTCHA Forms specification defines several others not shown here, such as picture recognition, speech recognition, and video recognition. For broader coverage, the challenger would offer several methods to the sender (e.g., one auditory test and one visual test). In any case, the sender would be expected to answer the test by returning a completed form:

```
<message from="knave@wonderland.lit/pda"
         to="alice@wonderland.lit/rabbithole"
         id="A4C7303D">
  <captcha xmlns="urn:xmpp:captcha">
    <x xmlns="jabber:x:data" type="submit">
      <field type="hidden" var="FORM_TYPE">
        <value>urn:xmpp:captcha</value>
      </field>
      <field type="hidden" var="challenge">
        <value>A4C7303D</value>
      </field>
      <field var="ocr">❶
        <value>tongue twister</value>
      </field>
    </x>
  </captcha>
</message>
```

❶ Although the `ocr` field in the presented form contained a media element, the response uses the default field type, which is `text-single`.

Summary

In this chapter, we covered the Data Forms extension (defined in [XEP-0004]), which provides a lightweight but powerful technology for offering and submitting information in semi-structured workflows. As we'll see in the next two chapters, Data Forms are used in a wide range of tasks, such as configuration of Multi-User Chat rooms and Publish-Subscribe nodes.

CHAPTER 7

Multi-Party Interactions

Starting the Party

Instant messaging as we've explored it to this point is a one-to-one interaction. But what if we want to communicate among multiple people, bots, or other entities at the same time? It would be nice if XMPP technologies included a real-time counterpart to email discussion lists, web forums, and other multi-party interactions. This feature would be similar to Internet Relay Chat (IRC), providing channels or rooms where people could exchange messages and see who else is present. Well, you're in luck, because XMPP includes just such a feature! The first iteration of this technology was called *groupchat*, while the more modern iteration is called *Multi-User Chat* (MUC) [XEP-0045].

The basic idea behind MUC is that people can join a room and send messages that are delivered to all the other participants. Thus the room acts as a kind of message "reflector" or "multiplier" (one incoming message is multiplied into many outgoing messages). You can see a typical interface for such a groupchat in an IM client in Figure 7-1.

Let's go over a few of the features:

- Messages are shared with all the participants (as we'll see, you can also send private messages to specific participants).
- There is a "room roster" of all the participants.
- The participants are identified by nicknames, not their real JabberIDs.
- The room shares presence information about the participants (in Figure 7-1, the user "Dormouse" is marked as "Do Not Disturb").
- The participants are not limited to mere humans. For example, in the room that we used while writing this book, a bot called "bookbot" provided helpful services, such as archiving the conversation and looking up URLs for XMPP specifications.

In the next section, we'll see how these features are implemented in XMPP.

Figure 7-1. A snippet of conversation from the tea party groupchat room

Groupchat Basics

The focus of groupchat is a particular room, which has its own JabberID. For example, the room shown in Figure 7-1 is `teaparty@conference.wonderland.lit`.

Components

The room is hosted at `teaparty@conference.wonderland.lit`, not `wonderland.lit`. This addressing is an artifact of the original `jabberd` server, wherein the only services handled by the core XMPP daemon were presence, rosters, one-to-one messages, and general stanza routing. Other services were handled by add-on modules called *components*. These components were assigned different domain names, such as `conference.jabber.org` for the groupchat service at `jabber.org`. These domain names were then used for internal routing, so that stanzas intended for any address at `conference.jabber.org` were automatically routed to the groupchat component. More modern XMPP server projects follow the same approach, although nothing in XMPP prevents an address such as `teaparty@wonderland.lit` from being a groupchat room.

To join a room, you send directed presence to the room, including your preferred nick-name as the resource identifier (this `room@domain.tld/nick` combination is known as your *room JID*). So, Alice would join our `teaparty` room as follows:

```
<presence from="alice@wonderland.lit/rabbithole"
          to="teaparty@conference.wonderland.lit/Alice"/>
```

The use of directed presence here ties in well with the more general concept of presence, because people in the room want to know your availability state just as people in your roster do. In addition, because you send directed presence, the room is automatically notified if you go offline unexpectedly, thus helping to prevent "ghost" users. (Such "ghosts" can still appear if a server-to-server link goes down.)

Several things happen when you join a room:

- The room sends a join notification (i.e., a presence stanza) from your room JID to the other participants.
- The room sends presence to you from the room JIDs of all the other participants so that your client can build a specialized "roster" of room occupants.
- The room will typically also send you some of the recent messages exchanged in the room so that you have a bit of context for discussion.

Let's see what these look like in protocol.

First, the participants of the room receive Alice's join notification:

```
<presence from="teaparty@conference.wonderland.lit/Alice"
          to="hatter@wonderland.lit/underahat"/>

<presence from="teaparty@conference.wonderland.lit/Alice"
          to="hare@wonderland.lit/chair"/>

<presence from="teaparty@conference.wonderland.lit/Alice"
          to="dormouse@wonderland.lit/sleepspace"/>
```

Next, Alice receives the room roster:

```
<presence from="teaparty@conference.wonderland.lit/Mad Hatter"
          to="alice@wonderland.lit/rabbithole"/>

<presence from="teaparty@conference.wonderland.lit/March Hare"
          to="alice@wonderland.lit/rabbithole"/>

<presence from="teaparty@conference.wonderland.lit/Dormouse"
          to="alice@wonderland.lit/rabbithole"/>
```

Then follows the room history. How many messages the room sends depends on the configuration. Notice these messages include a flag that they are sent with a delay—the timestamp shows the (UTC) time when each message was originally received by the room so that you can know how long ago the history messages were sent (and thus how busy the room is):

```
<message from="teaparty@conference.wonderland.lit/March Hare"
         to="alice@wonderland.lit/rabbithole"
         type="groupchat">
  <body>Have some wine,</body>
  <delay xmlns="urn:xmpp:delay" stamp="2008-11-07T18:42:03Z"/>
</message>

<message from="teaparty@conference.wonderland.lit/Mad Hatter"
         to="alice@wonderland.lit/rabbithole"
         type="groupchat">
  <body>Two days wrong!</body>
  <delay xmlns="urn:xmpp:delay" stamp="2008-11-07T18:42:17Z"/>
</message>

<message from="teaparty@conference.wonderland.lit/Mad Hatter"
         to="alice@wonderland.lit/rabbithole"
         type="groupchat">
  <body>March Hare: I told you butter wouldn't suit the works!</body>
  <delay xmlns="urn:xmpp:delay" stamp="2008-11-07T18:42:49Z"/>
</message>
```

As soon as you enter the room, you can join in the conversation by sending messages to the room itself. Because these messages are "live," they don't contain a delay flag:

```
<message from="alice@wonderland.lit/rabbithole"
         to="teaparty@conference.wonderland.lit"
         type="groupchat">
  <body>March Hare: There's PLENTY of room!</body>
</message>
```

Messages sent to the room are then reflected out to all the participants (including the party who sent the message):

```
<message from="teaparty@conference.wonderland.lit/Alice"
         to="hatter@wonderland.lit/underahat"
         type="groupchat">
  <body>March Hare: There's PLENTY of room!</body>
</message>

<message from="teaparty@conference.wonderland.lit/Alice"
         to="dormouse@wonderland.lit/sleepspace"
         type="groupchat">
  <body>March Hare: There's PLENTY of room!</body>
</message>

<message from="teaparty@conference.wonderland.lit/Alice"
         to="hare@wonderland.lit/chair"
         type="groupchat">
  <body>March Hare: There's PLENTY of room!</body>
</message>

<message from="teaparty@conference.wonderland.lit/Alice"
         to="alice@wonderland.lit/rabbithole"
         type="groupchat">
  <body>March Hare: There's PLENTY of room!</body>
</message>
```

The messages sent in a room are of type **groupchat**. Groupchat messages are specialized messages that are used only in the context of multi-party interactions. The main reason for the special message type is to differentiate between messages that are intended for the entire room and *private messages* sent from one participant to another (which are of type **chat** or **normal**). This enables the groupchat component to route messages appropriately and also enables the receiving client to show groupchat and chat messages separately.

To send a private message to the March Hare, Alice would send a message of type chat to the March Hare's *room JID*:

```
<message from="alice@wonderland.lit/rabbithole"
         to="teaparty@conference.wonderland.lit/March Hare"
         type="chat">
  <body>you silly Hare!</body>
</message>
```

Because the private message is sent to the March Hare's room JID, it is handled by the MUC service, which forwards the message from Alice to the March Hare. It does this by rewriting the **from** address so that the message appears to come from Alice's room JID and rewriting the **to** address so that the message is delivered to the March Hare's real JID:

```
<message from="teaparty@conference.wonderland.lit/Alice"
         to="hare@wonderland.lit/chair"
         type="chat">
  <body>you silly Hare!</body>
</message>
```

Alice and the Hare can hold an entire side conversation this way if they please (though if they wanted to invite a third person to their conversation, they would need to create another MUC room).

If you ever want to leave the room, you send unavailable presence to your current room JID (or your server sends it on your behalf when you go offline):

```
<presence from="dormouse@wonderland.lit/sleepspace"
          to="teaparty@conference.wonderland.lit/Dormouse"
          type="unavailable"/>
```

This presence too is broadcast to all the participants in the room so that they know you have left.

Crowd Control

It's an unfortunate fact of social dynamics that some people will misbehave in any given public space on the Internet, whether it is a Usenet channel, an email list, a web forum, or a chat room. This phenomenon always leads to social stratification, as people in authority (typically called moderators or admins) have special powers to kick out and ban those who misbehave (typically called trolls, abusers, spammers, and other such epithets).

XMPP groupchat is no exception. The full Multi-User Chat technology contains various tools for crowd control, including kick and ban commands, the ability to limit who can talk in an MUC room, and ways to restrict access entirely.

Crowd control measures follow a continuum from friendly warnings on up. If someone continues to cause trouble in a chat room after being verbally warned in the conversation, one of the room moderators might revoke the offender's ability to speak in the room (this works for moderated rooms but not unmoderated rooms, a distinction we discuss later). To revoke someone's "voice" in the room, the moderator changes the offender's role from participant to visitor. For example, it could be that someone with a JabberID of knave@wonderland.lit and a nickname of "The Knave" is causing trouble in the trial@conference.wonderland.lit chat room, so the King changes The Knave's role to visitor:

```
<iq from="king@wonderland.lit/throne"
    id="ks61f36g"
    to="trial@conference.wonderland.lit"
    type="set">
  <query xmlns="http://jabber.org/protocol/muc#admin">
    <item nick="The Knave" role="visitor"/>
  </query>
</iq>
```

The MUC service then informs everyone in the room (including the affected occupant) that the offender's status has been changed to visitor; it does this by sending updated presence from the offender including a notation of the user's new role:

```
<iq from="trial@conference.wonderland.lit"
    id="ks61f36g"
    to="king@wonderland.lit/throne"
    type="result"/>

<presence from="trial@conference.wonderland.lit/The Knave"
          to="knave@wonderland.lit/mobile">
  <x xmlns="http://jabber.org/protocol/muc#user">
    <item affiliation="none" role="visitor"/>❶
  </x>
</presence>
```

❶ In Multi-User Chat, presence notifications sent within the room contain an extension element that reports the user's long-term affiliation with the room and his short-term role within the room.

The offender can now no longer send messages to the entire room; if he tries to do so, the room will return a forbidden error:

```
<message from="knave@wonderland.lit/mobile"
         to="trial@conference.wonderland.lit"
         type="groupchat">
  <body>boo!</body>
```

```
      </message>

      <message from="trial@conference.wonderland.lit"
               to="knave@wonderland.lit/mobile"
               type="error">
        <body>boo!</body>
        <error type="auth">
          <forbidden xmlns="urn:ietf:params:xml:ns:xmpp-stanzas"/>
        </error>
      </message>
```

A somewhat stronger crowd control measure is to kick the offender out of the room.
When you kick someone from a room, he is temporarily removed from the room, but
he is free to join again later (sometimes this feature is used as a joke or even playfully).

In MUC, a person is kicked by changing his role in the room to none:

```
      <iq from="king@wonderland.lit/throne"
          id="u7r61fsv"
          to="trial@conference.wonderland.lit"
          type="set">
        <query xmlns="http://jabber.org/protocol/muc#admin">
          <item nick="The Knave" role="none"/>❶
        </query>
      </iq>
```

❶ Kicks and other temporary changes to roles are made based on the room nick of the
   occupant, not the real JID (primarily because room *moderators* cannot necessarily
   see the real JIDs of room occupants).

The service then removes the person from the room by sending presence of type unavailable from his room JID to everyone in the room, with a special status code to
indicate that he is leaving involuntarily:

```
      <presence from="trial@conference.wonderland.lit/The Knave"
                to="knave@wonderland.lit/mobile"
                type="unavailable">
        <x xmlns="http://jabber.org/protocol/muc#user">
          <item affiliation="none" role="none"/>
          <status code="307"/>❶
        </x>
      </presence>
```

❶ A status code of 307 means that the user has been temporarily kicked from the room.
   A full list of status codes is provided in the Multi-User Chat specification.

As mentioned, after being kicked, the offender can return to the room and cause more
trouble. If that happens, the admins can take more drastic action and ban the offender
entirely by changing the person's affiliation to outcast:

```
      <iq from="king@wonderland.lit/throne"
          id="d82csl87"
          to="trial@conference.wonderland.lit"
          type="set">
        <query xmlns="http://jabber.org/protocol/muc#admin">
```

```
            <item jid="knave@wonderland.lit" affiliation="outcast"/>❶
        </query>
    </iq>
```

❶ Bans and other changes to stable affiliations are made based on the real JID of the
   user, not the room nick.

The service then removes the person from the room by sending presence of type
unavailable from their room JID to everyone in the room, with a special status code to
indicate that he has been banned:

```
<presence from="trial@conference.wonderland.lit/The Knave"
          to="knave@wonderland.lit/mobile"
          type="unavailable">
    <x xmlns="http://jabber.org/protocol/muc#user">
      <item jid="knave@wonderland.lit" affiliation="outcast"/>
      <status code="301"/>❶
    </x>
</presence>
```

❶ A status code of 301 means that the user has been permanently banned from the
   room. A full list of status codes is provided in the Multi-User Chat specification.

Kicking and banning use one of the administrative features of the MUC protocol: roles
and affiliations. These are temporary or permanent associations between a JabberID
and the privileges that JID has in the room. For example, an affiliation of outcast is a
permanent association indicating that the user is not allowed to join the room.

Roles and Affiliations

Typically, roles are temporary (they last only as long as you are in the
room), whereas affiliations are permanent (they last across groupchat
sessions). However, MUC services are allowed to cache roles across
sessions, so in practice the distinction is not clear-cut. The important
point is that the pre-defined roles and affiliations provide all of the room
associations you might need to handle most multi-party scenarios.

The MUC specification defines the following roles and affiliations:

outcast
    Someone who can't even join the room.

visitor
    Someone who can join the room and listen to the conversation, but who can't
    speak.

participant
    Someone who can both listen and speak.

member
    Someone who can listen, speak, and join the room if it is members-only.

`moderator`
> Someone who can listen, speak, kick participants and visitors, and toggle others' ability to speak.

`admin`
> Someone who can listen, speak, kick and ban participants and visitors, toggle others' ability to speak, see the real JIDs of occupants, name new moderators and members, and reconfigure some room options.

`owner`
> Someone who can listen, speak, kick and ban participants and visitors, toggle others' ability to speak, see the real JIDs of occupants, name new moderators and members, reconfigure all room options, name new admins, and destroy the room.

As you can see, roles and affiliations are mostly arrayed in a hierarchy, from the all-powerful room owners down to the lowly outcasts. These room associations enable the room admins and owners not only to enforce decisions regarding individual participants, but also to configure some room-wide options, in particular the following dimensions:

- Can anyone speak in the room or can only certain restricted users join the conversation (i.e., is the room *unmoderated* or *moderated*)?

- Can anyone join the room or is the room restricted to only certain individuals (i.e., is the room *open* or *members-only*)?

These room types make it possible to exercise even greater control over a room than individual kicks and bans, because if only certain people can speak in the room, it is more difficult for spammers to attack, and if only room members can join, the room is even more strongly protected against abuse.

What's in a Nick?

When you join an MUC room, you specify your preferred nickname. These are handled a bit differently in MUC than in Internet Relay Chat (IRC):

- In IRC, your nick is limited to US-ASCII characters, whereas in MUC, your nick can contain just about any Unicode character.

- In IRC, people often change their nicks to things like "Alice|away," whereas in MUC such changes are unnecessary, because MUC natively passes along your XMPP presence information.

- In IRC, your nick is associated with your IP address, whereas in MUC, your nick is associated with your JabberID (and your IP address is not revealed to the other participants).

- In IRC, your nick applies globally to all the rooms at a service, whereas in MUC, your nick applies locally to a particular room at a service.

If you are a regular participant in a room, you might want to *reserve* your nickname so that no one else can masquerade as you. You do so using *In-Band Registration* [XEP-0077]. First, you need to find out what the registration requirements are, so you send an IQ-get to the room containing a `<query/>` element qualified by the `jabber:iq:register` namespace:

```
<iq from="hatter@wonderland.lit/home"
    id="g73hdn19"
    to="party@conference.wonderland.lit"
    type="get">
  <query xmlns="jabber:iq:register"/>
</iq>
```

The room then tells you what information you need to provide by returning an IQ-result that contains a data form of the kind we looked at in Chapter 6:

```
<iq from="party@conference.wonderland.lit"
    id="g73hdn19"
    to="hatter@wonderland.lit/home"
    type="result">
  <query xmlns="jabber:iq:register">
    <instructions>To register on the web, visit http://wonderland.lit/</instructions>❶
    <x xmlns="jabber:x:data" type="form">
      <title>Register with the Party!</title>
      <instructions>Please provide the following information to register with this room.
      </instructions>❷
      <field type="hidden" var="FORM_TYPE">
        <value>http://jabber.org/protocol/muc#register</value>
      </field>
      <field label="First Name" type="text-single" var="muc#register_first">
        <required/>
      </field>
      <field label="Last Name" type="text-single" var="muc#register_last">
        <required/>
      </field>
      <field label="Desired Nickname" type="text-single" var="muc#register_roomnick">
        <required/>
      </field>
      <field label="Email Address" type="text-single" var="muc#register_email"/>
    </x>
  </query>
</iq>
```

❶ The `<instructions/>` element qualified by the `jabber:iq:register` namespace provides human-readable text, often including an alternative registration method, such as a website URL; these instructions are provided in case the forms-requesting entity does not understand the `jabber:x:data` namespace.

❷ The `<instructions/>` element qualified by the `jabber:x:data` namespace provides human-readable text about how to fill out the form, which is presented in the form interface itself.

To finish the registration process, the user submits the completed form in an IQ-set:

```
<iq from="hatter@wonderland.lit/home"
    id="nb20aj39"
    to="party@conference.wonderland.lit"
    type="set">
  <query xmlns="jabber:iq:register">
    <x xmlns="jabber:x:data" type="form">
      <field type="hidden" var="FORM_TYPE">
        <value>http://jabber.org/protocol/muc#register</value>
      </field>
      <field var="muc#register_first"><value>Mad</value></field>
      <field var="muc#register_last"><value>Hatter</value></field>
      <field var="muc#register_roomnick"><value>The Mad Hatter</value></field>
    </x>
  </query>
</iq>
```

If the nick is available, the room informs the user that the registration is successful by returning an empty IQ-result:

```
<iq from="party@conference.wonderland.lit"
    id="nb20aj39"
    to="hatter@wonderland.lit/home"
    type="result"/>
```

Now if someone else attempts to join the room with that nick, the room will return a `conflict` error.

This nick registration applies only to the room in which it was completed (in this case, the `party@conference.wonderland.lit` room). To register the nick across the entire service, the user would complete the same registration process by interacting with the service instead of the room (in this case, with `conference.wonderland.lit`). However, that registration would not apply to another service on the network, such as the `conference.realworld.lit` service or any rooms at that service.

Configure This!

As discussed in Chapter 6, the Data Forms protocol defined in [XEP-0004] provides a lightweight, generic tool for configuration-related tasks. The data forms protocol is similar to HTML forms and is used throughout the XMPP protocol stack, including MUC.

When you attempt to join a room that doesn't exist yet, the MUC service will create that room on your behalf and lock the room until you configure it (either using manual configuration, or by automatically selecting the default room configuration). On large public MUC services hosted on the open Internet, that default configuration is typically a non-persistent, moderated room that anyone can join, where anyone can speak, where people's JabberIDs are revealed only to the room administrators, and where the conversations are not archived. On private MUC services behind company firewalls, the default configuration might be quite different (e.g., conversations might be archived by default, and participants' JabberIDs might be exposed for tracking purposes).

To change the default configuration, a room admin or owner requests the current configuration:

```
<iq from="queen@wonderland.lit/throne"
    id="zh93hs71"
    to="trial@conference.wonderland.lit"
    type="get">
  <query xmlns="http://jabber.org/protocol/muc#owner"/>
</iq>
```

The service then returns the configuration form to the room owner. This form can contain a large number of options, not all of which are shown here. In this example, the service needs to know whether the room owner wants to enable conversation logging, make the room persistent, enable or disable room moderation, and restrict the room to members only. These are all boolean fields, most of which default to false:

```
<iq from="trial@conference.wonderland.lit"
    id-"zh93hs71"
    to="queen@wonderland.lit/throne"
    type="result">
  <query xmlns="http://jabber.org/protocol/muc#owner">
    <x xmlns="jabber:x:data" type="form">
      <field type="hidden" var="FORM_TYPE">
        <value>http://jabber.org/protocol/muc#roomconfig</value>
      </field>
      <field label="Enable Public Logging?" type="boolean"
             var="muc#roomconfig_enablelogging">
        <value>0</value>
      </field>
      <field label="Make Room Persistent?" type="boolean"
             var="muc#roomconfig_persistentroom">
        <value>0</value>
      </field>
      <field label="Make Room Moderated?" type="boolean"
             var="muc#roomconfig_moderatedroom">
        <value>1</value>
      </field>
      <field label="Make Room Members Only?" type="boolean"
             var="muc#roomconfig_membersonly">
        <value>0</value>
      </field>
    </x>
  </query>
</iq>
```

Assuming that the room owner wants the room to be persistent, moderated, and open, but with no logging, she submits the following configuration to the room:

```
<iq from="queen@wonderland.lit/throne"
    id="rid18s76"
    to="trial@conference.wonderland.lit"
    type="set">
  <query xmlns="http://jabber.org/protocol/muc#owner">
    <x xmlns="jabber:x:data" type="submit">
      <field type="hidden" var="FORM_TYPE">
```

```
        <value>http://jabber.org/protocol/muc#roomconfig</value>
      </field>
      <field var="muc#roomconfig_enablelogging">
        <value>false</value>
      </field>
      <field var="muc#roomconfig_persistentroom">
        <value>true</value>
      </field>
      <field var="muc#roomconfig_moderatedroom">
        <value>true</value>
      </field>
      <field var="muc#roomconfig_membersonly">
        <value>false</value>
      </field>
    </x>
  </query>
</iq>
```

Because the room is now *moderated*, people who join the room will default to visitors, who have no voice (thus they can listen but they can't speak). This kind of room is easier to control, but it is clearly less user-friendly than an unmoderated room.

To exercise even more control, the room owner could change the room to members-only, which means that only people on the special members list are even allowed to join the room (for example, the authors chat room that we used while writing this book was members-only, because that gave us a private place to manage the project).

The most important configuration options are described next (we deleted the muc#room config_ "prefix" to make the list more readable). All of these options are boolean (true/false) unless otherwise noted:

allowinvites
> The allowinvites option defines whether non-admins are allowed to invite other people to the room.

changesubject
> The changesubject option defines whether non-admins are allowed to change the room subject.

enablelogging
> The enablelogging option defines whether the MUC service will store an archive of the discussions that occur in the room, typically to an HTML file or a database. On public MUC services, this option might be locked down so that only service-wide administrators (not merely room admins) can enable logging.

getmemberlist
> The list-multi getmemberlist option defines the roles (visitor, participant, or moderator) that are allowed to retrieve the list of registered members; this is comparable to the similar setting in discussion list software (e.g., Mailman) that determines whether the list of subscribers is public, available only to list members, or available only to list admins.

lang

> The `text-single` `lang` option defines the default human language "spoken" in the chat room.

maxusers

> The `text-single` `maxusers` option defines the maximum number of occupants allowed in the room (room admins and owners are excepted from this rule).

membersonly

> The `membersonly` option defines whether only registered members are allowed to enter the room or anyone may enter the room; this determines whether the room type is `members-only` or `open`.

moderatedroom

> The `moderatedroom` option defines whether only those with voice are allowed to post messages to the room or anyone can post; this determines whether the room type is `moderated` or `unmoderated`.

persistentroom

> The `persistentroom` option defines whether the room remains in existence even after the last person has left the room, or whether the room is automatically destroyed when the last person leaves; this determines whether the room type is `persistent` or `temporary`.

presencebroadcast

> The `list-multi` `presencebroadcast` option defines the roles (visitor, participant, moderator) for which presence is broadcast in the room. This is used mainly within rooms that have a large number of occupants, so that presence is sent only about the "important" people in the room (such as the speakers as opposed to the audience).

publicroom

> The `publicroom` option defines whether the room can be discovered via standard service discovery queries; this determines whether the room type is `public` or `hidden`.

roomadmins

> The `jid-multi` `roomadmins` option specifies the JabberIDs of the room admins.

roomdesc

> The `text-single` `roomdesc` option provides a natural-language description of the room.

roomname

> The `text-single` `roomname` option provides the natural-language name of the room, which is especially helpful if the JID of the room is automatically generated by the chat service.

roomowner

> The `jid-multi` `roomowner` option specifies the JabberIDs of the room owners.

whois

The `list-single whois` option defines whether only moderators or anyone is allowed to discover the real JabberIDs of the room occupants; this determines whether the room type is `semi-anonymous` or `anonymous` (no room is truly anonymous, because the room administrators need to be able to know who the occupants are so that they can exercise appropriate crowd control measures).

In addition to these standard room configuration options (specified by the `http://jabber.org/protocol/muc#roomconfig FORM_TYPE`, as described in Chapter 6), an MUC configuration form can also contain custom configuration options. For example, let's suppose that you have written a specialized bot for the rooms hosted at your service, which provides answers to frequently asked questions, along with other helpful services. Using a custom configuration option of `x-chatbot`, you might allow room admins to configure their rooms so that this ChatBot automatically joins their rooms:

```
<iq from="trial@conference.wonderland.lit"
    id="ks92h1n7"
    to="queen@wonderland.lit/throne"
    type="result">
  <query xmlns="http://jabber.org/protocol/muc#owner">
    <x xmlns="jabber:x:data" type="form">
      <field type="hidden" var="FORM_TYPE">
        <value>http://jabber.org/protocol/muc#roomconfig</value>
      </field>
      <field label="Load ChatBot by Default?" type="boolean" var="x-chatbot"/>
    </x>
  </query>
</iq>
```

Privacy, Security, and All That Jazz

Groupchat rooms are somewhat public spaces. When people join such rooms, they might think that they are completely anonymous and can say anything they please (perhaps this is why chat rooms have such a bad reputation). However, XMPP groupchat has built-in support for features that can make rooms less than completely anonymous, including:

- The room administrators can always see the real JabberIDs of users in the room; this enables them to deploy appropriate "crowd control" measures, as described earlier in this chapter. However, the room can also be configured so that all participants can view real JIDs by setting the `whois` configuration option to a value of "anyone" (this kind of transparency is important in certain deployment scenarios).

- If the room configuration sets the `enablelogging` option to `true`, the service will automatically archive all of the one-to-many conversations in the room. On public MUC services, users who are sensitive about privacy concerns may find this to be a breach of privacy, whereas within enterprise deployments, the lack of archiving might be considered a problem (e.g., archives might be used for incident reporting or regulatory compliance).

- Unless the room configuration sets the `publicroom` option to `false`, the service will enable entities to find the room using XMPP Service Discovery, as described in Chapter 5.

- Most MUC services will allow participants to send private, one-to-one messages to other participants in the room.

However, a user is warned about most of these features when joining the room. These warnings are provided as special status codes in the presence the user receives after joining, as documented in the Multi-User Chat specification:

```
<presence from="teaparty@conference.wonderland.lit/Alice"
          to="alice@wonderland.lit/rabbithole">
  <x xmlns="http://jabber.org/protocol/muc#user">
    <item affiliation="member" role="participant"/>
    <status code="100"/>❶
    <status code="110"/>❷
    <status code="170"/>❸
  </x>
</presence>
```

❶ This indicates that anyone can view the occupant's real JID.

❷ This indicates that the presence stanza refers to the JID itself (i.e., this is your own presence information); the room might want to include this if it rewrites the user's room nick on entry.

❸ This indicates that conversation logging is enabled.

Although some of these features may seem like privacy intrusions, they can be quite beneficial (e.g., some public meeting rooms need a record of the conversations for archival purposes). The fact that users are warned when these features are in force enables them to avoid such rooms if desired.

MUC As a Data Transport

Up to this point, we have focused on MUC as a way to exchange textual messages. But as we've already seen, XMPP is an extensible way to send any kind of payload (as long as the resulting messages are of some reasonable size). Here are some payload types that might be of interest:

- Geolocation data for tracking vehicles, packages, and the like, using the format defined in [XEP-0080].

- Atom (or RSS) data for following syndicated feeds, using the format defined in [RFC 4287].

- Tune data for a jukebox or radio application, using the format defined in [XEP-0118].

- Alerting data for real-time emergency notifications, using the format defined in [XEP-0127].
- Signaling data for setting up multi-party media sessions, using the format defined in [XEP-0166], [XEP-0167], and related specifications (we discuss this further in Chapter 9).

MUC rooms can also be used to transport custom application data. One popular example of this is the Chesspark gaming service, which uses XMPP to send all of the chess moves between two players (with an in-room bot to enforce the rules of chess so that neither player can cheat).

In fact, nothing says that an MUC room needs to contain any people whatsoever! A chat room might include automated processes that exchange machine-readable data without any interaction from humans. Here the data formats used might be things like remote procedure calls as specified in *Jabber RPC* [XEP-0009], *SOAP over XMPP* [XEP-0072], *IO Data* [XEP-0244], or plain old *Data Forms* [XEP-0004].

Some of these uses shade over into a kind of "poor man's pubsub" because in essence multiuser chat follows the same "observer" or "publish-subscribe" design pattern as the XMPP PubSub extension. Although we discuss XMPP PubSub in more detail in Chapter 8, here we at least note that MUC is more appropriate for scenarios in which human users are involved (since messages of type groupchat are associated with a particular kind of user interface) or in which it is expected that the entities need to communicate among themselves in a stable venue of the kind provided by a persistent chat room with automatic archiving to a discussion log. By contrast, PubSub is usually more appropriate for one-to-many communication from a single publisher (or a few publishers) to a set of passive subscribers who merely listen for events, especially when no human subscribers are involved.

Summary

In this chapter, we provided an overview of multi-party interactions using XMPP groupchat, including the processes for joining, participating in, and leaving a chat room; sending and receiving messages; delayed delivery of the room history; reserving a nickname using the In-Band Registration protocol; configuring a room using the Data Forms extension; and enforcing appropriate security and privacy measures, such as kicking and banning users, disabling room logging, and preventing anyone except registered room members from joining the room. We also saw how the Multi-User Chat (MUC) protocol can be used to exchange not only human-readable messages, but any XML payload, such as syndicated data feeds, geolocation information, multimedia signaling messages, and even custom data for application, such as multiplayer games. Refer to *Multi-User Chat* [XEP-0045] for details about even more features, including changing your in-room nickname, modifying the room subject, inviting users, and adding or removing moderators and admins.

CHAPTER 8

Publish/Subscribe

Why It Matters

"Are we there yet?" asks a small boy in the back seat of a car. "No, not yet," answers the adult. Some minutes later, the child asks, "Are we there *now*?" This short but frequently repeated exchange is a real-world example of a *polling* system: the child won't know when the vehicle is approaching its destination, so he frequently checks with the adult driving the car. That is, the child is polling for information.

Usually it doesn't take long for the adult to reply, "I'll tell you when we're there." This is an example of a *publish/subscribe* system: here, the boy has expressed an interest in (*subscribed to*) a piece of information, and the adult will tell the child once the information changes (i.e., once updated information is *published*). Publish/subscribe systems avoid the need to frequently poll for updates. In this example, this helps the adult traveling with a young boy to stay sane; on the Internet, it serves the dual purpose of saving bandwidth and server resources (there are no more "has it changed?", "no, it hasn't" exchanges), and ensuring that the subscriber receives updates as quickly as the network can deliver them, rather than only the next time the subscriber polls the source.

As in real life, polling over the Internet is painful, especially for the server. Imagine that you have 100 "followers" on a microblogging service, each of whom polls the server every 10 minutes on the off chance that you have said something interesting (indeed, they would poll even more frequently if the server allowed them to). The server will receive 600 polls for information every hour, which works out to 10 polls per minute or one poll every 6 seconds for just one microblogging publisher! And the shame of it is that the vast majority of the polling requests result in the same answer: "Sorry to disappoint you, but there's nothing new to report." Multiply this scenario by 10,000 or 100,000 publishers, and it quickly becomes apparent that a polling architecture simply won't scale up as needed to deploy the kind of responsive social networking or "lifestreaming" services that end users demand on today's real-time Internet.

The pain of polling can be removed by a shift in mental models: a lifestreaming service such as microblogging or geolocation or social music is not a set of mini-websites (one for each publisher) that followers must poll for changes, but instead is a kind of micro-messaging service where each publisher is a node or channel for real-time notifications that are automatically sent to subscribers. Figure 8-1 illustrates the vast difference in traffic between a polling system and a pubsub system.

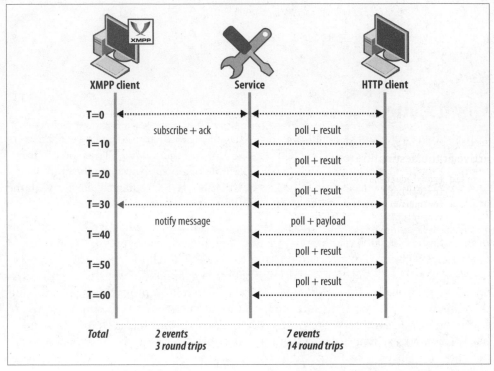

Figure 8-1. If a web client polls once every 10 minutes for a notification that occurs once an hour, the difference between polling and pubsub is significant

This publish/subscribe model is already familiar to you in the XMPP world because *presence* (described in Chapter 3) is a specialized form of publish/subscribe. A more generalized form of the publish/subscribe model is provided by a dedicated XMPP extension known as *PubSub* and defined in [XEP-0060]. As you will see throughout this chapter, PubSub enables you to build many dynamic applications that are difficult to build in a scalable manner with existing polling-based technologies.

After walking through a simple example to outline the flow of PubSub services, we delve into the details of XMPP PubSub before discussing some of the more advanced uses. Finally, we discuss the use of PubSub for extending the presence mechanisms of XMPP with "rich presence" constructs.

Quickstart

Although PubSub has many options and nuances that make it powerful enough for almost anything you'll want to do with it, the premises are simple enough that we can jump straight in. If the adult in the earlier example is publishing to the `are-we-there-yet` node on the `pubsub.holiday.lit` service, the child can simply subscribe to that node with the following stanza:

```
<iq from="child@holiday.lit/car"
    id="bnx2hd03"
    to="pubsub.holiday.lit"
    type="set">
  <pubsub xmlns="http://jabber.org/protocol/pubsub">
    <subscribe node="are-we-there-yet" jid="child@holiday.lit"/>
  </pubsub>
</iq>
```

After a successful IQ reply from the server, the child is now subscribed to the PubSub node, and will be notified when any new items are published to it. Finally, the car will arrive at the destination and the adult can publish their arrival with:

```
<iq from="adult@holiday.lit/car"
    id="wpd7x937"
    to="pubsub.holiday.lit"
    type="set">
  <pubsub xmlns="http://jabber.org/protocol/pubsub">
    <publish node="are-we-there-yet">
      <item>
        <there xmlns="http://holiday.lit/there-yet" status="true"/>
      </item>
    </publish>
  </pubsub>
</iq>
```

And the child receives a notification:

```
<message from="pubsub.holiday.lit" to="child@holiday.lit">
  <event xmlns="http://jabber.org/protocol/pubsub#event">
    <items node="are-we-there-yet">
      <item id="bc42su0a93">
        <there xmlns="http://holiday.lit/there-yet" status="true"/>
      </item>
    </items>
  </event>
</message>
```

This simple example of PubSub is a bit contrived, but it illustrates the three main aspects of PubSub: *subscribing* to a node, *publishing* to a node, and receiving *notifications* from a node. We build on these concepts through the remainder of this chapter.

Is Everything PubSub?

You may notice that the publish-subscribe pattern is used implicitly elsewhere in XMPP. As we've noted, in XMPP presence entities subscribe to each other's presence and receive publish notifications. A multi-user chat room can be seen as a channel where all the participants are publishers. And so on. In fact, it has been joked that all of XMPP could be modeled on top of [XEP-0060]. There even exists a (humorous) "XMPP Eventing via Pubsub" specification [XEP-0207] defining just that, written for the XSF's annual "April Fool" XEP.

Subscriptions

We now look at some of the common operations you will use while working with PubSub systems. The examples that follow were built around weblogs published by the Queen and by Alice. Notifications of new entries at these weblogs are posted to XMPP PubSub nodes at the `notify.wonderland.lit` service. Let's start with Alice trying to subscribe to the Queen's blog, `queenly_proclamations`:

```
<iq from="alice@wonderland.lit/rabbithole"
    id="gh921nx3"
    to="notify.wonderland.lit"
    type="set">
  <pubsub xmlns="http://jabber.org/protocol/pubsub">
    <subscribe node="queenly_proclamations" jid="alice@wonderland.lit"/>❶
  </pubsub>
</iq>
```

❶ Including the JID in the `<subscribe/>` enables the subscriber to register a subscription either from her bare JID (so that all her resources can receive notifications) or from a specific full JID (to limit notifications to only that resource).

In this stanza, you can see that Alice is trying to subscribe from her `alice@wonderland.lit` JID to the `queenly_proclamations` node on the `notify.wonderland.lit` PubSub service, which is where the Queen announces updates to her blog. The `<subscribe/>` element specifies both the node to subscribe to, and Alice's own JID for the subscription.

PubSub Addressing

Although the examples in this chapter use the `node` attribute to select a specific node of a PubSub service, it is also possible to address nodes by using the name of the node as the resource identifier of the service (e.g., `notify.wonderland.lit/alices_blog`). However, this form is often avoided, perhaps because JabberIDs of the form `domain.tld/resource` somehow look unnatural.

We don't want our story to have an unhappy ending before it's begun, so the subscription succeeds:

```
<iq from="notify.wonderland.lit"
    id="gh921nx3"
    to="alice@wonderland.lit/rabbithole"
    type="result">
  <pubsub xmlns="http://jabber.org/protocol/pubsub">
    <subscription node="queenly_proclamations" jid="alice@wonderland.lit"
                  subscription="subscribed"/>
  </pubsub>
</iq>
```

This stanza mostly mirrors the original request in content, with the addition of a subscription attribute whose value here is subscribed to signal that the subscription request succeeded. It is also possible that the server will include an optional subid attribute, which is used to differentiate between multiple subscriptions to the same node from the same JID.

Usually, a subscription request will succeed without any errors or further action required. At that point, the subscriber will begin to receive notifications from the node, as explained in the next section of this chapter. However, as with any other type of IQ request, a request can fail. Besides standard errors (such as permission errors or nonexistent nodes), it is also possible that the node may require the subscriber to configure the subscription before notifications can be delivered. This alternate flow is signaled by the following reply:

```
<iq from="notify.wonderland.lit"
    id="gh921nx3"
    to="alice@wonderland.lit/rabbithole"
    type="result">
  <pubsub xmlns="http://jabber.org/protocol/pubsub">
    <subscription node="queenly_proclamations" jid="alice@wonderland.lit"
                  subscription="unconfigured">
      <subscribe-options>
        <required/>❶
      </subscribe-options>
    </subscription>
  </pubsub>
</iq>
```

❶ The <required/> element signals, reasonably enough, that the subscriber must configure their subscription options before the request will be applied.

In this case, the subscription state remains unconfigured until the subscriber completes the subscription configuration form. Therefore, Alice would request the configuration options:

```
<iq from="alice@wonderland.lit/rabbithole"
    id="hu48s01m"
    to="notify.wonderland.lit"
    type="get">
  <pubsub xmlns="http://jabber.org/protocol/pubsub">
```

```
            <options node="queenly_proclamations" jid="alice@wonderland.lit" />
        </pubsub>
    </iq>
```

The PubSub service would then return the configuration form (here a very simple single-option reply). The configuration form is another example of the data forms that we discussed in Chapter 6:

```
<iq from="notify.wonderland.lit"
    id="hu48s01m"
    to="alice@wonderland.lit/rabbithole"
    type="result">
  <pubsub xmlns="http://jabber.org/protocol/pubsub">
    <options node="queenly_proclamations" jid="alice@wonderland.lit" >
      <x xmlns="jabber:x:data" type="form">
        <field var="FORM_TYPE" type="hidden">
          <value>http://jabber.org/protocol/pubsub#subscribe_options</value>
        </field>
        <field var="pubsub#digest" type="boolean"
               label="Receive digest notifications (approx. one per day)?">
          <value>0</value>
        </field>
      </x>
    </options>
  </pubsub>
</iq>
```

Of course, it does you no good to subscribe if you can't also unsubscribe. So let us imagine that Alice has been subscribed to the Queen's blog for a few days and has grown quite tired of hearing "Off with his/her head!" in one way or another. She therefore unsubscribes from the node by sending a simple `<unsubscribe/>` request:

```
<iq from="alice@wonderland.lit/rabbithole"
    id="vd923k66"
    to="notify.wonderland.lit"
    type="set">
  <pubsub xmlns="http://jabber.org/protocol/pubsub">
    <unsubscribe node="queenly_proclamations" jid="alice@wonderland.lit"/>
  </pubsub>
</iq>
```

In return, the server acknowledges the unsubscription:

```
<iq from="notify.wonderland.lit"
    id="vd923k66"
    to="alice@wonderland.lit/rabbithole"
    type="result"/>
```

Publishing and Receiving Notifications

By now, you're fully conversant with subscribing to and unsubscribing from nodes, so all that remains is to do something interesting with them. Let's start with the Queen publishing some proclamations to her blog:

```
<iq from="queen@wonderland.lit/croquetlawn"
    id="ma019r58"
    to="notify.wonderland.lit"
    type="set">
  <pubsub xmlns="http://jabber.org/protocol/pubsub">
    <publish node="queenly_proclamations">❶
      <item>❷
        <entry xmlns="http://www.w3.org/2005/Atom">❸
          <title>A new thought</title>
          <summary>Off with their heads!</summary>
          <link rel="alternate" type="text/html" href="http://wonderland.lit/1865/"/>
          <id>tag:wonderland.lit,1865:entry-42</id>
          <published>1865-12-13T18:30:02Z</published>
          <updated>1865-12-13T18:30:02Z</updated>
        </entry>
      </item>
    </publish>
  </pubsub>
</iq>
```

❶ The `<publish/>` element indicates that the Queen wants to publish an item.

❷ The `<item/>` element surrounds the *payload* that the Queen is publishing.

❸ The `<entry/>` element here is the payload of the publication—the thing getting published. This particular payload is a standard Atom notification, as described in [RFC 4287]. However, PubSub isn't concerned about the nature of the payload, since it's simply a routing mechanism. This is why any (custom "namespaced") XML element can be a payload.

Now that the Queen has published this item to the node, the service sends Alice a notification (if she's not gotten bored and unsubscribed yet):

```
<message from="notify.wonderland.lit" to="alice@wonderland.lit">❶
  <body>A new thought: off with their heads!</body>
  <event xmlns="http://jabber.org/protocol/pubsub#event">❷
    <items node="queenly_proclamations"  id="bl38pahu98h">
      <item id="zi2ba967">
        <entry xmlns="http://www.w3.org/2005/Atom">❸
          <title>A new thought</title>
          <summary>Off with their heads!</summary>
          <link rel="alternate" type="text/html" href="http://wonderland.lit/1865/"/>
          <id>tag:wonderland.lit,1865:entry-42</id>
          <published>1865-12-13T18:30:02Z</published>
          <updated>1865-12-13T18:30:02Z</updated>
        </entry>
      </item>
    </items>
  </event>
</message>
```

❶ PubSub notifications are sent via the XMPP `<message/>` stanza, just like normal IM messages, mainly because the PubSub service doesn't necessarily know whether the subscriber is online and which of the subscriber's resources might be best for sending; it's best to leave those delivery details up to the subscriber's XMPP server and not try to second-guess the delivery logic at the PubSub service. However, if the PubSub service does have presence information, it can optimize delivery according to the `presence_based_delivery` configuration option (see "Creating and Deleting Nodes" on page 107).

❷ The `<event/>` element sent to Alice almost mirrors the `<publish/>` element from the Queen's submission, with a slightly modified namespace.

❸ The `entry` payload will be quite familiar, as it's the same payload the Queen submitted in the previous stanza.

Payloads: To Send or Not to Send?

When configuring a PubSub node, you face two fundamental choices:

- Whether notifications sent from the node will include the payload
- Whether items published at the node will be stored for later retrieval

PubSub nodes can be configured in any combination of these facets. In this section, we discuss whether to include the payload, and in the next section, we discuss whether to store the items.

It may seem odd not to include the payload. Surely everyone wants to receive the complete notification, such as the Atom data that defines the blog post!

Not always. Sometimes the items published to a PubSub node don't even contain a payload. Consider the example of a doorbell node: all you want to know is that someone is ringing the doorbell so that you can answer the door. When your client receives this event, it can play an appropriate sound, so no payload is necessary.

Another example is the "metadata" node for user avatars, as defined in [XEP-0084]. Here, the notifications do not include a payload, because the image data itself (which might be quite large) is hosted at a different node (the "data" node).

Whether payloads are sent or not sent is controlled by the `deliver_payloads` configuration option; the resulting node types are called *payload-included* nodes and *notification-only* nodes, respectively. (We discuss node configuration a bit later in this chapter.)

If the `queenly_proclamations` node we've been considering were configured to not include payloads, the notification would have looked like this:

```
<message from="notify.wonderland.lit" to="alice@wonderland.lit">
  <event xmlns="http://jabber.org/protocol/pubsub#event">
    <items node="queenly_proclamations">
      <item id="zi2ba967"/>❶
    </items>
  </event>
</message>
```

❶ The <item/> element has an id attribute in this example, providing a key for fetching the payload if needed.

Items: To Store or Not to Store?

The other primary configurable facet defines whether to store the items or not (this is controlled by the persist_items configuration option). When the XMPP community originally discussed publish-subscribe technologies, some developers insisted that it might be valuable to keep a history of published items (e.g., for traceability), whereas other developers just as strongly argued that the publish-subscribe design pattern is a pure eventing system with no history required. To satisfy both groups, it was decided to make this a configuration option. The resulting node types are called *persistent* nodes and *transient* nodes, respectively.

To use the example of the doorbell node, it is quite possible that you don't need an archive of when the doorbell rang—you just want to subscribe to the stream of people who arrive at your front door. In this case, the notifications would not even include an ItemID, because there is nothing to track or retrieve later.

For something more significant, such as notifications related to the queenly_proclama tions blog, there is value in keeping a history—for example, so that new subscribers can request some past notifications to gain some context for current postings.

If Alice subscribed to the queenly_proclamations node with a notifications-only configuration, she might want to retrieve the payload corresponding to a particular item. She would do so using the retrieve items feature:

```
<iq from="alice@wonderland.lit/rabbithole"
    id="ka03p485"
    to="notify.wonderland.lit"
    type="get">❶
  <pubsub xmlns="http://jabber.org/protocol/pubsub">
    <items node="queenly_proclamations">
      <item id="zi2ba967"/>❷
    </items>
  </pubsub>
</iq>
```

❶ The items are fetched using an IQ-get, to which the service replies with an error or an IQ-result. If the fetch is successful, the service will send one message for each notification (or, optionally, multiple notifications per message).

❷ Each <item/> element requests an item with a specified ItemID (you can request multiple items at once).

Or, if she was feeling particularly heavy-handed (or forgetful), she could ask for all the items:

```
<iq from="alice@wonderland.lit/rabbithole"
    to="notify.wonderland.lit"
```

```
        id="vru42mn"
        type="get">
    <pubsub xmlns="http://jabber.org/protocol/pubsub">
      <items node="queenly_proclamations" />❶
    </pubsub>
  </iq>
```

❶ The empty <items/> element requests all available items.

However, the service might not return the complete history (too many items!), or it might have kept only a certain number of items in storage (as set by the max_items configuration option discussed in "Node Configuration" on page 108).

Discovering Nodes

Suppose you have heard that the Queen has built up a collection of blog posts, and you would like to discover more about this service. First, you could verify that you have the address of the PubSub service correct, as the Knave does in the following disco#info exchange (we discussed service discovery in Chapter 5):

```
<iq from="knave@wonderland.lit/croquetlawn"
    to="notify.wonderland.lit"
    id="d1nfg39e"
    type="get">
  <query xmlns="http://jabber.org/protocol/disco#info"/>
</iq>

<iq from="notify.wonderland.lit"
    id="d1nfg39e"
    to="knave@wonderland.lit/croquetlawn"
    type="result">
  <query xmlns="http://jabber.org/protocol/disco#info">
    <identity category="pubsub" type="service"/>
    <feature var="http://jabber.org/protocol/pubsub"/>
  </query>
</iq>
```

You've discovered that notify.wonderland.lit is, indeed, a PubSub service—a good start. Now, to discover the (top-level) nodes available at this service, you can send a disco#items query to the service, as the Knave does here:

```
<iq from="knave@wonderland.lit/croquetlawn"
    id="nb74fg13"
    to="notify.wonderland.lit"
    type="get">
  <query xmlns="http://jabber.org/protocol/disco#items"/>
</iq>

<iq from="notify.wonderland.lit"
    id="nb74fg13"
    to="knave@wonderland.lit/croquetlawn"
    type="result">
  <query xmlns="http://jabber.org/protocol/disco#items">
```

```
        <item jid="notify.wonderland.lit"
              node="blogregator"
              name="Weblogs"/>❶
        <item jid="notify.wonderland.lit"
              node="croquet_results"
              name="Results from croquet games"/>❷
    </query>
  </iq>
```

❶ The blog entries we were looking for.

❷ You may find other nodes as well, such as this one.

With these service discovery requests, you've identified the weblogs node you're interested in. The next step of interest is to discover information about the node, which you can do in the same way as for the service—that is, by sending a `disco#info` query to the service, but this time specifying the particular node you're interested in:

```
<iq from="knave@wonderland.lit/croquetlawn"
    id="hl43fy32"
    to="notify.wonderland.lit"
    type="get">
  <query xmlns="http://jabber.org/protocol/disco#info" node="blogregator"❶/>
</iq>

<iq from="notify.wonderland.lit"
    id="hl43fy32"
    to="knave@wonderland.lit/croquetlawn"
    type="result">
  <query xmlns="http://jabber.org/protocol/disco#info" node="blogregator">
    <identity category="pubsub" type="collection"❷/>
  </query>
</iq>
```

❶ Adding the node attribute gets you results about a specific node, rather than the root node of the service.

❷ The type attribute tells you what kind of node this is. In this case, the node is a collection, as described in [XEP-0248].

There are two kinds of pubsub nodes: leaf nodes and collection nodes. A leaf node is a node to which items are published, whereas a collection node is a kind of aggregator for leaf nodes. (We discuss collection nodes more fully when we address item aggregation later in this chapter.) Because the blogregator node is a collection node, you can ask it about its associated nodes in the same manner as querying the service:

```
<iq from="knave@wonderland.lit/croquetlawn"
    id="xvp29fh7"
    to="notify.wonderland.lit"
    type="get">
  <query xmlns="http://jabber.org/protocol/disco#items" node="blogregator"/>
</iq>

<iq from="notify.wonderland.lit"
    id="xvp29fh7"
```

```
        to="knave@wonderland.lit/croquetlawn"
        type="result">
    <query xmlns="http://jabber.org/protocol/disco#items" node="blogregator">
      <item jid="notify.wonderland.lit" node="queenly_proclamations"/>
      <item jid="notify.wonderland.lit" node="alices_blog" />
    </query>
</iq>
```

Here, the reply to your query shows two available weblogs in the collection node: Alice's blog and the Queenly Proclamations blog that you've seen throughout the chapter. Since you're interested in hearing what the Queen has to say, let's perform a final query for information about this blog (which happens to be a leaf node):

```
<iq from="knave@wonderland.lit/croquetlawn"
    id="dge834wi"
    to="notify.wonderland.lit"
    type="get">
  <query xmlns="http://jabber.org/protocol/disco#items" node="queenly_proclamations"/>
</iq>

<iq from="notify.wonderland.lit"
    id="dge834wi"
    to="knave@wonderland.lit/croquetlawn"
    type="result">
  <query xmlns="http://jabber.org/protocol/disco#items" node="queenly_proclamations">
    <identity category="pubsub" type="leaf"/>
    <feature var="http://jabber.org/protocol/pubsub"/>
    <x xmlns="jabber:x:data" type="result">
      <field var="FORM_TYPE" type="hidden">
        <value>http://jabber.org/protocol/pubsub#meta-data</value>
      </field>
      <field var="pubsub#type" label="Payload type">
        <value>http://www.w3.org/2005/Atom</value>
      </field>
      <field var="pubsub#creator" label="Node creator">
        <value>queen@wonderland.lit</value>
      </field>
      <field var="pubsub#creation_date" label="Creation date">
        <value>1865-05-04T10:00Z</value>
      </field>
      <field var="pubsub#title" label="A short name for the node">
        <value>Queenly Proclamations (A Blog)</value>
      </field>
      <field var="pubsub#description" label="A description of the node">
        <value>The Queen's blog, home of beheadings.</value>
      </field>
      <field var="pubsub#language" label="Default language">
        <value>en</value>
      </field>
      <field var="pubsub#owner" label="Node owners">
        <value>queen@wonderland.lit</value>
      </field>
      <field var="pubsub#publisher" label="Publishers to this node">
        <value>queen@wonderland.lit</value>
      </field>
```

```
        <field var="pubsub#num_subscribers"
              label="Number of subscribers to this node">
          <value>42</value>
        </field>
      </x>
    </query>
  </iq>
```

As we've already seen for Multi-User Chat rooms, here again a data form is used to
include extended information in the service discovery result. In particular, this form
provides some interesting statistics (such as the creation date and the number of subscribers). It also discloses node management details, such as the list of publishing JIDs
and the node owners. You can also find out what kind of payload is published here—
in this case, your old data syndication friend http://www.w3.org/2005/Atom for the Atom
format. Now that you're armed with all this information, you can decide whether you
want to subscribe to this node, tell your friends about it, and so on.

Node Management

So far you've seen how to both Publish and Subscribe to nodes, and also how to discover
nodes. Now we'll cover the node management features available in PubSub: creating
nodes, deleting nodes, configuring nodes, and managing relationships with the node
(subscriptions and affiliations).

Creating and Deleting Nodes

Although many PubSub services will automatically create a node the first time you
publish to it, some services will require you to explicitly create the node first (and
sometimes you may want to, regardless). The auto-creation feature can be detected by
the inclusion or exclusion of the http://jabber.org/protocol/pubsub#auto-create entry in the disco#info results you receive from the service.

If the Queen wants to create her "Queenly Proclamations" node, she can do it with the
following stanza:

```
<iq from="queen@wonderland.lit/throne"
    id="cr561nd0"
    to="notify.wonderland.lit"
    type="set">
  <pubsub xmlns="http://jabber.org/protocol/pubsub">
    <create node="queenly_proclamations"/>
  </pubsub>
</iq>
```

PubSub Takes a REST

When a PubSub node is associated with a resource that is also available on the World Wide Web, it makes sense for the XMPP NodeID to be the same as the HTTP URL of the web resource. This simple practice is consistent with the representational state transfer (REST) architectural style and helps to ensure information coherence because the same data will appear via the Web and via XMPP. For instance, if the Queen's weblog is hosted at `http://blogs.wonderland.lit/queenly_proclama tions/`, then it would be appropriate to use that string as the ID of the node where her blog posts appear on the XMPP network.

If the pressures of public disclosure become too much for the Queen, she can delete her node entirely:

```
<iq from="queen@wonderland.lit/throne"
    id="d3l3t41t"
    to="notify.wonderland.lit"
    type="set">
  <pubsub xmlns="http://jabber.org/protocol/pubsub#owner">
    <delete node="queenly_proclamations"/>
  </pubsub>
</iq>
```

Because the Knave earlier subscribed to this node, he then receives a notification upon its deletion:

```
<message from="notify.wonderland.lit" to="knave@wonderland.lit">
  <event xmlns="http://jabber.org/protocol/pubsub#event">
    <delete node="queenly_proclamations"/>
  </event>
</message>
```

Node Configuration

Just as there are configuration options for subscriptions, there are also configuration options for nodes. Configuration options can be included at node creation time if the PubSub service supports the `create-and-configure` feature (which can be determined via the `disco#info` result you receive from the service). For example, the following stanza simultaneously creates the Queenly Proclamations node and sets two configuration options, the title of the node and the payload type:

```
<iq from="queen@wonderland.lit/throne"
    id="cr34t32o"
    to="notify.wonderland.lit"
    type="set">
  <pubsub xmlns="http://jabber.org/protocol/pubsub">
    <create node="queenly_proclamations"/>
    <configure>
      <x xmlns="jabber:x:data" type="submit">
        <field var="FORM_TYPE">
          <value>http://jabber.org/protocol/pubsub#node_config</value>❶
```

```
        </field>
        <field var="pubsub#title">
          <value>Queenly Proclamations - A Blog.</value>
        </field>
        <field var="pubsub#type">
          <value>http://www.w3.org/2005/Atom</value>
        </field>
      </x>
    </configure>
  </pubsub>
</iq>
```

❶ As we discussed in Chapter 6, the FORM_TYPE scopes the data for the node configuration form, which means that the client creating the node can know ahead of time which fields are supported.

To reconfigure the node after initial creation, the Queen queries the node for the full list of configuration options by sending an IQ-get to the server:

```
<iq from="queen@wonderland.lit/throne"
    id="kj2gs891"
    to="notify.wonderland.lit"
    type="get">
  <pubsub xmlns="http://jabber.org/protocol/pubsub#owner">❶
    <configure node="queenly_proclamations"/>
  </pubsub>
</iq>
```

❶ Here, the namespace is http://jabber.org/protocol/pubsub#owner because the action is related to actions taken by node owners.

The server then returns a complete node configuration form to the Queen, with the current node configuration choices set as the default values. The complete form is quite long because there are so many node configuration options, so here we show a truncated version:

```
<iq from="notify.wonderland.lit"
    id="kj2gs891"
    to="queen@wonderland.lit/throne"
    type="result">
  <pubsub xmlns="http://jabber.org/protocol/pubsub#owner">
    <configure node="queenly_proclamations">
      <x xmlns="jabber:x:data" type="form">
        <field var="FORM_TYPE" type="hidden">
          <value>http://jabber.org/protocol/pubsub#node_config</value>
        </field>
        <field var="pubsub#title" type="text-single"
               label="A friendly name for the node">
          <value>Queenly Proclamations - A Blog.</value>
        </field>
        <field var="pubsub#deliver_payloads" type="boolean"
               label="Whether to deliver payloads with event notifications">
          <value>true</value>
        </field>
        <field var="pubsub#persist_items" type="boolean"
```

```
                 label="Persist items to storage">
        <value>1</value>
      </field>
      <field var="pubsub#max_items" type="text-single"
             label="Max # of items to persist">
        <value>10</value>
      </field>
      <field var="pubsub#access_model" type="list-single"
             label="Specify the subscriber model">
        <option><value>authorize</value></option>
        <option><value>open</value></option>
        <option><value>presence</value></option>
        <option><value>roster</value></option>
        <option><value>whitelist</value></option>
        <value>open</value>
      </field>
      <field var="pubsub#roster_groups_allowed" type="list-multi"
             label="Roster groups allowed to subscribe">
        <option><value>friends</value></option>
        <option><value>courtiers</value></option>
        <option><value>servants</value></option>
        <option><value>enemies</value></option>
      </field>
      <field var="pubsub#send_last_published_item" type="list-single"
             label="When to send the last published item">
        <option label="Never"><value>never</value></option>
        <option label="When a new subscription is processed"><value>on_sub</value>
        </option>
        <option label="When a new subscription is processed and
         whenever a subscriber comes online">
          <value>on_sub_and_presence</value>
        </option>
        <value>never</value>
      </field>
      <field var="pubsub#type" type="text-single"
             label="Specify the type of payload data to be provided at this node">
        <value>http://www.w3.org/2005/Atom</value>
      </field>
    </x>
  </configure>
 </pubsub>
</iq>
```

The Queen then completes the node configuration form, and submits it to the server by sending an IQ-set with a data form of type submit.

Fire and Forget

It is also possible to include the configuration element when publishing an item, in which case the service will either reconfigure the node with the new settings, or treat them as a precondition to publishing and thus reject the publish request if the options don't match those currently in force at the node. Support for this publish-options feature can be determined via the disco#info result you receive from the service.

As you can see, there are many node configuration options. The most important configuration options are described next (we have deleted the `pubsub#` "prefix" to make the list more readable). See [XEP-0060] for a complete list of node configuration options.

- The `list-single access_model` option defines whether subscriptions are `open` to anyone, restricted to a `whitelist` controlled by the node owner, limited to those who have a `presence` subscription to the node owner or who are in a particular group in the owner's `roster`, or whether the node owner must explicitly `authorize` all subscription requests. We discuss this setting in the next section.

- The `list-multi collection` option defines which collection node(s) another node is affiliated with.

- The boolean `deliver_notifications` option defines whether notifications are sent at all (setting this to false results in a "quiet" node from which entities must explicitly pull information, which goes against the PubSub philosophy, but is useful in some scenarios; naturally, it defaults to `true`).

- The boolean `deliver_payloads` option defines whether payloads are included in notifications. We discussed this setting earlier in the chapter.

- The `text-single max_items` option defines the maximum number of published items that the service will store in the "history" of the node; typically, publication of a new item will result in deletion of the oldest item (consistent with the policy of "first in, first out").

- The `text-single max_payload_size` option defines the largest allowable payload (in bytes).

- The `list-single node_type` option defines whether the node is a `leaf` or a `collection`.

- The boolean `notify_config`, `notify_delete`, and `notify_retract` options define whether subscribers receive a notification when the node configuration is changed, when an item is deleted, or when an item is retracted.

- The boolean `notify_sub` option defines whether the node owner receives a notification when new entities subscribe to the node.

- The boolean `persist_items` option defines whether items published to the node are kept in persistent storage (up to the `max_items` number) or the node does not persist items and therefore is `transient`. We discussed this setting earlier in this chapter.

- The boolean `presence_based_delivery` option defines whether the service will send notifications if it has presence information about the subscriber. For a standalone pubsub service, this will require the subscriber to register with the service, but if the pubsub service is associated with an IM user's JID in the Personal Eventing Protocol, then the service might already have this information, thus enabling it to optimize the delivery of notifications.

- The `list-single publish_model` option defines who is allowed to publish to the node: `publishers` only, `subscribers`, or anyone (an `open` publication model).

- The `list-multi roster_groups_allowed` option specifies exactly which roster group or groups can subscribe to and retrieve items from the node. It is used together with an `access_model` setting of `roster`.

- The `list-single send_last_published_item` option defines when the node will automatically send at least the last published item to a subscriber: `never`, when the subscriber is newly subscribed (the `on_sub` value), or when the entity is newly subscribed or sends presence to the node or service (the `on_sub_and_presence` value).

- The boolean `subscribe` option defines whether subscriptions are allowed.

- The `title` option defines a human-readable name for the node.

- The `type` option defines the XML namespace of the payloads that are generated at the node.

Managing Node Access

All that remains before you have the full PubSub arsenal at your disposal is a quick look at managing the way a node is accessed.

You can choose from several access schemes for PubSub nodes in [XEP-0060]:

- The *Open* access model allows anyone to subscribe.

- The *Whitelist* access model allows only preselected JIDs to subscribe or to retrieve the node.

- The *Authorize* access model requires the node owner to approve any subscription requests.

- The *Presence* access model allows subscriptions only from JIDs that already have a presence subscription to the node owner.

- The *Roster* access model enables you to limit subscriptions to JIDs that are in specific roster groups (e.g., you might specify that only people in your Friends group can access information about your physical location).

Alice and the Queen have decided that they want to limit access to their weblogs using these node access models. Alice wants to whitelist only her friends, whereas the Queen wants to vet each subscription with the Authorize model (she is a bit of a control freak). Alice first checks the JIDs currently affiliated with her blog:

```
<iq from="alice@wonderland.lit/rabbithole"
    id="wl62hf87"
    to="notify.wonderland.lit"
    type="get">
  <pubsub xmlns="http://jabber.org/protocol/pubsub#owner">
    <affiliations node="alices_blog"/>
  </pubsub>
</iq>
```

```
<iq from="notify.wonderland.lit"
    id="wl62hf87"
    to="alice@wonderland.lit/rabbithole"
    type="result">
  <pubsub xmlns="http://jabber.org/protocol/pubsub#owner">
    <affiliations node="alices_blog">
      <affiliation jid="alice@wonderland.lit" affiliation="owner"/>
      <affiliation jid="rabbit@wonderland.lit" affiliation="member"/>
    </affiliations>
  </pubsub>
</iq>
```

Currently Alice owns the blog node, and the White Rabbit is whitelisted for access (an affiliation of `member`). She can add more JIDs to the whitelist at any time, as she now does with the Mad Hatter:

```
<iq from="alice@wonderland.lit/rabbithole"
    id="ad4ui81nk"
    to="notify.wonderland.lit"
    type="set">
  <pubsub xmlns="http://jabber.org/protocol/pubsub#owner">
    <affiliations node="alices_blog">
      <affiliation jid="hatter@wonderland.lit" affiliation="member"/>
    </affiliations>
  </pubsub>
</iq>
```

The Queen, with her Authorized access model, might receive notice that the Duchess wants to subscribe to her blog (here we see yet another use of data forms):

```
<message from="notify.wonderland.lit" to="queen@wonderland.lit">
  <x xmlns="jabber:x:data" type="form">
    <title>PubSub subscriber request</title>
    <instructions>
      To approve this entity's subscription request,
      set the "Allow this JID..." field to true.
    </instructions>
    <field var="FORM_TYPE" type="hidden">
      <value>http://jabber.org/protocol/pubsub#subscribe_authorization</value>
    </field>
    <field var="pubsub#subid" type="hidden"><value>subscription-001</value></field>
    <field var="pubsub#node" type="text-single" label="Node ID">
      <value>queenly_proclamations</value>
    </field>
    <field var="pusub#subscriber_jid" type="jid-single" label="Subscriber Address">
      <value>duchess@wonderland.lit</value>
    </field>
    <field var="pubsub#allow" type="boolean"
           label="Allow this JID to subscribe to this pubsub node?">
      <value>false</value>
    </field>
  </x>
</message>
```

At this point, the Duchess has a subscription state of pending. The Queen denies the request, as she's about to have the Duchess beheaded:

```
<message from="queen@wonderland.lit/croquetlawn" to="notify.wonderland.lit">
  <x xmlns="jabber:x:data" type="submit">
    <field var="FORM_TYPE">
      <value>http://jabber.org/protocol/pubsub#subscribe_authorization</value>
    </field>
    <field var="pubsub#subid">
      <value>subscription-001</value>
    </field>
    <field var="pubsub#node">
      <value>queenly_proclamations</value>
    </field>
    <field var="pubsub#subscriber_jid">
      <value>duchess@wonderland.lit</value>
    </field>
    <field var="pubsub#allow">
      <value>false</value>
    </field>
  </x>
</message>
```

The Duchess is then notified of the fact that her subscription request has been denied:

```
<message from="notify.wonderland.lit" to="duchess@wonderland.lit">
  <pubsub xmlns="http://jabber.org/protocol/pubsub">
    <subscription jid="duchess@wonderland.lit"
                  node="queenly_proclamations"
                  subscription="none"/>
  </pubsub>
</message>
```

In addition to the subscriber affiliation, a JID can be affiliated with a PubSub node in several ways (these affiliations might look familiar, since they are quite similar to the multiuser chat affiliations we described in Chapter 7). While [XEP-0060] defines these, and the possible transitions between them, in some detail, they can be quickly summarized: An owner has full control over a node, whereas an outcast is banned from access to a node, and an affiliation of none means there is no connection between a JID and a node. Between these, there are also publishers, who can publish to the node but not control it, and members, who can subscribe to the node and fetch data from it. You can set these in the same way as Alice set the Mad Hatter to be a member.

Item Aggregation via Collection Nodes

You've already met collection nodes, such as the one containing the Queen's and Alice's weblogs, but we didn't say much about them. A collection node is like a folder on a file system: it can contain files (leaf nodes) and other folders (collection nodes), but not the text that goes into a file (items). In XMPP PubSub, when a leaf node is *associated* with a collection node, the items that are published to the leaf node are also pushed to entities that have subscribed to the collection node. Thus collection nodes are a powerful mechanism for aggregation of notifications.

Subscribing to a collection node is no different from subscribing to a leaf node, so the examples we've already looked at still apply. And creating a collection node is as simple as sending a `create` request while specifying a `node_type` of `collection`:

```
<iq from="queen@wonderland.lit/croquetlawn"
    id="kip71j8r"
    to="notify.wonderland.lit"
    type="set">
  <pubsub xmlns="http://jabber.org/protocol/pubsub">
    <create node="blogregator"/>
    <configure>
      <x xmlns="jabber:x:data" type="submit">
        <field var="FORM_TYPE">
          <value>http://jabber.org/protocol/pubsub#node_config</value>
        </field>
        <field var="pubsub#node_type"><value>collection</value></field>
      </x>
    </configure>
  </pubsub>
</iq>
```

There are two ways to associate a leaf with a collection node: the owner of the leaf node can modify the `pubsub#collection` configuration option, or the owner of the collection node can modify the `pubsub#children` configuration option. Because the same rules apply to associating one collection node with another collection node, XMPP developers tend to call the associated leaf (or collection) node a *child node* and the collection node to which the leaf (or collection) node has been associated a *parent node*.

For example, Alice can associate her blog with the `blogregator` node, as shown in the following example, thus making her `alices_blog` node a *child* of the `blogregator` collection node:

```
<iq from="alice@wonderland.lit/rabbithole"
    id="buq73bn9"
    to="notify.wonderland.lit"
    type="set">
  <pubsub xmlns="http://jabber.org/protocol/pubsub">
    <create node="alices_blog"/>
    <configure>
      <x xmlns="jabber:x:data" type="submit">
        <field var="FORM_TYPE">
          <value>http://jabber.org/protocol/pubsub#node_config</value>
        </field>
        <field var="pubsub#collection"><value>blogregator</value></field>
      </x>
    </configure>
  </pubsub>
</iq>
```

Because the Queen created the `blogregator` collection node, she can make her `queenly_proclamations` node a child of the `blogregator` node by modifying the configuration of the collection node:

```
<iq from="queen@wonderland.lit/croquetlawn"
    id="vc91hs63"
    to="notify.wonderland.lit"
    type="set">
  <pubsub xmlns="http://jabber.org/protocol/pubsub#owner">
    <configure node="blogregator">
      <x xmlns="jabber:x:data" type="submit">
        <field var="FORM_TYPE">
          <value>http://jabber.org/protocol/pubsub#node_config</value>
        </field>
        <field var="pubsub#children">
          <value>alices_blog</value>
          <value>queenly_proclamations</value>
        </field>
      </x>
    </configure>
  </pubsub>
</iq>
```

Once a node has been associated with a collection, the owner of the parent node can disassociate the child node by again modifying the `pubsub#children` configuration option of the parent node. Here, the Queen removes her own blog from the `blogregator` collection node:

```
<iq from="queen@wonderland.lit/croquetlawn"
    id="sl8eo3i8"
    to="notify.wonderland.lit"
    type="set">
  <pubsub xmlns="http://jabber.org/protocol/pubsub#owner">
    <configure node="blogregator">
      <x xmlns="jabber:x:data" type="submit">
        <field var="FORM_TYPE">
          <value>http://jabber.org/protocol/pubsub#node_config</value>
        </field>
        <field var="pubsub#children">
          <value>alices_blog</value>
        </field>
      </x>
    </configure>
  </pubsub>
</iq>
```

The owner of the child node can terminate the association by again modifying the `pubsub#collection` configuration option for the child node:

```
<iq from="alice@wonderland.lit/rabbithole"
    id="kqid71n7"
    to="notify.wonderland.lit"
    type="set">
  <pubsub xmlns="http://jabber.org/protocol/pubsub">
    <configure node="alices_blog">
```

```
              <x xmlns="jabber:x:data" type="submit">
                <field var="FORM_TYPE">
                  <value>http://jabber.org/protocol/pubsub#node_config</value>
                </field>
                <field var="pubsub#collection"/>❶
              </x>
            </configure>
          </pubsub>
        </iq>
```

❶ Because Alice is removing all associations, she sends an empty `<field/>` element.

Collection nodes can be arranged and associated in a wide variety of ways that have not yet been widely explored within the XMPP developer community. [XEP-0248] describes some of these possibilities, but in many ways, collection nodes are on the cutting edge of XMPP technologies, so expect to see more development in this area after this book has been published.

Personal Eventing: PubSub Simplified

Although the XMPP PubSub extension has many advanced features, the basic idea is really quite simple: if you subscribe to a node, you will receive a notification whenever a publisher posts an item to the node. However, this presupposes that you have found a node you're interested in. When XMPP developers started working on publish-subscribe technologies in 2002, they thought in terms of the component model we've seen in Multi-User Chat: nodes would be hosted at a specialized component such as `notify.wonderland.lit`, and users would explore such a component to find nodes of interest.

Unfortunately, this model is not very user-friendly nor very personal. What if a typical IM user wants to publish information about her mood or the tunes she listens to, or perhaps some other form of rich presence? Does she really need to create multiple nodes at a large service? And how do her friends discover these nodes? Do they need to explore that service to find them, or wait for her to tell them explicitly? That seems like a roundabout way of creating and discovering personal information sources.

However, some clever XMPP developers realized that this model could be simplified quite a bit if the IM user's own JabberID could be a virtual PubSub service. Instead of forcing Alice to create nodes at `notify.wonderland.lit` and forcing her friends to find those nodes, the JID `alice@wonderland.lit` could function as a collection node for all sorts of information about Alice. And the model could be simplified even further if Alice's friends could advertise their interests in the presence information they are already sharing with Alice.

The result of these simplifications is a profile of PubSub called *Personal Eventing Protocol*, or PEP [XEP-0163]. In essence, PEP assumes that potential subscribers have two kinds of interests:

- If you use an IM system, then you're interested in certain *people*, namely the people in your roster.

- If you're interested in certain people, then you're probably interested in more than just their network availability; you might also be interested in their thoughts, their activities, their whereabouts, what music they listen to, etc.

These two assumptions underlie the explosion of "lifestreaming" services on the Internet today—microblogging services, geolocation services, social music services, and all the rest. XMPP's PubSub technology (especially the PEP subset) provides a perfect foundation for streaming interesting data about the people you want to know about. Let's explore how.

PEP leverages presence by enabling you to tell your friends what payloads you would like to receive. It does this using a clever hack to the Entity Capabilities protocol we look at in Chapter 5: if you are interested in receiving, say, tunes data, your client advertises support for the `http://jabber.org/protocol/tune+notify` feature, where the `+notify` suffix means that you want to receive notifications about the string that precedes the suffix. Your interest in that data is then encapsulated into the Entity Capabilities format and advertised in the presence notifications that you send to your friends.

When your friend's XMPP server receives your specially marked presence notification, it sees that you are interested in receiving tunes data. It then checks to see whether you are authorized to receive that data from your friend. If so, it automatically starts sending you tune notifications, with no explicit discovery or subscription processes required on your part.

So far, PEP is mainly used for rich presence. What follows is a catalog of several types of rich presence extensions, available at the time of this writing. In the following examples, we omit the surrounding publish (or notification) elements, which are exactly as the previous examples, and show only the actual payload:

User Tune [XEP-0118]
> Enables you to publish the music you are listening to, including the track number, the length (in seconds), a rating of the played track, and a URI to visit for extra information about the track:

```
<tune xmlns="http://jabber.org/protocol/tune">
  <artist>Pink Floyd</artist>
  <title>Dogs</title>
  <source>Animals</source>
  <track>2</track>
  <length>1024</length>
  <rating>8</rating>
  <uri>http://pinkfloyd.com</uri>
</tune>
```

User Location [XEP-0080]
> Provides information about your current location. The exact description of your location can be given using different properties, from the exact positioning

parameters (such as latitude, longitude and altitude) to more abstract descriptions (such as country, region, city, street, and building). On top of this, a textual description can be given to describe your current location in a more general way:

```
<geoloc xmlns="http://jabber.org/protocol/geoloc">
  <country>Italy</country>
  <lat>45.44</lat>
  <locality>Venice</locality>
  <lon>12.33</lon>
  <alt>2</alt>
</geoloc>
```

User Activity [XEP-0108]

Basic presence provides only a small set of status types: away, extended away, and do not disturb. User Activity provides a taxonomy of extra types that further describe the actual activity, such as <eating/>, <working/>, and <relaxing/>. These types can be further specified using sub-types and a generic description, for example:

```
<activity xmlns="http://jabber.org/protocol/activity">
  <relaxing>
    <partying/>
  </relaxing>
  <text>My sister's birthday!</text>
</activity>
```

User Mood [XEP-0107]

Communicates information about your current mood. Besides a fixed taxonomy of types of moods (such as *happy*, *hungry*, and *proud*), you can specify your mood with a textual description. For example:

```
<mood xmlns="http://jabber.org/protocol/mood">
  <annoyed/>
  <text>Curse the Queen!</text>
</mood>
```

User Nickname [XEP-0172]

Allows you to publish your nickname. This enables your contacts to display the nickname you chose in addition to (or instead of) the name they assigned themselves when adding you to their roster. A nickname specification is very simple:

```
<nick xmlns="http://jabber.org/protocol/nick">The Knave</nick>
```

Besides being used with the publish/subscribe protocol described throughout this section, nickname information can also appear in other contexts. A nickname can be added to the presence subscription requests from Chapter 3, in order to suggest a nickname for adding the contact to the roster. For example:

```
<presence from="knave@wonderland.lit/pda"
          to="alice@wonderland.lit"
          type="subscribe">
  <nick xmlns="http://jabber.org/protocol/nick">The Knave</nick>
</presence>
```

Nickname information can also be added to messages. This is useful in a conversation between people who don't have presence (and therefore extended presence) information about each other (e.g., because they are not subscribed to each other's presence). The following is an example of such an annotated message:

```
<message from="alice@wonderland.lit/rabbithole"
         to="whiterabbit@wonderland.lit"
         type="chat">
  <body>If you please, sir--</body>
  <nick xmlns="http://jabber.org/protocol/nick">Alice</nick>
</message>
```

User Avatar [XEP-0084]

Another way of distinguishing people, besides nicknames, is by using pictures. Such a picture or photograph is also called an "avatar." In XMPP, you can publish your avatar using PEP as well, by embedding the raw image data as a Base64 string:

```
<iq from="alice@wonderland.lit/rabbithole" id="krw7361g" type="set">
  <pubsub xmlns="http://jabber.org/protocol/pubsub">
    <publish node="urn:xmpp:avatar:data">
      <item id="111f4b3c50d7b0df729d299bc6f8e9ef9066971f">
        <data xmlns="urn:xmpp:avatar:data">
          qANQR1DBwU4DX7jmYZnncm...
        </data>
      </item>
    </publish>
  </pubsub>
</iq>
```

However, there's a catch here. Not only will all your interested contacts get this chunk of image data when you change it, but your server will send it to them every time they log onto the network, so that they will have up-to-date versions of your avatar. Since your avatar changes infrequently, this would result in a waste of bandwidth. To avoid this, you publish the metadata of your avatar, including a (SHA-1) hash of the image data:

```
<iq from="alice@wonderland.lit/rabbithole" id="cqo82g57" type="set">
  <pubsub xmlns="http://jabber.org/protocol/pubsub">
    <publish node="urn:xmpp:avatar:metadata">
      <item id="111f4b3c50d7b0df729d299bc6f8e9ef9066971f">
        <metadata xmlns="urn:xmpp:avatar:metadata">
          <info width="64" height="64" type="image/png" bytes="12345"
                id="111f4b3c50d7b0df729d299bc6f8e9ef9066971f"/>
        </metadata>
      </item>
    </publish>
  </pubsub>
</iq>
```

When your contacts now subscribe to your metadata node (instead of to your actual data node), they get much more concise information about your avatar every time they receive an update:

```
<message from="alice@wonderland.lit" to="sister@realworld.lit">
  <event xmlns="http://jabber.org/protocol/pubsub#event">
    <items node="urn:xmpp:avatar:metadata">
      <item id="111f4b3c50d7b0df729d299bc6f8e9ef9066971f">
        <metadata xmlns="urn:xmpp:avatar:metadata">
          <info width="64" height="64" type="image/png" bytes="12345"
                id="111f4b3c50d7b0df729d299bc6f8e9ef9066971f"/>
        </metadata>
      </item>
    </items>
  </event>
</message>
```

When their client receives an avatar hash it has not seen before, the client requests the image from the data node:

```
<iq from="sister@realworld.lit/home"
    id="hf387ir4"
    to="juliet@capulet.lit"
    type="set">
  <pubsub xmlns="http://jabber.org/protocol/pubsub">
    <items node="urn:xmpp:avatar:data">
      <item id="111f4b3c50d7b0df729d299bc6f8e9ef9066971f"/>
    </items>
  </pubsub>
</iq>
```

As a result, your server replies with your published data:

```
<iq from="juliet@capulet.lit"
    to="sister@realworld.lit/home"
    id="hf387ir4"
    type="result">
  <pubsub xmlns="http://jabber.org/protocol/pubsub">
    <items node="urn:xmpp:avatar:data">
      <item id="111f4b3c50d7b0df729d299bc6f8e9ef9066971f">
        <data xmlns="urn:xmpp:avatar:data">
          qANQR1DBwU4DX7jmYZnncm...
        </data>
      </item>
    </items>
  </pubsub>
</iq>
```

The list of applications of extended presence goes on: publishing the chat rooms you visit, the videos you watch, the games you play, you name it. All these applications use the same principles as the ones mentioned in this chapter, so we do not provide detailed descriptions here.

Summary

As we've seen, the model of *subscribing* to an information node and then receiving a notification only when an entity *publishes* an item to that node provides a scalable, real-time alternative to the pain of constant polling for updates. The XMPP PubSub extension supports these core publish and subscribe semantics, as well as a broad range of ancillary use cases, such as node configuration, subscription configuration, several helpful node access models, item persistence, and aggregation of items via collection nodes. And the PubSub specification [XEP-0060] defines additional use cases we don't have space for in this book. Furthermore, the Personal Eventing Protocol, or PEP [XEP-0163], specifies a slimmed-down profile of PubSub that simplifies the processes of discovering and subscribing to nodes associated with accounts registered on an XMPP server. PEP is mainly used for communicating "rich presence," such as moods, and exchanging "lifestreaming" data, such as microblogs, but is also being applied to storing personal data, such as bookmarks and client preferences. PubSub is an exciting addition to the XMPP toolkit that will be used for years to come in building out the real-time Internet.

CHAPTER 9

Jingle: Jabber Does Multimedia

To Instant Messaging and Beyond

So far we've seen how XMPP can be used to exchange one-to-one messages, participate in multi-user chat rooms, and send alerts and notifications. But what if text is not enough? Sometimes there is no replacement for voice, video, and other rich media interactions.

Enter Jingle, defined in [XEP-0166] and a number of related specifications. After several years of experimentation, in 2005 the XMPP developer community finally got serious about adding support for voice chat, spurred on by the launch of Google Talk, an XMPP-based service for instant messaging and Voice over Internet Protocol (VoIP). In fact, the Google Talk team worked with developers in the community to define Jingle as a refinement of the Google Talk protocol (similar to the way in which XMPP is a refinement of the original Jabber protocol or Multi-User Chat is a refinement of the original groupchat protocol).

Jingle Versioning

The original protocol deployed at the Google Talk service has some subtle differences from the protocol that has been formalized by the XMPP Standards Foundation (with many contributions from members of the Google Talk team and other developers). You can think of that original protocol as "Jingle 0.9," but by the time you read this book, the version to implement will be "Jingle 1.0," as published in the relevant XEPs.

Jingle provides a reliable mechanism for setting up voice calls over the Internet (see [XEP-0167] for details). Even more interesting, the same basic Jingle methods can be used to negotiate and manage any kind of media session, including video chat, file transfer, and screen sharing. This makes Jingle yet another powerful building block in the XMPP toolkit.

Jingle provides a pluggable model for both application types and transport methods. Typically, Jingle is used to set up sessions that are not appropriate over XMPP itself. As we've discussed, XMPP is optimized for the exchange of many small snippets of XML, not data-heavy media streams. The Internet community has defined perfectly good technologies for the transport of voice, video, files, and other application types. Jingle therefore simply reuses those technologies for "heavy lifting" rich media sessions. The basic idea is that Jingle uses XMPP as the *signaling* channel to set up, manage, and terminate media sessions, whereas the media data itself is sent either *peer-to-peer* or *mediated* through a dedicated media relay.

Channels and Connections

There are two kinds of channels in Jingle, SIP, and other multimedia technologies: the *signaling channel* is used to send messages for overall session management, whereas the *media channel* is used to send the media data itself. Furthermore, the media channel itself can result in a connection that is either *peer-to-peer* (a direct connection between two clients) or *mediated* (the data is sent through a relay server).

There are exceptions to this pattern, which we explore in upcoming chapters, but for now you can think of Jingle as a way to set up media sessions that go outside the normal XMPP channel. Let's see how it works.

The Jingle Model

In a Jingle negotiation, one party (the *initiator*) offers to start a session, and the other party (the *responder*) answers the offer by either agreeing to proceed or declining the invitation. An offer has two parts:

Application type
    States *what* is going to be exchanged in the session—for example, voice chat via the Real-time Transport Protocol (RTP).

Transport method
    Describes *how* data is going to be sent—for example, using the User Datagram Protocol (UDP).

The offer triggers a flurry of XMPP traffic between the initiator and the responder, as their XMPP clients negotiate various parameters related to the application type (e.g., audio codecs) and the transport method (e.g., IP addresses and port numbers to check for connectivity). Once both parties agree on these parameters and the responder sends a Jingle session-accept message, the session transitions from the pending phase to the active phase. At this point, the XMPP signaling traffic quiets down as the parties exchange media data (XMPP stanzas can still be exchanged during the active phase as well, for example, to renegotiate parameters, or to add a new application type such as video to an existing session). Thus, the overall flow of a Jingle session is as follows:

1. The initiator sends an offer to the responder.
2. The offer consists of one or more application types (voice, video, file transfer, screen sharing, etc.) and one or more transport methods (UDP, ICE, TCP, etc.).
3. The parties negotiate parameters related to the application type(s) and work to set up the transport(s).
4. The responder either accepts or declines the offer.
5. If the offer is accepted, the parties exchange data related to the application type(s) over the negotiated transport method(s).
6. If needed, the parties can modify certain parameters during the life of the session (e.g., by adding video to a voice chat or switching to a better transport candidate).
7. Eventually, the session ends and the parties go on with their lives.

This flow is illustrated in Figure 9-1.

The following simplified example illustrates the format of an offer using "stubs" for the application type and transport method:

```
<iq from="alice@wonderland.lit/rabbithole"
    id="jah28fh1"
    to="sister@realworld.lit/home"
    type="set">
  <jingle xmlns="urn:xmpp:jingle:1">
          action="session-initiate"❶
          initiator="alice@wonderland.lit/rabbithole"
          sid="a73sjjvkla37jfea">❷
      <content creator="initiator" name="just-an-example">
        <description xmlns="urn:xmpp:jingle:apps:stub:0"/>❸
          <transport xmlns="urn:xmpp:jingle:transports:stub:0"/>❹
      </content>
  </jingle>
</iq>
```

❶ The action attribute specifies the particular request or notification; here a request to initiate a session.

❷ The sid attribute specifies a unique Session ID for this Jingle session, which is generated by the initiator.

❸ The <description/> element always defines the application type; particular application types are differentiated by the XML namespace of the <description/> element and, for some application types, by the media attribute (e.g., "audio" or "video").

❹ The <transport/> element always defines a transport method; particular transport methods are differentiated by the XML namespace of the <transport/> element.

After the responder acknowledges receipt of the session-initiate and the parties negotiate some parameters related to the application type and the transport method (we

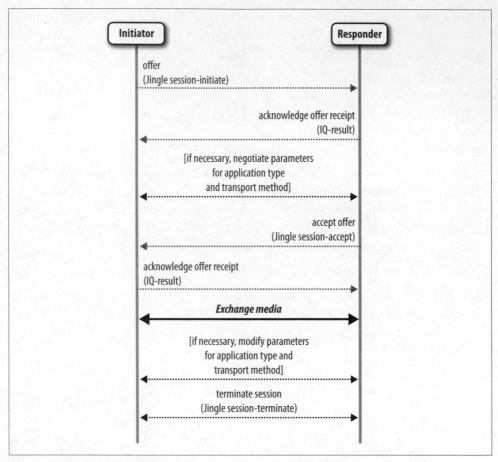

Figure 9-1. Jingle defines a state machine for the flow of a peer-to-peer multimedia session

explore these processes later), the responder would eventually send a `session-accept` to the initiator:

```
<iq from="sister@realworld.lit/home"
    id="b18dh29f"
    to="alice@wonderland.lit/rabbithole"
    type="set">❶
  <jingle xmlns="urn:xmpp:jingle:1"
          action="session-accept"❷
          initiator="alice@wonderland.lit/rabbithole"
          responder="sister@realworld.lit/home"
          sid="a73sjjvkla37jfea">
    <content creator="initiator" name="just-an-example">
      <description xmlns="urn:xmpp:jingle:apps:stub:0"/>
      <transport xmlns="urn:xmpp:jingle:transports:stub:0"/>
    </content>
  </jingle>
</iq>
```

❶ The `session-accept` action is a new IQ-set, not an IQ-result sent in response to the session-initiate; each Jingle action is a separate IQ-set so that it can be immediately acknowledged with an IQ-result and thus keep the negotiation moving forward as fast as possible.

❷ A Jingle action of `session-accept` is used to definitively accept the offer. The acceptance usually will include the precise application parameters and transport candidate that is acceptable to the responder.

The initiator acknowledges receipt of the `session-accept` (a simple IQ-result, not shown here) and the parties can exchange "stub" media data over the "stub" transport.

Eventually, one of the parties (here the responder) will terminate the session:

```
<iq from="sister@realworld.lit/home"
    id="g91hs73n"
    to="alice@wonderland.lit/rabbithole"
    type="set">
  <jingle xmlns="urn:xmpp:jingle:1"
          action="session-terminate"❶
          initiator="alice@wonderland.lit/rabbithole"
          responder="sister@realworld.lit/home"
          sid="a73sjjvkla37jfea">
    <reason>❷
      <success/>❸
    </reason>
  </jingle>
</iq>
```

❶ A Jingle action of `session-terminate` is used to formally end the session.

❷ The `<reason/>` element is used to specify why this particular Jingle action is being sent; it contains a predefined condition and, optionally, a human-readable `<text/>` element.

❸ The `<success/>` element implies that no error has occurred, or that the session has completed successfully.

The recipient acknowledges receipt of the `session-terminate` (a simple IQ-result, not shown here), and the session is ended.

Now that we've looked at the overall session flow at a high level using a stub example, let's look at how real Jingle sessions are established to fill in the blanks for the `<description/>` and `<transport/>` elements.

Making a Call

Jingle was first developed for one-to-one voice chat over the Internet. In this case, the application type is a Jingle RTP session, as defined in [XEP-0167] using a *datagram* transport method that is appropriate for voice data.

Transport Types: Datagram and Streaming

There are two basic kinds of transport methods: datagram and streaming. A datagram transport is suitable for applications where some packet loss is tolerable, such as voice and video (if you lose some packets of audio or video data, you can interpolate without seriously degrading the quality). A streaming transport is suitable for applications where packet loss is not tolerable, such as file transfer (if you lose some packets of file data, you can't correctly construct the file). The canonical examples of datagram and streaming transports are UDP and TCP, respectively.

Here the offered transport method is the simplest one-to-one UDP association, negotiated using the *Jingle Raw UDP Transport* [XEP-0177]:

```
<iq from="alice@wonderland.lit/rabbithole"
    id="v73hwcx9"
    to="sister@realworld.lit/home"
    type="set">
  <jingle xmlns="urn:xmpp:jingle:1"
          action="session-initiate"
          initiator="alice@wonderland.lit/rabbithole"
          sid="a73sjjvkla37jfea">
    <content creator="initiator" name="voice">
      <description xmlns="urn:xmpp:jingle:apps:rtp:1" media="audio">
        <payload-type id="96" name="speex" clockrate="16000"/>❶
        <payload-type id="97" name="speex" clockrate="8000"/>
        <payload-type id="0" name="PCMU"/>
        <payload-type id="8" name="PCMA"/>
      </description>
      <transport xmlns="urn:xmpp:jingle:transports:raw-udp:1">
        <candidate candidate="1"
                   generation="0"
                   id="a9j3mnbtu1"
                   ip="10.1.1.104"
                   port="13540"/>❷
      </transport>
    </content>
  </jingle>
</iq>
```

❶ For RTP sessions, each `<payload-type/>` element defines an audio or video codec and some associated information, such as the clockrate and the number of channels (e.g., two for stereo).

❷ For many transport methods, each `<candidate/>` element defines an IP address and port that can be attempted for direct or mediated communication of media data.

In this case, the initiator's client wishes to establish an RTP session using any of four audio codecs in the following preference order:

1. The open source Speex codec at a clockrate of 8,000 Hertz.

2. The open source Speex codec at a clockrate of 16,000 Hertz (this is a "wideband" codec with higher audio quality).

3. The "PCMU," or μ-law, flavor of the ITU's G.719 codec, which is supported in traditional telephony systems in the U.S. and Japan.

4. The "PCMA," or a-law, flavor of the ITU's G.719 codec, which is supported in telephony systems in the rest of the world.

The initiator's client also wishes to use the Raw UDP transport, which is defined in [XEP-0177], with an IP address of 10.1.1.104 and a port of 13540. (We don't need to concern ourselves here with each and every parameter communicated in the Jingle stanzas, such as the candidate numbers and IDs or the generation numbers; refer to the Jingle specifications for all the details.)

Because the response to an XMPP IQ stanza must be either an IQ-result or an IQ-error, the responder's client immediately acknowledges receipt (but not yet acceptance) of the offer:

```
<iq from="sister@realworld.lit/home"
    id="v73hwcx9"
    to="alice@wonderland.lit/rabbithole"
    type="result"/>
```

As mentioned, the parties must now negotiate parameters related to the application type and the transport method. In this case, the responder's client performs a few actions:

- Checks the offered codecs against the list of codecs it supports.
- Optionally sends an informational "ringing" notification to the initiator.
- When it accepts the session, optionally offers an IP address and port number of its own as another connectivity candidate (e.g., this might be a relay server that the responder knows about).

The following two examples show the "ringing" notification and the candidate offer:

```
<iq from="sister@realworld.lit/home"
    id="k3d7abv8"
    to="alice@wonderland.lit/rabbithole"
    type="set">
  <jingle xmlns="urn:xmpp:jingle:1"
          action="session-info"❶
          initiator="alice@wonderland.lit/rabbithole"
          responder="sister@realworld.lit/home"
          sid="a73sjjvkla37jfea">
    <ringing xmlns="urn:xmpp:jingle:apps:rtp:info:1"/>❷
  </jingle>
</iq>
```

❶ Here the Jingle action is `session-info`, which is used to send informational messages throughout the life of the session.

❷ This informational message is a simple notification that the other party's device is ringing.

And, of course, the responder's client asks the human user controlling the client if she wants to accept a voice call from the initiator!

If the responding user wants to talk, the responding client accepts the session by sending the codecs it supports (here only Speex at a clockrate of 8,000 Hertz) along with an IP address and port that the responder offers for connectivity checking:

```
<iq from="sister@realworld.lit/home"
    id="ikw71b54"
    to="alice@wonderland.lit/rabbithole"
    type="set">
  <jingle xmlns="urn:xmpp:jingle:1"
          action="session-accept"
          initiator="alice@wonderland.lit/rabbithole"
          responder="sister@realworld.lit/home"
          sid="a73sjjvkla37jfea">
    <content creator="initiator" name="voice">
      <description xmlns="urn:xmpp:jingle:apps:rtp:1" media="audio">
        <payload-type id="97" name="speex" clockrate="8000"/>❶
      </description>
      <transport xmlns="urn:xmpp:jingle:transports:raw-udp:1">
        <candidate candidate="1"
                   generation="0"
                   id="z7sdjb01hf"
                   ip="208.68.163.214"
                   port="9876"/>
      </transport>
    </content>
  </jingle>
</iq>
```

❶ The only payload-type that this responder supports (from among those offered by the initiator) is the open source Speex codec at a clockrate of 8,000 Hertz.

Now the parties can begin to chat over the negotiated voice channel, using the Speex codec in RTP over a raw UDP connection. Here we leave the world of XMPP behind, because the media data is sent peer-to-peer or through a media relay, not through the XMPP servers used by the initiator and responder for call setup. This is the beauty of Jingle: it uses XMPP for call management but more appropriate transport methods for voice, video, files, and other binary data.

Eventually, one of the parties will want to end the call. Since this is a call management action, it is completed over the XMPP signaling channel using a Jingle action of session-terminate:

```
<iq from="sister@realworld.lit/home"
    id="ip71v3fz"
    to="alice@wonderland.lit/rabbithole"
    type="set">
  <jingle xmlns="urn:xmpp:jingle:1"
```

```
      action="session-terminate"
      initiator="alice@wonderland.lit/rabbithole"
      responder="sister@realworld.lit/home"
      sid="a73sjjvkla37jfea">
  <reason><success/></reason>
</jingle>
</iq>
```

A Swarm of NATs

That was rather painless, wasn't it? Well, not so fast! Life on the Internet is never quite as easy as it seems. The problem arises from that little part about the initiator and responder exchanging IP addresses where they could be contacted. In today's world, you need to be extremely careful about allowing connections to your computer on random ports. As a result, your computer probably lives behind a firewall to protect itself from the big, bad Internet. Furthermore, your firewall probably includes something called a Network Address Translator, or NAT. This means that devices inside the firewall (including your Jabber client) think they have one IP address, whereas devices outside the network see a different IP address.

As you can see in Figure 9-2, Party 1 thinks his IP address is "1.2.3.4". However, the NAT has translated that IP address to "10.0.0.1" for use by outside entities such as Party 2. If Party 1 tells Party 2 that his IP address is "1.2.3.4" and Party 2 then tries to contact him at "1.2.3.4" instead of "10.0.0.1", her communication attempt might fail.

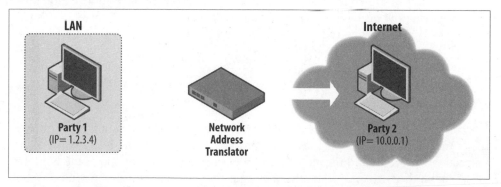

Figure 9-2. Network Address Translators (NATs) make it difficult to establish peer-to-peer media sessions

Even this description simplifies the problem quite a bit, because there are many different kinds of NATs. Although we need not worry about all the details here, we do need a solution to the problem of NAT traversal in order for media to flow reliably. And when it comes to features like voice chat, reliability matters (if your phone worked only 90% of the time, you might not use it!).

Thankfully, the smart people at the IETF have defined several technologies for NAT traversal, with catchy names like STUN, TURN, and ICE. XMPP reuses these technologies so that Jingle clients can seamlessly interact with devices that implement the Session Initiation Protocol (SIP). Here's a brief overview of these three technologies:

- STUN ("Session Traversal Utilities for NAT") provides a way for you to find out what your IP address and port look like from outside your firewall (if, that is, you are able to contact a STUN server for address lookups).

- TURN ("Traversal Using Relays around NAT") provides a way for you to relay media data in case you can't set up a direct, peer-to-peer connection with the other party (if, that is, you are able to find a TURN server for media relaying).

- ICE ("Interactive Connectivity Establishment") provides a consistent way for two endpoints to rank, communicate, and negotiate all the possible combinations of direct and mediated connections between them.

These technologies come together in the *Jingle ICE-UDP Transport* [XEP-0176]. This transport method results in a lot more XMPP traffic than the Raw UDP method we looked at in the last section, mainly because there are many more "candidates" (IP addresses and ports) to be checked. However, the result is greater reliability.

You'll also notice that STUN and TURN both require additional infrastructure. So far, Jingle hasn't even required special XMPP server modules, because the clients have done all the work. (It may seem that this goes against the original Jabber philosophy of "simple clients, complex servers," but the story here is that clients really do know best when it comes to the codecs they support and the exchange of IP+port candidates.) However, we now need some server-side help, which is provided not by the XMPP server itself but by specialized STUN servers and TURN relays.

The next section explains the ICE methodology in greater detail.

Jingle on ICE

Interactive Connectivity Establishment is a powerful methodology for figuring out how to set up media sessions (such as voice and video calls) over the Internet while still respecting the NATs and firewalls that may exist in a given network. Some NAT traversal methods try to "fake out" firewalls, and therefore are frowned upon by system administrators, but in contrast, ICE tries to work with NATs.

This "kindler, gentler" approach to NAT traversal requires quite a bit of up-front negotiation between the parties, as they exchange IP+port pairs for UDP.

But before the parties can communicate that information, they need to create their preferred list of candidates. There are four candidate types (see the ICE specification for complete details):

Host

> This is an IP+port hosted on the device itself (e.g., as obtained via Ethernet, a Wi-Fi hotspot, or a VPN).

Server reflexive

> This is an IP+port for a party's device, but translated into a public IP address by a NAT when the party sends a packet through the NAT to a STUN server or a TURN server. The party then discovers the server reflexive address for a specific candidate by contacting the STUN server or TURN server.

Peer reflexive

> A peer reflexive candidate is similar to a server reflexive candidate, except that the mapping of addresses happens in the NAT when the party sends a STUN binding request to a peer instead of directly to a STUN or TURN server. The party discovers the peer reflexive address as a result of connectivity checks later in the negotiation process.

Relayed

> This is the IP+port of a relay server (e.g., as hosted by an ISP). Typically, such a relay implements TURN, but it could implement some other data-relaying technology.

Once a Jingle client gathers these candidates, it prioritizes them according to the ICE rules, and then includes its highest-priority candidates in the session offer it sends to the responder. The session offer is rather large because it specifies both the payload types and transport candidates, but for our purposes here, the key aspect of the offer is the IP address and port of each candidate, along with its priority (candidates with higher numbers are more highly preferred):

```
<iq from="alice@wonderland.lit/rabbithole"
    id="xle82n56"
    to="sister@realworld.lit/home"
    type="set">
  <jingle xmlns="urn:xmpp:jingle:1">
        action="session-initiate"
        initiator="alice@wonderland.lit/rabbithole"
        sid="a73sjjvkla37jfea">
    <content creator="initiator" name="voice">
      <description xmlns="urn:xmpp:jingle:apps:rtp:1" media="audio">
        <payload-type id="96" name="speex" clockrate="16000"/>
        <payload-type id="97" name="speex" clockrate="8000"/>
        <payload-type id="0" name="PCMU"/>
        <payload-type id="8" name="PCMA"/>
      </description>
      <transport xmlns="urn:xmpp:jingle:transports:ice-udp:1"
                 pwd="asd88fgpdd777uzjYhagZg"
                 ufrag="8hhy">
        <candidate component="1"
                   foundation="1"
                   generation="0"
                   ip="10.0.1.1"
                   network="1"
```

```
                    port="8998"
                    priority="2130706431"❶
                    protocol="udp"❷
                    type="host"/>
          <candidate component="1"
                    foundation="2"
                    generation="0"
                    ip="192.0.2.3"❸
                    network="1"
                    port="45664"
                    priority="1694498815"
                    protocol="udp"
                    rel-addr="10.0.1.1"❹
                    rel-port="8998"
                    type="srflx"/>
      </content>
    </jingle>
  </iq>
```

❶ Don't worry about how these big numbers are generated! All you need to know is that a candidate with a larger value for the `priority` element is preferred in relation to a candidate with a small value for the `priority` attribute.

❷ The only protocol supported by ICE is UDP. However, work on an ICE profile for TCP is ongoing, so the `protocol` attribute might accept other values in the future.

❸ For server reflexive and peer reflexive candidates, the IP address and port describe the network address of the party outside the local network the party is on (i.e., as discovered via STUN). For a relayed candidate, the IP address and port describe the address of the relay server.

❹ The `rel-addr` and `rel-port` are used for diagnostic purposes; they specify the IP address and port of the host candidate from which the server reflexive, peer reflexive, or relayed candidate was derived.

When the responder sends its `session-accept` to the initiator, it also sends a set of possible candidates from its perspective (e.g., it may know about different relay servers). The parties then send connectivity checks over each pair of possible IP addresses and ports. More specifically, the responder sends one check from each of its IP+port candidates to each of the IP+port candidates sent by the initiator, and vice versa. This results in even more traffic between the parties, but this time outside the XMPP channel because the XMPP channel uses TCP, whereas ICE uses UDP. (After the parties exchange their highest-priority candidates in the `session-initiate` and `session-accept` messages, they can also send lower-priority candidates using Jingle `transport-info` messages.)

For example, the initiator offered the candidates 10.0.1.1:8998 and 192.0.2.3:45664. If the responder offered the candidates 192.0.2.1:3478 and 10.0.1.2:15999, the parties would try the following connectivity checks over UDP:

- The initiator sends connectivity checks from 10.0.1.1:8998 to 192.0.2.1:3478, from 10.0.1.1:8998 to 10.0.1.2:15999, from 192.0.2.3:45664 to 192.0.2.1:3478, and from 192.0.2.3:45664 to 10.0.1.2:15999.

- The responder sends connectivity checks from 192.0.2.1:3478 to 10.0.1.1:8998, from 192.0.2.1:3478 to 192.0.2.3:45664, from 10.0.1.2:15999 to 10.0.1.1:8998, and from 10.0.1.2:15999 to 192.0.2.3:45664.

Eventually, these connectivity checks will yield results, because connectivity checks will reveal the candidate pairs that succeed. And given the large number of candidates exchanged, the parties are almost guaranteed that at least one of the candidates pairs will succeed, thus leading to reliable call setup.

Additional Jingle Actions

So far, we've looked at the core Jingle actions: `session-initiate`, `session-accept`, `session-info`, `transport-info`, and `session-terminate`. However, several other Jingle actions enable you to modify a session while it is in progress:

content-add
> The `content-add` action enables you to add an entire content-type to a session (e.g., to add video to a voice call); this action is accepted or rejected using the `content-accept` action or the `content-reject` action.

content-remove
> The `content-remove` action enables you to delete an entire content-type from a session (e.g., to remove video from a combined voice-and-video session); the `content-replace` action is silently accepted.

content-modify
> The rarely used `content-modify` action changes the directionality of media exchange (from sender-only to both, receiver-only to both, etc.).

description-info
> The `description-info` action enables you to send hints about application parameters within a session (e.g., to provide suggestions about the height and width of a video feed).

transport-replace
> The `transport-replace` action enables you to redefine a transport method while it is in use (e.g., to change an IP address or port); this action is accepted or rejected using the `transport-accept` action or the `transport-reject` action.

We show how some of these are used in Chapter 10.

Summary

Jingle is a relatively recent addition to the XMPP toolkit. Although it provides a flexible framework for the negotiation and management of peer-to-peer media sessions, to date it has mostly been used for one-to-one voice chat. At the time of this writing, the Google Talk service and several open source XMPP clients have also added video support. Moreover, the same basic session-management pattern can be applied to many different kinds of negotiation (for example, Chapter 10 explains how to use Jingle for file transfer).

You probably noticed that Jingle uses IQ stanzas between two parties in order to negotiate a one-to-one session. But what if you want to set up a multi-party session, such as a conference call? In fact, a number of Jingle developers are exploring the potential of sending Jingle signaling through the Multi-User Chat (MUC) rooms we discussed in Chapter 7, resulting in a hybrid of Jingle and MUC. You'll need to check out *http://xmpp.org* for all the details, because they are being defined as we go to press.

The potential of Jingle is just starting to be explored, and the next few years promise to bring new Jingle applications for features, such as torrents, screen sharing, and virtual private networks (VPNs).

CHAPTER 10

Sending Binary Data

So far, we have mainly considered the exchange of small pieces of structured information: sending and receiving of messages (with or without markup, to one or more parties), broadcasting information about various forms of presence, sending alerts using PubSub, and the like. In Chapter 9, we delved into the Jingle framework for session negotiation, but we focused on the structured signaling messages rather than binary media data such as voice and video chats. In this chapter, we look at sending other kinds of binary data, especially files. We'll proceed in ascending order from small pieces of binary data up to large files.

Starting Small: Bits of Binary

As we have noted, XMPP is not optimized for sending binary data. But sometimes the data you want to send is so small and seemingly insignificant that you figure there must be a way to send it in-band. Why should those XML zealots prevent you from sharing, say, a small image file? Such images can be quite useful when you want to send an emoticon (those "smiley" and "frowny" faces that kids of all ages exchange over IM systems), a CAPTCHA ("Completely Automated Public Turing Test to Tell Computers and Humans Apart") to prevent malicious bots from overwhelming your XMPP server with new account registrations, and so on.

The XMPP developer community lacked such a method for a long time, so in 2008 they finally defined one, called *Bits of Binary* [XEP-0231], or BOB for short. The approach is simple: include a unique reference to the data in a message or other stanza, and enable the recipient to retrieve the data from the sender if the recipient has not already cached it.

One way to reference the data is by including an XHTML `<img/>` element in a message. The `src` attribute of the `<img/>` element contains a "cid:" URL, as defined in [RFC 2111] and illustrated in the following example:

```
<message from="mouse@wonderland.lit/foo"
         to="lory@wonderland.lit/bar"
         type="chat">
```

```
        <body>I beg your pardon! :( Did you speak?</body>
        <html xmlns="http://jabber.org/protocol/xhtml-im">
          <body xmlns="http://www.w3.org/1999/xhtml">
            <p>I beg your pardon!
              <img src="cid:sha1+5fb0482ba7f9a01b54a1af25060f7c783fd390af@bob.xmpp.org"/>❶
              Did you speak?
            </p>
          </body>
        </html>
      </message>
```

❶ A "cid:" URL has a special format when included in the Bits of Binary protocol: it consists of the hashing algorithm used (here sha1), a hash of the binary data itself, the at-sign, and the domain bob.xmpp.org (which might be used in the future for archiving and publishing common data files).

Here we assume that the recipient does not have the data cached, so it requests the data from the sender. This is done by sending an IQ-get that specifies the referenced cid:

```
      <iq from="lory@wonderland.lit/bar"
          id="vh39akj2"
          to="mouse@wonderland.lit/foo"
          type="get">
        <data xmlns="urn:xmpp:bob"
              cid="sha1+5fb0482ba7f9a01b54a1af25060f7c783fd390af@bob.xmpp.org"/>
      </iq>
```

The sender then returns the Base64-encoded data in the IQ-result (to improve readability, the data includes line breaks, but these would not occur in the stanza sent over the wire):

```
      <iq from="mouse@wonderland.lit/foo"
          to="lory@wonderland.lit/bar"
          id="vh39akj2"
          type="result">
        <data xmlns="urn:xmpp:bob"
              cid="sha1+5fb0482ba7f9a01b54a1af25060f7c783fd390af@bob.xmpp.org"
              type="image/png">
          iVBORwOKGgoAAAANSUhEUgAAADIAAAAyCAYAAAAeP4ixAAAABmJLR0QA/wD/AP+g
          ...
          mOjs3AAAAABJRU5ErkJggg==
        </data>
      </iq>
```

Now the recipient has the referenced data and can render the image in the original message (this is not unlike fetching an image to display in a web page).

The Bits of Binary approach is appropriate only for very small pieces of binary data (typically limited to 8 kilobytes). If you have more data to send, you need to use different methods, as we discuss next.

Moving On Up: Transferring Midsize Files In-Band

Let's say that Alice has a small camera with her when she takes her trip down the rabbit hole. She feels compelled to share some pictures with her sister, who otherwise simply wouldn't believe her story. So she picks the best picture and her XMPP client prepares to send all 400 KB of the file to her sister. There are three steps involved in this preparation:

1. Because XMPP has strict rules about what types of data it can carry, the first step of sending binary data is Base64-encoding it, such that it consists only of alpha-numeric characters.

2. Alice's XMPP server doesn't allow her to send stanzas that are larger than 64k, and her sister's server might be even more restrictive (there are good security and per-formance reasons for these restrictions, so Alice and her sister will have to live with them). Because the smallest allowable number of bytes for a server-enforced max-imum stanza size is only 10,000 (i.e., 10 kilobytes), Alice's XMPP client needs to break the 400 KB picture into smaller chunks. That is, it will chop up the data *stream* that it reads from the file into a number of smaller pieces, called *blocks*.

3. Because her sister's client will reconstruct the file from these data blocks, Alice's client needs to indicate that these blocks belong together, and that together they form one piece of data. Her client therefore announces to her sister that she is going to send a stream of data that is chunked into blocks of a certain size (here 4,096 bytes per block).

Let's see how this translates into XMPP, specifically *In-Band Bytestreams*, or IBB [XEP-0047]. First, Alice sends a request to initiate an in-band bytestream:

```
<iq from="alice@wonderland.lit/rabbithole"
    id="iy2s986q"
    to="sister@realworld.lit/home"
    type="set">
  <open sid="dv917fb4"❶
        block-size="4096"
        xmlns="http://jabber.org/protocol/ibb"/>
</iq>
```

❶ The `sid` attribute specifies a unique identifier for this bytestream.

After Alice sends her initiation request, her sister accepts the request:

```
<iq from="sister@realworld.lit/home"
    id="iy2s986q"
    to="alice@wonderland.lit/rabbithole"
    type="result"/>
```

Alice's client can now start sending packets. In order to do so, it chops up the Base64-encoded stream into 4,096-byte blocks (as it promised when opening the bytestream) and puts them inside a series of message stanzas (here again the line breaks are included only for readability):

```
<message from="alice@wonderland.lit/rabbithole"
         to="sister@realworld.lit/home"
         id="ck39fg47">
  <data xmlns="http://jabber.org/protocol/ibb"
        sid="dv917fb4"
        seq="0">❶
    qANQR1DBwU4DX7jmYZnncmUQB/9KuKBddzQH+tZ1ZywKKOyHKnq57kWq+RFtQdCJ
    WpdWpROuQsuJe7+vh3NWn59/gTc5MDlX8dS9pOovStmNcyLhxVgmqS8ZKhsblVeu
    IpQOJgavABqibJolc3BKrVtVV1igKiX/N7Pi8RtY1K18toaMDhdEfhBRzO/XBO+P
    AQhYlRjNacGcslkhXqNjK5Va4tuOAPy2n1Q8UUrHbUdOg+xJ9BmoGOLZXyvCWyKH
    kuNEHFQiLuCY6IvOmyq6iX6tjuHehZlFSh8Ob5BVV9tNLwNR5Eqz1klxMhoghJOA
  </data>
</message>
```

❶ For every block Alice sends, she adds a sequence number such that her sister can detect missing blocks. The sequence starts at zero, and increments by one with each block.

After sending the first block, Alice's client then continues to send message stanzas, incrementing the seq attribute by one each time:

```
<message from="alice@wonderland.lit/rabbithole"
         to="sister@realworld.lit/home"
         id="fh91f36s">
  <data xmlns="http://jabber.org/protocol/ibb"
        sid="dv917fb4"
        seq="1">
    dNADE1QOjH4QK7wzLMaapzHDO/9XhXOqqmDU+gM1MljXXOlUXad57xJd+ESgDqPW
    JcqJcEOhDfhWr7+iu3AJa59/tGp5ZQyK8qF9cObiFgzAplYukItzdF8MXufoyIrh
    VcDOWtniNOdvoWbyp3OXeIgII1vtXvK/A7Cv8EgL1X18gbnZQuqRsuOEmB/KOO+C
    NDuLyEwAnpTpfyxuKdAwX5In4ghBNCl2a1D8HHeUoHqOt+kW9OzOTOYMKliPJlXU
    xhARUSDvYhPL6ViOzld6vK6gwhUruMySFu80o5OII9gAYjAE5Rdm1xykZubtuWBN
  </data>
</message>
```

And so on until reaching the end of the file. After sending the last packet, Alice's client closes the in-band bytestream:

```
<iq from="alice@wonderland.lit/rabbithole"
    id="fr61g835"
    to="sister@realworld.lit/home"
    type="set">
  <close xmlns="http://jabber.org/protocol/ibb" sid="dv917fb4"/>
</iq>
```

Because a reply must be sent to all IQ-sets and IQ-gets, her sister's client sends an IQ-result indicating receipt:

```
<iq from="sister@realworld.lit/home"
    id="fr61g835"
    to="alice@wonderland.lit/rabbithole"
    type="result"/>
```

The picture was sent successfully.

There's one caveat with this approach: we assume that every packet we send will be immediately received and processed by the other side. However, there are several situations where this assumption is not true: both XMPP servers could be under heavy load, there might be a lot of traffic on your contact's connection, or your contact might be using a device that has minimal computing power. In this case, firing all these messages one after the other could cause you to "flood" one of the servers or your contact's client, as they would not be able to process all this data. To solve this problem, we can wait until the other party has acknowledged receipt of the current packet before sending the next one. This gives your contact as well as the intermediate servers the chance to control the rate at which it receives the packets. To get feedback about when to send new packets, we embed our blocks not in message stanzas but in IQ stanzas:

```
<iq from="alice@wonderland.lit/rabbithole"
    id="u46sf1b9"
    to="sister@realworld.lit/home"
    type="set">
  <data xmlns="http://jabber.org/protocol/ibb" sid="dv917fb4" seq="0">
    qANQR1DBwU4DX7jmYZnncmUQB/9KuKBddzQH+tZ1ZywKKOyHKnq57kWq+RTtQdCJ
    WpdWpROuQsuJe7+vh3NWn59/gTc5MDlX8d59pOovStmNcyLhxVgmqS8ZKhsblVeu
    IpQOJgavABqibJolc3BKrVtVV1igKiX/N7Pi8RtY1K18toaMDhdEfhBRzO/XBO+P
    AQhYlRjNacGcslkhXqNjK5Va4tuOAPy2n1Q8UUrIlbUdOg+xJ9BmOGOLZXyvCWyKH
    kuNEIlFQiLuCY6lvOmyq6iX6tjuHehZlFSh8Ob5BVV9tNLwNR5Eqz1klxMhoghJOA
  </data>
</iq>
```

After a while, the response packet filters through:

```
<iq from="sister@realworld.lit/home"
    id="u46sf1b9"
    to="alice@wonderland.lit/rabbithole"
    type="result"/>
```

We can now send our next packet:

```
<iq from="alice@wonderland.lit/rabbithole"
    id="y71fskn7"
    to="sister@realworld.lit/home"
    type="set">
  <data xmlns="http://jabber.org/protocol/ibb" sid="dv917fb4" seq="1">
    dNADE1QOjH4QK7wzLMaapzHDO/9XhXOqqmDU+gM1MljXXOlUXad57xJd+ESgDqPW
    JcqJcEOhDfhWr7+iu3AJa59/tGp5ZQyK8qF9cObiFgzAplYukItzdF8MXufoyIrh
    VcDOWtniNOdvoWbyp3OXeIgII1vtXvK/A7Cv8EgL1X18gbnZQuqRsuOEmB/KOO+C
    NDuLyEwAnpTpfyxuKdAwX5In4ghBNCl2a1D8HHeUoHqOt+kW9OzOTOYMKliPJlXU
    xhARUSDvYhPL6ViOzld6vK6gwhUruMySFu8Oo5OII9gAYjAE5Rdm1xykZubtuWBN
  </data>
</iq>
```

And so on, until the entire file has been transferred.

Unfortunately, sending binary files over XMPP using the in-band bytestreams method has some severe drawbacks. First, all binary data needs to be encoded and put inside a message or IQ stanza. This introduces some overhead, both in speed and in generated traffic: besides the increased size of the encoded data, both sides need to encode and decode the data and process the XMPP stanzas for all blocks.

However, there's an even more severe problem than mere speed and size overhead. Imagine someone in Europe sending a file to his friend, who happens to be sitting at a desk right next to him. The file's data needs to travel all the way to the sender's server in the U.S., over to the recipient's server in Japan, back to the desk in Europe. Not only does this slow down the transfer quite a bit, it also generates excessive traffic and a high processing load on both servers. Especially when servers have many users, this quickly becomes problematic. In practice, servers typically put a limit on the amount of data a user can send; this practice (called "rate limiting" or "karma") can make in-band transfers fail for larger files. Therefore, files are usually sent out-of-band, which we describe in the next section.

In-Band and Out-of-Band

XMPP developers typically use the phrase *in-band* to refer to data sent within the XMPP streams negotiated between a server and a client. By contrast, the phrase *out-of-band* (or OOB) indicates that we are sending data using a non-XMPP method, such as a peer-to-peer connection or a channel established through a media relay.

Thinking Big: Sending Large Files Out-of-Band

When sending data out-of-band, there are two options: sending the data directly from one entity to another over a connection that has no intermediaries or sending the data through a third-party proxy or relay. We discuss each of these methods in turn.

Sending Data Directly

Alice's trip down the rabbit hole results in more than just one picture. Indeed, she comes home with a gazillion photos, all taken at the highest resolution (it's good that she always carries a few extra memory sticks with her). Since Alice's best friend at school is also curious, she decides to make a decent selection of her pictures, package them up, and send them to her friend directly. Given the size of her selection, she doesn't want to send this data through a series of servers, as we discussed in the previous section. Instead, Alice is going to tell her friend's client to connect to her computer directly, and she will send the raw data through the direct connection. This approach re-uses the SOCKS5 protocol originally defined in [RFC 1928], in particular a special profile that is specified in *SOCKS5 Bytestreams* [XEP-0065].

To begin transferring her package of photos, Alice's client first informs her friend's client of the network address (192.168.4.1) and port (5086) on which it can connect, and on which she will serve the stream of data:

```
<iq from="alice@realworld.lit/home-at-last"
    id="p9735fg1"
    to="bestfriend@school.lit/laptop"
    type="set">
  <query xmlns="http://jabber.org/protocol/bytestreams"❶
         sid="dv917fb4"
         mode="tcp">
    <streamhost
         jid="alice@realworld.lit/home-at-last"
         host="192.168.4.1"
         port="5086"/>
  </query>
</iq>
```

❶ Although this protocol namespace is `http://jabber.org/protocol/bytestreams`, these are no longer in-band bytestreams, but instead SOCKS5 bytestreams.

After her friend's client successfully connects on the given address and port, it acknowledges Alice's request:

```
<iq from="bestfriend@school.lit/laptop"
    id="p9735fg1"
    to="alice@realworld.lit/home-at-last"
    type="result">
  <query xmlns="http://jabber.org/protocol/bytestreams">
    <streamhost-used jid="alice@realworld.lit/home-at-last"/>
  </query>
</iq>
```

After Alice receives the acknowledgment, her client starts sending the data. This happens directly over a raw bytestream at the IP address and port that Alice advertised (192.168.4.1:5086), so there is no need to chunk the stream into blocks as we did for in-band bytestreams.

Sending Data Through a Proxy

Alice's tech-savvy sister has installed some new security software, and now all the machines at their house are firewalled. As a result, nobody outside the house is able to connect directly to Alice's PC, which means that she can't send her pictures through a direct connection to her best friend anymore. This is where a proxy comes into play: instead of having her friend connect directly to her machine, Alice and her friend both connect to a third host, which transfers the data she sends to her friend.

Therefore, when Alice's client sends the SOCKS5 Bytestreams offer, it includes the IP address (24.24.24.1) and port (5999) of a bytestreams proxy service, in addition to Alice's home computer:

```
<iq from="alice@realworld.lit/home-at-last"
    id="uy461vfw"
    to="bestfriend@school.lit/laptop"
    type="set">
  <query xmlns="http://jabber.org/protocol/bytestreams"
```

```
              sid="dv917fb4"
              mode="tcp">
          <streamhost
              jid="alice@realworld.lit/home-at-last"
              host="192.168.4.1"
              port="5086"/>
          <streamhost
              jid="streamhostproxy.realworld.lit"
              host="24.24.24.1"
              port="5999"/>
      </query>
  </iq>
```

Her friend's client now tries to connect to both hosts. When it discovers that Alice's host (the first entry) is unreachable, it tries the proxy and finds it can connect to that. Her friend's client therefore informs Alice's client that it has connected to the proxy and is waiting for data there:

```
<iq from="bestfriend@school.lit/laptop"
    id="uy461vfw"
    to="alice@realworld.lit/home-at-last"
    type="result">
    <query xmlns="http://jabber.org/protocol/bytestreams">
        <streamhost-used jid="streamhostproxy.realworld.lit"/>
    </query>
</iq>
```

At this point, Alice's client connects to the proxy as well. Before sending the data over this connection, Alice's client first needs to activate the stream, allowing the proxy to identify her:

```
<iq from="alice@realworld.lit/home-at-last"
    id="dl4wr217"
    to="streamhostproxy.realworld.lit"
    type="set">
    <query xmlns="http://jabber.org/protocol/bytestreams" sid="dv917fb4">
        <activate>bestfriend@school.lit/laptop</activate>
    </query>
</iq>
```

After this request has been acknowledged by the proxy, Alice's client can start sending data over the open connection.

Note that, in the previous example, we assumed that Alice specified the proxy herself. However, it is possible for a client to automatically detect whether a proxy is available on her server. This is done using service discovery, which we discussed in Chapter 5. Here we look for an item in the **proxy** category that advertises support for the bytestreams protocol:

```
<iq from="alice@realworld.lit/home-at-last"
    id="o6y1g48s"
    to="example.com"
    type="get">
    <query xmlns="http://jabber.org/protocol/disco#items"/>
</iq>
```

```
<iq from="example.com"
    id="o6y1g48s"
    to="alice@realworld.lit/home-at-last"
    type="result">
  <query xmlns="http://jabber.org/protocol/disco#items">
    <item jid="streamhostproxy.realworld.lit" name="Bytestreams Proxy"/>
  </query>
</iq>
```

Alice's client continues to "walk the tree" of entities, so it queries `streamhostproxy.real world.lit`:

```
<iq from="alice@realworld.lit/home-at-last"
    id="r81g33fv"
    to="streamhostproxy.realworld.lit"
    type="get">
  <query xmlns="http://jabber.org/protocol/disco#info"/>
</iq>

<iq from="streamhostproxy.realworld.lit"
    id="r81g33fv"
    to="alice@realworld.lit/home-at-last"
    type="result">
  <query xmlns="http://jabber.org/protocol/disco#info">
    <identity category="proxy"
              type="bytestreams"
              name="SOCKS5 Bytestreams Service"/>
    <feature var="http://jabber.org/protocol/bytestreams"/>
  </query>
</iq>
```

Voilà, a SOCKS5 Bytestreams proxy!

Unfortunately, not every server on the XMPP network deploys a bytestreams proxy. For one thing, such proxies have the potential to use a lot of bandwidth. Thankfully, IM users don't send files all that often, so in practice, the bandwidth requirements are quite reasonable. And sending data through a dedicated bytestreams proxy is much more efficient than sending it in-band, as the proxy can be hosted on a separate machine, thus lightening the load on the XMPP daemon.

Negotiating File Transfer

Let's take another look at the foregoing scenario. Alice starts her conversation by announcing that she is going to send some pictures:

Alice: Hey, I just finished processing those pictures from my trip down the rabbit hole!

Friend: Wow, cool! How do you want to send them?

Alice: Well, I have quite a few, so let's send them out-of-band.

Friend: OK, works for me!

Then, Alice instructs her client to start sending the files out-of-band using SOCKS5 Bytestreams. Unfortunately, her attempt fails: it seems that both Alice and her friend are firewalled, and Alice doesn't have access to a SOCKS5 Bytestreams proxy. Time to revisit the plan:

> Friend: Hmm, it seems we're both firewalled. Can you send them in-band instead?
>
> Alice: Sure, let's try that!

Alice then instructs her client to send the files in-band, which *does* succeed.

What just happened is that Alice negotiated with her friend that she was going to send a file, and told her how she wanted to send it. When finding out that the negotiated way of sending the file didn't work out, Alice and her friend re-negotiated how to send the file.

However, we want to automate these negotiations in our XMPP clients, instead of having to do this through a natural-language conversation between error-prone and easily confused humans. In XMPP, there are two ways to do this: the older way using the Stream Initiation protocol defined in [XEP-0095] and [XEP-0096], and the newer way using the Jingle negotiation framework, as discussed in Chapter 9. We will explore each in turn.

File Transfer Using Stream Initiation

The *Stream Initiation* (SI) protocol was the XMPP community's first attempt at defining a generalized media negotiation technology. Although it was never used for anything other than file transfer, many clients support it for just that function. Over time, it is likely that clients will transition to using Jingle for file transfer, as described in the next section. However, we include coverage of the older method because it will probably be in use for some time to come.

Stream initiation begins when the person who wants to transfer the file sends an offer to the other person. This offer consists of two things: a definition of the data to be exchanged (via the `<file/>` element), and some possible transport methods (here SOCKS5 Bytestreams and In-Band Bytestreams), encapsulated via a Data Form inside a feature negotiation wrapper element, as described in [XEP-0050]. The entire offer is then wrapped in an `<si/>` element. (Yes, that's a good example of XML namespaces and XMPP extensibility in action!)

```
<iq from="alice@realworld.lit/home-at-last"
    id="pe72ndg9"
    to="bestfriend@school.lit/laptop"
    type="set">
  <si xmlns="http://jabber.org/protocol/si"
      id="a0b2n44k"
      mime-type="text/plain"
      profile="http://jabber.org/protocol/si/profile/file-transfer">
    <file xmlns="http://jabber.org/protocol/si/profile/file-transfer"
          name="test.txt"
```

```
          size="1022"/>
      <feature xmlns="http://jabber.org/protocol/feature-neg">
        <x xmlns="jabber:x:data" type="form">
          <field var="stream-method" type="list-single">
            <option>
              <value>http://jabber.org/protocol/bytestreams</value>
            </option>
            <option>
              <value>http://jabber.org/protocol/ibb</value>
            </option>
          </field>
        </x>
      </feature>
    </si>
  </iq>
```

The recipient now needs to decide which of the offered transport methods it prefers.
Typically, this preference will be configured into a client (as this is more user-friendly
than asking an end user to choose). Here, the preference is SOCKS5 Bytestreams:

```
<iq from="bestfriend@school.lit/laptop"
    id="pe72ndg9"
    to="alice@realworld.lit/home-at-last"
    type="result">
  <si xmlns="http://jabber.org/protocol/si" id="a0b2n44k">
    <feature xmlns="http://jabber.org/protocol/feature-neg">
      <x xmlns="jabber:x:data" type="submit">
        <field var="stream-method">
          <value>http://jabber.org/protocol/bytestreams</value>
        </field>
      </x>
    </feature>
  </si>
</iq>
```

Both clients now attempt to set up use of SOCKS5 bytestreams. In particular, the sending client initiates the SOCKS5 negotiation process by sending a set of possible stream-
hosts to the recipient:

```
<iq from="alice@realworld.lit/home-at-last"
    to="bestfriend@school.lit/laptop"
    id="u7yr51v4"
    type="set">
  <query xmlns="http://jabber.org/protocol/bytestreams"
         sid="dv917fb4"
         mode="tcp">
    <streamhost
        jid="alice@realworld.lit/home-at-last"
        host="192.168.4.1"
        port="5086"/>
    <streamhost
        jid="streamhostproxy.realworld.lit"
        host="24.24.24.1"
        zeroconf="_jabber.bytestreams"/>
```

```
    </query>
  </iq>
```

However, as described in the foregoing negotiation narrative, we assume that the
SOCKS5 negotiation fails, so the friend's client returns a `<remote-server-not-found/>`
error to Alice in accordance with the definition of SOCKS5 Bytestreams:

```
<iq from="bestfriend@school.lit/laptop"
    id="u7yr51v4"
    to="alice@realworld.lit/home-at-last"
    type="error">
  <error type="cancel">
    <remote-server-not-found xmlns="urn:ietf:params:xml:ns:xmpp-stanzas"/>
  </error>
</iq>
```

Now that the SOCKS5 Bytestreams negotiation has failed, the clients need to negotiate
the use of in-band bytestreams instead. However, in the stream initiation protocol,
there is no way to fall back from SOCKS5 to in-band bytestreams, so the sender generates a new stream initiation request unconnected to the original request, this time
specifying only one transport method, in-band bytestreams:

```
<iq from="alice@realworld.lit/home-at-last"
    id="b93cvr3t"
    to="bestfriend@school.lit/laptop"
    type="set">
  <si xmlns="http://jabber.org/protocol/si"
      id="a0b2n44k"
    mime-type="text/plain"
    profile="http://jabber.org/protocol/si/profile/file-transfer">
    <file xmlns="http://jabber.org/protocol/si/profile/file-transfer"
        name="test.txt"
        size="1022"/>
    <feature xmlns="http://jabber.org/protocol/feature-neg">
      <x xmlns="jabber:x:data" type="form">
        <field var="stream-method" type="list-single">
          <option>
            <value>http://jabber.org/protocol/ibb</value>
          </option>
        </field>
      </x>
    </feature>
  </si>
</iq>
```

The recipient has no choice but to either accept the offer and try in-band bytestreams
or reject the offer and not receive the file. Here we assume that the recipient decides to
try in-band bytestreams:

```
<iq from="bestfriend@school.lit/laptop"
    id="b93cvr3t"
    to="alice@realworld.lit/home-at-last"
    type="result">
  <si xmlns="http://jabber.org/protocol/si" id="a0b2n44k">
    <feature xmlns="http://jabber.org/protocol/feature-neg">
```

```
        <x xmlns="jabber:x:data" type="submit">
          <field var="stream-method">
            <value>http://jabber.org/protocol/ibb</value>
          </field>
        </x>
      </feature>
    </si>
  </iq>
```

As you can see, in stream initiation, the only way to "fall back" to a different data transfer method is by sending a completely new offer. This is one of the reasons why the XMPP community is moving to the Jingle method described in the next section (another good reason is code reuse; it's not efficient to have two different ways to negotiate sessions, and Jingle is the go-forward technology for negotiating voice, video, and other session types).

Session Negotiation Using Jingle

The Jingle technology was originally defined for the setup and management of voice (and more recently, video) sessions. However, Jingle can also be used to negotiate a file transfer "session"; this usage is currently defined in [XEP-0234].

Give Me a Jingle?

The use of Jingle for file transfer is still a bit experimental at the time of this writing. In particular, it is quite possible that more advanced methods will be defined, both for content description (e.g., to reference multiple files and include thumbnails for certain file types) and the data transport (e.g., the use of BitTorrent or ICE-TCP). Check *http://xmpp .org* and the discussion lists for the most up-to-date information.

Alice starts her Jingle negotiation by offering to send a file to her friend. Upon starting a new file transfer session, Alice's client sends a *description* of the file she is about to send and the *transport* she wants to use (here the SOCKS5 Bytestreams protocol). Thus, Jingle performs the same media negotiation function as the Stream Initiation protocol we looked at in the last section, albeit in a more modern, extensible format, as defined in [XEP-0260]:

```
<iq from="alice@realworld.lit/home-at-last"
    id="fi8g376r"
    to="bestfriend@school.lit/laptop"
    type="set">
  <jingle xmlns="urn:xmpp:jingle:1"
          action="session-initiate"
          initiator="alice@realworld.lit/home-at-last"
          sid="851ba2g">
    <content creator="initiator" name="a-file">
      <description xmlns="urn:xmpp:jingle:apps:file-transfer:1">
        <file xmlns="http://jabber.org/protocol/si/profile/file-transfer"
              name="TripPictures.zip">
```

```
                    size="400000"
                    hash="552da749930852c69ae5d2141d3766b1">
                <desc>Lots of crazy photos!</desc>
            </file>
        </description>
        <transport xmlns="urn:xmpp:jingle:transports:s5b:0">
          <streamhost
              jid="alice@realworld.lit/home-at-last"
              host="192.168.4.1"
              port="5086"/>
          <streamhost
              jid="streamhostproxy.realworld.lit"
              host="24.24.24.1"
              zeroconf="_jabber.bytestreams"/>
        </transport>
      </content>
    </jingle>
  </iq>
```

When Alice's best friend approves the file transfer request, her client sends a **session-accept** message to Alice:

```
  <iq from="bestfriend@school.lit/laptop"
      id="krw927s0"
      to="alice@realworld.lit/home-at-last"
      type="set">
    <jingle xmlns="urn:xmpp:jingle:1"
            action="session-accept"
            initiator="alice@realworld.lit/home-at-last"
            responder="bestfriend@school.lit/laptop"
            sid="851ba2g">
      <content creator="initiator" name="a-file">
        <description xmlns="urn:xmpp:jingle:apps:file-transfer:1">
        <file xmlns="http://jabber.org/protocol/si/profile/file-transfer"
            name="TripPictures.zip"
            size="400000"
            hash="552da749930852c69ae5d2141d3766b1">
            <desc>Lots of crazy photos!</desc>
        </file>
        </description>
        <transport xmlns="urn:xmpp:jingle:transports:bytestreams:0">
          <streamhost
              jid="alice@realworld.lit/home-at-last"
              host="192.168.4.1"
              port="5086"/>
          <streamhost
              jid="streamhostproxy.realworld.lit"
              host="24.24.24.1"
              zeroconf="_jabber.bytestreams"/>
        </transport>
      </content>
    </jingle>
  </iq>
```

After the initiator acknowledges the `session-accept` message, the parties will attempt to set up a SOCKS5 bytestream between themselves. However, here again, we assume that the SOCKS5 negotiation fails, so the friend's client returns a `<remote-server-not-found/>` error to Alice:

```
<iq from="bestfriend@school.lit/laptop"
    id="od7v46xh"
    to="alice@realworld.lit/home-at-last"
    type="error">
  <error type="cancel">
    <remote-server-not-found xmlns="urn:ietf:params:xml:ns:xmpp-stanzas"/>
  </error>
</iq>
```

Now that the SOCKS5 Bytestreams negotiation has failed, the clients need to negotiate the use of in-band bytestreams instead. This is done using the Jingle `transport-replace` action mentioned in Chapter 9. The `transport-replace` message defines the new transport to be attempted, in this case IBB:

```
<iq from="bestfriend@school.lit/laptop"
    id="gu72vsl9"
    to="alice@realworld.lit/home-at-last"
    type="set">
  <jingle xmlns="urn:xmpp:jingle:1"
          action="transport-replace"
          initiator="alice@realworld.lit/home-at-last"
          responder="bestfriend@school.lit/laptop"
          sid="851ba2g">
    <content creator="initiator" name="a-file">
      <transport xmlns="urn:xmpp:jingle:transports:ibb:0"/>
    </content>
  </jingle>
</iq>
```

Based on its supported transport methods and configured transport preferences, Alice's client accepts the request to try a new transport method by sending a `transport-accept` message:

```
<iq from="alice@realworld.lit/home-at-last"
    id="yt481nf0"
    to="bestfriend@school.lit/laptop"
    type="set">
  <jingle xmlns="urn:xmpp:jingle:1"
          action="transport-accept"
          initiator="alice@realworld.lit/home-at-last"
          responder="bestfriend@school.lit/laptop"
          sid="851ba2g">
    <content creator="initiator" name="a-file">
      <description xmlns="urn:xmpp:jingle:apps:file-transfer:1">
        <file xmlns="http://jabber.org/protocol/si/profile/file-transfer"
              hash="552da749930852c69ae5d2141d3766b1"
              name="test.txt"/>
      </description>
      <transport xmlns="urn:xmpp:jingle:transports:ibb:0"
          block-size="4096"
```

```
        sid="dv917fb4"/>
    </content>
  </jingle>
</iq>
```

Now Alice sends the file to her friend over the IBB transport as previously described.

Summary

In this chapter, we covered a lot of ground. First, we looked at a lightweight method for sending very small "bits of binary" over XMPP. This method is mainly used to send in-line images within XHTML messages and data forms (which we discussed in Chapter 6). Then we looked at in-band bytestreams, a way to break down a binary file into smaller chunks so that it can be sent in an ordered sequence of multiple stanzas (either messages or IQ stanzas). While IBB provides a reliable (if slow) mechanism when all else fails, it's not necessarily appropriate for sending larger files; in this case, the "out-of-band" SOCKS5 bytestreams method is more network-friendly. In the future, additional methods might be defined, such as a way to initiate a BitTorrent over XMPP.

Given the existence of multiple file transfer methods, we need a good way to negotiate which method to use, and to fall back from one method to another if necessary. The original Stream Initiation negotiation method used in the XMPP developer community lacks some flexibility and has never been used for anything except file transfer. Specifically, it was not adapted for multimedia session management; instead, the community has defined the Jingle technology for more modern negotiation scenarios, and is working to migrate file transfer negotiation to use Jingle as well.

CHAPTER 11

Remote Commands

XMPP includes several technologies used to send commands to other entities. These technologies enable you to remotely control servers and clients—for example, to add users to a server, configure a multiuser chat room or a pubsub node, tell another client of yours to go offline, or define the fields needed to register an account on a server or other service. In Chapter 6 and subsequent chapters, we've seen some of these technologies in action through the use of the Data Forms extension. In this chapter, we take that knowledge further to explore more advanced workflow applications.

Controlling Clients

Picture the situation: Alice is expecting an important message to come in through her Jabber client, but she is running late for a very important date, so she sets off in a hurry for the party. Once she arrives at the party, she logs in again with her mobile phone but realizes that she left her other client logged in. Her urgent message has probably been sent to her other client, and she needs it now! What does she do? Using a combination of XMPP technologies, she can command her other client to forward the messages to her at the party and then to go offline so that no further messages will be sent to the wrong resource.

The key piece here is the Ad-Hoc Commands protocol, defined in [XEP-0050]. This XMPP extension provides workflow capabilities that can be used for any structured interaction between two XMPP entities, called the *requester* (the entity that requests completion of the commands) and the *responder* (the entity where the commands will be performed).

The basic flow in an ad-hoc commands interaction is shown in Figure 11-1.

Typically, such a workflow uses either a single-stage, standalone command (with no payload) or a multi-stage command that includes a data form of the kind we saw in Chapter 6.

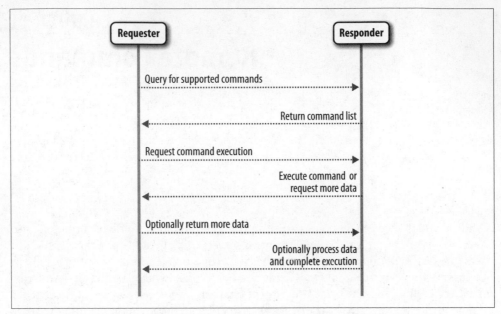

Figure 11-1. The Ad-Hoc Commands protocol provides a relatively simple workflow engine

A Simple Command

In Alice's party scenario, she wants to forward messages received by her first client (the `rabbithole` resource, which is the responder here) to her second (the `party` resource, which is the requester). To do this, she first queries her `rabbithole` client for all the available commands by sending a service discovery query to its `http://jabber.org/protocol/commands` node, as we did in Chapter 5:

```
<iq from="alice@wonderland.lit/party"
    id="a1266a"
    to="alice@wonderland.lit/rabbithole"
    type="get">
  <query xmlns="http://jabber.org/protocol/disco#items"
         node="http://jabber.org/protocol/commands"/>❶
</iq>
```

❶ By including a service discovery node of `http://jabber.org/protocol/commands`, the requester is saying "please send me all of the ad-hoc commands that you support."

Her `rabbithole` resource then returns the following list of commands:

```
<iq from="alice@wonderland.lit/rabbithole"
    id="a1266a"
    to="alice@wonderland.lit/party"
    type="result">
  <query xmlns="http://jabber.org/protocol/disco#items"
         node="http://jabber.org/protocol/commands">
    <item node="http://jabber.org/protocol/rc#set-status"❶
          name="Set Status">
```

```
                    jid="alice@wonderland.lit/rabbithole"/>
        <item node="http://jabber.org/protocol/rc#forward"
              name="Forward Messages"
              jid="alice@wonderland.lit/rabbithole"/>
        <item node="http://jabber.org/protocol/rc#set-options"
              name="Set Options"
              jid="alice@wonderland.lit/rabbithole"/>
      </query>
    </iq>
```

❶ Each command supported by the responder is specified as a particular service discovery node associated with the generic `http://jabber.org/protocol/commands` node.

This reveals that her **rabbithole** resource supports, amongst others, the **set-status** and **forward** commands that Alice is interested in. She can now ask her first client to forward messages to her second client by executing the **forward** command:

```
    <iq from="alice@wonderland.lit/party"
        id="a126aa"
        to="alice@wonderland.lit/rabbithole"
        type="set">
      <command xmlns="http://jabber.org/protocol/commands"
               node="http://jabber.org/protocol/rc#forward"
               action="execute"/>❶
    </iq>
```

❶ The **action** attribute is included in IQ-set stanzas that the requester sends to the responder. This tells the responder what to do (here, to execute the command).

In response, the **rabbithole** client starts sending its pending messages to Alice's mobile phone at the party:

```
    <message from="alice@wonderland.lit/rabbithole"
             id="a1268a"
             to="alice@wonderland.lit/party">
      <body>I"m late, I"m late, for a very important date.</body>
      <delay xmlns="urn:xmpp:delay"
             from="alice@wonderland.lit/rabbithole"
             stamp="2008-11-12T13:05:00Z"/>❶
      <addresses xmlns="http://jabber.org/protocol/address">❷
        <address type="ofrom" jid="rabbit@wonderland.lit/transit"/>
        <address type="oto" jid="alice@wonderland.lit"/>
      </addresses>
    </message>
```

❶ As we've already seen in Chapter 7, the **delay** element (defined in *Delayed Delivery* [XEP-0203]) is used to annotate messages where delivery is delayed (such as forwarded messages, messages stored offline by a server, or chat room history).

❷ The **addresses** element (defined in *Extended Stanza Addressing* [XEP-0033]) stores the original sender and destination of the forwarded message.

Once all of Alice's messages have been sent, the `rabbithole` client sends a response back, saying that the command has been successfully processed (this is indicated by setting the `status` attribute to a value of `completed`):

```
<iq from="alice@wonderland.lit/rabbithole"
    id="a126aa"
    to="alice@wonderland.lit/party"
    type="result">
  <command xmlns="http://jabber.org/protocol/commands"
           node="http://jabber.org/protocol/rc#forward"
           status="completed"/>❶
</iq>
```

❶ The `status` attribute is included in IQ-result stanzas that the responder returns to the requester. Here the status is `completed`, indicating that the single-stage command has been processed successfully and that no further interaction is expected.

Commands and Data Forms

Now that the messages have been forwarded from her `rabbithole` client, Alice can ask that client to go offline, thus preventing any other misdirected messages. She does this by issuing a second command, this time `set-status`:

```
<iq from="alice@wonderland.lit/party"
    id="afd4a"
    to="alice@wonderland.lit/rabbithole"
    type="set">
  <command xmlns="http://jabber.org/protocol/commands"
           node="http://jabber.org/protocol/rc#set-status"
           action="execute"/>
</iq>
```

However, in order to change status, the `rabbithole` client needs to have a bit more information. It should at least know what status needs to be set (e.g., a `<show/>` value of `away` or `dnd`), the presence priority, and the resulting status message. Therefore, the `rabbithole` client responds with a *Data Form* containing all the fields that Alice needs to fill in to provide the missing information:

```
<iq from="alice@wonderland.lit/rabbithole"
    id="afd4a"
    to="alice@wonderland.lit/party"
    type="result">
  <command xmlns="http://jabber.org/protocol/commands"
           node="http://jabber.org/protocol/rc#set-status">
           sessionid="b82nsd82nfdos51vs9"❶
           status="executing">❷
    <x xmlns="jabber:x:data" type="form">
      <title>Set Status</title>
      <instructions>Choose the status and status message</instructions>
      <field type="hidden" var="FORM_TYPE">
        <value>http://jabber.org/protocol/rc</value>
      </field>
      <field type="list-single" label="Status" var="status">
```

```
            <required/>
            <option label="Online">
               <value>online</value>
            </option>
            <option label="Away">
               <value>away</value>
            </option>
            <option label="Extended Away">
               <value>xa</value>
            </option>
            <option label="Offline">
               <value>offline</value>
            </option>
            <value>online</value>❸
         </field>
         <field type="text-single" label="Priority" var="status-priority">❹
            <value>5</value>
         </field>
         <field type="text-multi" label="Message" var="status-message">❺
            <value/>
         </field>
      </x>
   </command>
</iq>
```

❶ The session ID is generated by the responder for tracking commands and results sent in the context of an ad-hoc commands session. The responder didn't include a session ID in the simple command we discussed earlier, because it did not require further input from the requester. However, in the set-status scenario, the responder does include the session ID because additional steps are required. Furthermore, the use of session IDs makes it possible to execute several instances of the same command among the same parties at the same time.

❷ The executing status indicates that the command is in the middle of execution.

❸ This value element provides the current value of the field (that is, the remote client currently has a state of online).

❹ Th status-priority field specifiesproxies the <priority/> element of the new presence stanza; because the value must be between −127 and +128, the client or server will enforce this range of values.

❺ The status-message field specifies the value of the <status/> element within the presence stanza.

Alice's mobile client will now render the form (e.g., as in Figure 11-2) so that she can complete the required fields.

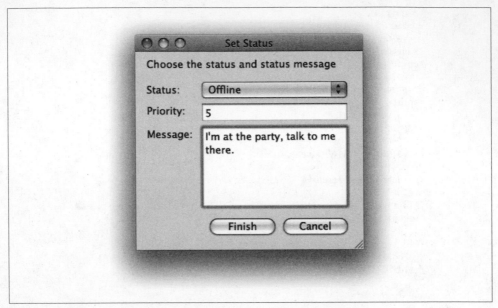

Figure 11-2. The status change command form, as rendered by the Psi client

Once Alice fills out the form, the client on her mobile phone submits the form to the remote client. This form mirrors that requested in the previous stanza, with the values included:

```
<iq from="alice@wonderland.lit/party"
    id="afd5a"
    to="alice@wonderland.lit/rabbithole"
    type="set">
  <command xmlns="http://jabber.org/protocol/commands"
           action="complete"❶
           sessionid="b82nsd82nfdos51vs9"❷
           node="http://jabber.org/protocol/rc#set-status">
    <x xmlns="jabber:x:data" type="submit">
      <field type="hidden" var="FORM_TYPE">
        <value>http://jabber.org/protocol/rc</value>
      </field>
      <field var="status">
        <value>offline</value>
      </field>
      <field var="status-priority">
        <value>5</value>
      </field>
      <field var="status-message">
        <value>I'm at the party, talk to me there.</value>
      </field>
    </x>
  </command>
</iq>
```

❶ The requester specifies an `action` of `complete` because it has provided all required information and therefore is asking the responder to complete the command session if possible.

❷ The requester copies back the `sessionid` generated by the responder so that the responder can maintain state regarding the interaction.

Stating the Obvious

In a multi-stage interaction, the responder might need to maintain some state regarding command processing. Typically, it does this using the `sessionid` attribute. However, the responder can avoid the need to maintain state by including data form fields of type `hidden`, which the requester must return without modification. (This is similar to an `<INPUT>` tag of type `hidden` in HTML forms.)

As previously, Alice's remote client now confirms that the command has been successfully processed:

```
<iq from="alice@wonderland.lit/rabbithole"
    id="afd5a"
    to="alice@wonderland.lit/party"
    type="result">
  <command xmlns="http://jabber.org/protocol/commands"
           node="http://jabber.org/protocol/rc#set-status"
           sessionid="b02n3d02nfdus5ivsy"
           status="completed"/>
</iq>
```

Finally, because the remote client was asked to go offline, the `rabbithole` resource now goes offline and Alice's `party` resource receives the `unavailable` presence stanza:

```
<presence from="alice@wonderland.lit/rabbithole"
          to="alice@wonderland.lit/party"
          type="unavailable">
  <status>I'm at the party, talk to me there.</status>
</presence>
```

You just saw two of the commands described in *Remote Controlling Clients* [XEP-0146]. Other commands include accepting file transfer requests, leaving groupchats, and changing run-time options remotely using the same techniques. *Service Administration* [XEP-0133] is another XEP that uses ad-hoc commands for entity control, and can be thought of as the server counterpart of the client remote controlling commands we've just seen; it basically follows the same flow, which is common to all ad-hoc commands. In the next section, we explore how to define custom commands that use the same workflow engine.

Providing Custom Commands

Suppose that Alice has just stumbled across the `bookstore.wonderland.lit` service, which sells books through an Ad-Hoc Commands interface. Having already registered with the service and given it her payment details (Alice is very trusting, and Wonderland suffers a very low fraud rate), she is now ready to begin her book-buying adventures.

Having found the command she wants to execute, Alice can now begin buying books by sending a command element with an action of `execute` to the node she has discovered:

```
<iq from="alice@wonderland.lit/party"
    id="bs3m20oa"
    to="bookstore.wonderland.lit"
    type="set">
  <command xmlns="http://jabber.org/protocol/commands"
           action="execute"
           node="http://wonderland.lit/books/buy"/>
</iq>
```

The service then returns a data form to fill in (including, as before, a session ID because a multistage process is required to complete the transaction):

```
<iq from="bookstore.wonderland.lit"
    id="bs3m20oa"
    to="alice@wonderland.lit/party"
    type="result">
<command xmlns="http://jabber.org/protocol/commands"
         node="http://wonderland.lit/books/buy"
         sessionid="uaroeb3eub3920ubon"
         status="executing">
  <actions execute="next">
    <next/>
  </actions>
  <x xmlns="jabber:x:data" type="form">
    <title>Choosing your author</title>
    <instructions>
        Please choose an author from the list.
    </instructions>
    <field label="Authors" type="list-single" var="author">
      <option label="Jane Austen"><value>Jane Austen</value></option>
      <option label="Lewis Carroll"><value>Lewis Carroll</value></option>
      <option label="William Shakespeare"><value>William Shakespeare</value></option>
    </field>
  </x>
</command>
</iq>
```

Then, just as for the remote control commands earlier, Alice can submit the form:

```
<iq from="alice@wonderland.lit/party"
    id="laulm029"
    to="bookstore.wonderland.lit"
    type="set">
  <command xmlns="http://jabber.org/protocol/commands"
```

```
                action="complete"
                node="http://wonderland.lit/books/buy"
                sessionid="uaroeb3eub3920ubon">
      <x xmlns="jabber:x:data" type="submit">
        <field var="author">
          <value>William Shakespeare</value>
        </field>
      </x>
    </command>
  </iq>
```

However, because this is a multistage command, the responder returns not a
completed result but the next stage of the command:

```
<iq from="bookstore.wonderland.lit"
    id="laulm029"
    to="alice@wonderland.lit/party"
    type="result">
  <command xmlns="http://jabber.org/protocol/commands"
           node="http://wonderland.lit/books/buy"
           sessionid="uaroeb3eub3920ubon"
           status="executing">
    <actions execute="next">
      <next/>
      <prev/>
    </actions>
    <x xmlns="jabber:x:data" type="form">
      <title>Choosing your book</title>
      <instructions>
          Please choose a book by William Shakespeare from the list.
      </instructions>
      <field label="Titles" type="list-single" var="author">
        <option label="The Complete Works"><value>The Complete Works</value></option>
      </field>
    </x>
  </command>
</iq>
```

Here you see an action element, which describes the actions that can be taken. The ad-
hoc commands protocol is stateful when dealing with multistage forms, and by including <prev/> as a permitted action, the service is allowing the client to travel back
to the previous stage in the command. As Alice didn't mean to select Shakespeare's
collection, she avails herself of this feature and goes back to select Lewis Carroll:

```
<iq from="alice@wonderland.lit/party"
    id="uagdbal2"
    to="bookstorewonderland.lit"
    type="set">
  <command xmlns="http://jabber.org/protocol/commands"
           sessionid="uaroeb3eub3920ubon"
           node="http://wonderland.lit/books/buy"
           action="prev"/>
</iq>
```

The service would now resend the list of authors, but we quickly skip over that (in case you're getting bored of so many angle brackets). After selecting Lewis Carroll from the list of authors, the service will send Alice the appropriate book list:

```
<iq from="bookstore.wonderland.lit"
    id="ua38bana"
    to="alice@wonderland.lit/party"
    type="result">
  <command xmlns="http://jabber.org/protocol/commands"
           node="http://wonderland.lit/books/buy"
           sessionid="uaroeb3eub3920ubon"
           status="executing">
    <actions execute="next">
      <next/>
      <prev/>
    </actions>
    <x xmlns="jabber:x:data" type="form">
      <title>Choosing your book</title>
      <instructions>
        Please choose a book by Lewis Carroll from the list.
      </instructions>
      <field label="Titles" type="list-single" var="author">
        <option label="Alice's Adventures in Wonderland">
          <value>Alice's Adventures in Wonderland</value>
        </option>
        <option label="Through the Looking-Glass">
          <value>Through the Looking-Glass</value>
        </option>
        <option label="The Hunting of the Snark">
          <value>The Hunting of the Snark</value>
        </option>
        <option label="Jabberwocky">
          <value>Jabberwocky</value>
        </option>
      </field>
    </x>
  </command>
</iq>
```

Just as she's about to buy a copy of *Jabberwocky*, Alice decides to save her money instead, and cancels the transaction. Alice does so by setting the value of the action attribute to cancel:

```
<iq from="alice@wonderland.lit/party"
    id="ulamabam"
    to="bookstore.wonderland.lit"
    type="set">
  <command xmlns="http://jabber.org/protocol/commands"
           sessionid="uaroeb3eub3920ubon"
           node="http://wonderland.lit/books/buy"
           action="cancel"/>
</iq>
```

The service acknowledges that request by returning an IQ-result with the value of the status attribute set to a value of canceled:

```
<iq from="bookstore.wonderland.lit"
    id="ulamabam"
    to="alice@wonderland.lit/party"
    type="result">
  <command xmlns="http://jabber.org/protocol/commands"
           sessionid="uaroeb3eub3920ubon"
           node="http://wonderland.lit/books/buy"
           status="canceled"/>
</iq>
```

And so ends Alice's book-buying adventure.

Advanced Workflows: SOAP, RPC, IO Data

If ad-hoc commands and data forms won't solve the workflow needs of your application, XMPP contains support for several more advanced workflow technologies.

First, ad-hoc commands are not tightly coupled with data forms: the `<command/>` element can contain data qualified by any XML namespace, not just the `jabber:x:data` namespace. You can take advantage of this extensibility to define your own "payload" for the `<command/>` element. Alternatively, you can re-use an existing payload format, such as the one defined in the *IO Data* [XEP-0244]. The intention behind IO Data is to provide a more generic, XML-friendly payload format than Data Forms, including the ability to specify XML data types and include data that can be checked against an XML schema.

Second, the XMPP Standards Foundation has worked with the World Wide Web Consortium (W3C) to define an official binding of SOAP to XMPP. The SOAP standard [SOAP] is widely used in web services deployments across the Internet. Although typically SOAP workflows are sent over HTTP, the XMPP binding has several inherent advantages, including strong identity on the part of the XMPP sender (not just the receiver, as in HTTP) and presence information to dynamically redirect workflows in response to network availability. The XMPP binding, which is defined in [XEP-0072], is supported in several SOAP libraries.

For those desiring a workflow technology that is a bit more lightweight than SOAP, many years ago the XMPP developer community also defined a binding of [XML-RPC] for remote procedure calls between XMPP entities. This "Jabber-RPC" technology is described in [XEP-0009], and has been used in online gaming networks, integration with enterprise resource planning (ERP) systems, and other applications.

Summary

This chapter has covered *Ad-Hoc Commands* [XEP-0050], revisited *Data Forms* [XEP-0004], which are typically contained in an ad-hoc commands interaction, looked at the use of ad-hoc commands in *Remote Controlling Clients* [XEP-0146], and illustrated a custom workflow with a book-buying example. In using these, you've learned about the various steps involved in sending commands, from discovery of commands, command and data form details, how to require the submission of particular fields, the types of fields available, submission of completed forms, and the workflows used to move through an ad-hoc commands session. We've also looked at some specialized uses of data forms and the potential of more advanced workflow technologies. All of these methods can be used in a wide variety of scenarios, including game management, remote instrument monitoring, machine-to-machine communication, and cloud computing.

CHAPTER 12

Connection Methods and Security

Most of the chapters in this book focus on describing the high-level XMPP protocols in terms of stanzas sent and received, without talking about the XML streaming layer that handles the sending and receiving of stanzas over the wire. To round out our coverage of XMPP, we focus on the lower layers of the XMPP protocol stack in this chapter.

XMPP provides a great deal of flexibility regarding connection methods, authentication, encryption, and other fundamentals. This chapter walks you through some of these fundamentals, showing how you can use them to build more powerful and secure applications. First, we describe standard client-to-server connections over TCP, including techniques for securing those connections. We then illustrate the power of the network by explaining how server-to-server connections work, and how servers can be extended using external components. We then look at an alternative binding that enables you to send XMPP traffic over HTTP for web applications and for mobile devices that have intermittent network connectivity. Going even farther afield, we explore how to set up serverless messaging between clients on ad-hoc local networks. Finally, we provide an overview of some of the key security issues to consider when deploying XMPP-based systems.

Negotiating an XMPP Stream

The fundamental building block of XMPP is the XML stream, which in client-to-server communication equates to a *session*. A client session starts by connecting to a server and negotiating the session details, after which the client can send message, presence, and IQ stanzas to other entities on the network. The session ends when the client (or the server) decides to close the stream. In this section, we focus on how the client and server work together to set up the XML stream; what happens after that is the topic of the other chapters in Part II.

In broad outline, setting up a client-to-server session consists of the following phases:

1. Initiating a TCP connection to the server
2. Opening an XML stream
3. Negotiating various stream features
4. Authenticating with the server
5. Selecting a resource
6. For IM applications, requesting the roster and sending initial presence

After the session has been started, the actual XMPP communication (consisting of message, IQ, and presence stanzas) can start happening.

Let's say that our friend `alice@wonderland.lit` wants to connect to her server. She first needs to find out which physical machine is providing XMPP services for that domain. You might expect that Alice can simply connect to the machine `wonderland.lit`. However, XMPP allows you to run your XMPP service for a given domain on any host you choose, so this guess isn't necessarily correct (although it's a good fallback method).

To find out the machine name of the XMPP service for `wonderland.lit`, Alice needs to do a DNS *Service* lookup. This means that she queries the DNS SRV record for the `_xmpp-client._tcp.wonderland.lit.` service (i.e., the machine that services XMPP clients over TCP at the `wonderland.lit` domain). The DNS answer yields the following result:

```
_xmpp-client._tcp.wonderland.lit. 86400 IN SRV 10 20 5222 xmpp1.wonderland.lit
_xmpp-client._tcp.wonderland.lit. 86400 IN SRV 10 5 5222 xmpp2.wonderland.lit
```

It seems that there are two XMPP servers available for the `wonderland.lit` service, `xmpp1` and `xmpp2`, and that both of them are running on port 5222 (which is the standard port used for receiving XMPP client connections). To proceed, Alice's does the following:

1. Based on the priority and weight of the records, picks one of these machines (here, `xmpp1.wonderland.lit`).
2. Performs a standard "A" (or "AAAA") lookup to determine the IP address of the chosen machine.
3. Opens a TCP connection to that IP address and port.

Now the XMPP negotiation begins. Alice's client sends an initial *stream header* to the server:

```
<?xml version="1.0"?>❶
<stream:stream❷ to="wonderland.lit"❸
               version="1.0"❹
               xmlns="jabber:client"❺
               xmlns:stream="http://etherx.jabber.org/streams">❻
```

❶ This is the XML text declaration. It is optional to include it before sending the stream header itself.

❷ Elements qualified by the `http://etherx.jabber.org/streams` namespace must always be prefixed with `stream:` (e.g., an opening stream tag of `<stream:stream>`).

❸ The `to` attribute contains the domain part of Alice's JID. It is the logical domain name, which might not be the same as the physical machine used for connecting.

❹ The `version` attribute indicates the version of the XMPP protocol. This is always `1.0`.

❺ The `xmlns` attribute specifies the default namespace for all XML sent over the stream (i.e., the namespace that applies if no other namespace is noted). Because this is a client-to-server stream, the default namespace is `jabber:client`.

❻ The `<stream/>` element is not closed. At this point the client sends only the opening tag to start the stream, i.e., `<stream:stream>`. From now on, all subsequent XML elements will be sent as children of this root element, until the session ends by closing the root element with the ending `</stream:stream>` tag.

In response, the server opens a *response stream* in the opposite direction by sending an opening `<stream:stream>` tag to Alice (as mentioned, there is one stream in each direction):

```
<?xml version="1.0"?>
<stream:stream from="wonderland.lit"
               id="k0d1m43rt53ht"❶
               version="1.0"
               xmlns="jabber:client"
               xmlns:stream="http://etherx.jabber.org/streams">
```

❶ Before sending the response stream header, the server generates a unique stream ID for this session.

Immediately after opening the response stream, the server tries to reach agreement with the client on how the connection will proceed. First, the server tells the client about the *stream features* it supports:

```
<stream:features>
  <starttls xmlns="urn:ietf:params:xml:ns:xmpp-tls">
    <optional/>
  </starttls>
  <mechanisms xmlns="urn:ietf:params:xml:ns:xmpp-sasl">
    <mechanism>PLAIN</mechanism>
    <mechanism>DIGEST-MD5</mechanism>
    <required/>
  </mechanisms>
  <compression xmlns="http://jabber.org/features/compress">
    <method>zlib</method>
  </compression>
</stream:features>
```

In this case, the server supports the following features:

- Encrypted connections with the XMPP profile of *Transport Layer Security (TLS)* [RFC 5246]. The `wonderland.lit` server says that TLS negotiation is *optional*, but in general it is recommended for all XML streams (we discuss TLS in "Encrypting the Connection" on page 172).

- Authentication via the *Simple Authentication and Security Layer (SASL)* [RFC 4422]. In this case, the only supported authentication methods are the PLAIN mechanism and the DIGEST-MD5 mechanism. The `wonderland.lit` server says that SASL negotiation is required.

- Stream compression for more optimal bandwidth usage, as described in [XEP-0138]; this too is optional here (the `wonderland.lit` server has not included an `<optional/>` child element, but features default to optional).

Optional Features

RFC 3920 defined the `<required/>` flag only for the TLS stream feature, and did not define the `<optional/>` flag at all. Implementation experience has indicated the need for consistent flagging of which stream features are required and which are optional, so the document that captures ongoing revisions to RFC 3920 (known as [rfc3920bis]) specifies that all stream features must indicate whether they are required or optional.

Because Alice isn't interested in securing or compressing her connection at this point, she proceeds directly to the authentication step. In this step, she *logs in* to her account by passing her credentials to the server, proving to the server that she really is Alice.

Since the `wonderland.lit` service supports both DIGEST-MD5 and PLAIN, Alice chooses the simplest alternative, and authenticates herself using the PLAIN mechanism (this is for demonstration purposes only—don't do this over an unencrypted connection, because your password will be sent in the clear!). Alice does this by sending a Base64-encoded version of a string containing her username and her password, separated by a 0 byte:

```
<auth xmlns="urn:ietf:params:xml:ns:xmpp-sasl" mechanism="PLAIN">
  AGFsaWNlAHBhc3N3b3JkCg==
</auth>
```

(The Base64-decoded string is `<0>alice<0>password`—clearly Alice needs some instruction on best practices for information security.)

Alice's server responds with the message that her authentication was successful:

```
<success xmlns="urn:ietf:params:xml:ns:xmpp-sasl"/>
```

SASL Challenges

Unlike the PLAIN authentication mechanism, most SASL authentication mechanisms typically consist of more than one step. In those cases, the server and client send each other different subsequent challenges and responses (embedded in `<challenge/>` and `<response/>` elements), until the authentication has been established.

Immediately following the notification of successful authentication, the server resets the session by sending a new stream header (with a new Stream ID). This time, however, it announces different stream features:

```
<?xml version="1.0"?>
<stream:stream from="wonderland.lit"
               id="d1r3ht0n4"
               version="1.0"
               xmlns="jabber:client"
               xmlns:stream="http://etherx.jabber.org/streams">
  <stream:features>
    <compression xmlns="http://jabber.org/features/compress">
      <method>zlib</method>
    </compression>
    <bind xmlns="urn:ietf:params:xml:ns:xmpp-bind">
      <required/>
    </bind>
    <session xmlns="urn:ietf:params:xml:ns:xmpp-session">
      <optional/>
    </session>
  </stream:features>
```

SASL negotiation has been completed, so the authentication feature is no longer advertised. However, two other features are now included: support for *resource binding* and support for formally starting an XMPP session.

Before starting the XMPP session, Alice requests a resource from the server, since this is necessary for proper routing of XMPP stanzas. Because Alice is currently in the rabbit hole, she decides to ask for a resource called `rabbithole`:

```
<iq id="b1h4r9rx" type="set">
  <bind xmlns="urn:ietf:params:xml:ns:xmpp-bind">
    <resource>rabbithole</resource>
  </bind>
</iq>
```

The server acknowledges this request, which means that Alice's full JID on the XMPP network is now `alice@wonderland.lit/rabbithole`:

```
<iq id="b1h4r9rx" type="result">
  <bind xmlns="urn:ietf:params:xml:ns:xmpp-bind">
    <jid>alice@wonderland.lit/rabbithole</jid>
  </bind>
</iq>
```

Resource Assignment

When a client requests a specific resource, most servers grant the requested resource unchanged if it is available, or fail if it is not. However, servers are always free to assign a different resource than the one requested. For example, when requesting the `rabbithole` resource, the server could have returned `alice@wonderland.lit/rabbithole-1` in its response, binding the session to the `rabbithole-1` resource instead. A possible reason for doing this is to avoid collisions between resources, or to randomize resource IDs for security purposes.

Finally, Alice seals the deal by explicitly starting an XMPP session:

```
<iq id="uyq6z751" type="set">
  <session xmlns="urn:ietf:params:xml:ns:xmpp-session"/>
</iq>
```

And the server responds with success:

```
<iq id="uyq6z751" type="result"/>
```

The Session No-Op

After the XMPP RFCs were published in October 2004, the XMPP developer community realized that the `xmpp-session` step of the stream negotiation was unnecessary, so most clients and servers now treat it as a "no-op," advertise it only for backward compatibility, and proceed normally if the step is skipped.

Alice can now begin sending messages and presence notifications. She will typically start by retrieving her roster and sending initial presence, as we discussed in Chapter 3:

```
<iq from="alice@wonderland.lit/rabbithole"
    id="hr71vl77"
    to="alice@wonderland.lit"
    type="get">
  <query xmlns="jabber:iq:roster"/>
</iq>

<iq from="alice@wonderland.lit"
    id="hr71vl77"
    to="alice@wonderland.lit/rabbithole"
    type="result">
  <query xmlns="jabber:iq:roster">
    <item jid="whiterabbit@wonderland.lit"/>
    <item jid="lory@wonderland.lit"/>
    <item jid="mouse@wonderland.lit"/>
    <item jid="sister@realworld.lit"/>
  </query>
</iq>

<presence/>
```

Now that Alice has logged in, retrieved her roster, and sent initial presence, she can chat with friends, join chat rooms, and interact with other entities on the network.

Authentication Options

The PLAIN mechanism illustrated in the previous section is the very simplest (and least secure) of SASL mechanism. One benefit of the SASL framework is that it enables application developers and service administrators to support many different authentication mechanisms depending on their requirements. Here are some of the SASL mechanisms that are currently used or planned for deployment within the XMPP community:

PLAIN

As we've seen, the PLAIN mechanism [RFC 4616] provides a very simple password-based authentication method. Because the password is sent without any security protection, the PLAIN mechanism is safe to use only if the underlying XML stream is protected using Transport Layer Security (TLS).

DIGEST-MD5

The DIGEST-MD5 mechanism [RFC 2831] provides stronger security than the PLAIN mechanism, since the password is encrypted in transit (thus the channel does not require TLS security). Unfortunately, many interoperability problems have arisen for DIGEST-MD5, not just in XMPP but in other uses of SASL, such as IMAP. Therefore, the IETF has deprecated DIGEST-MD5 in favor of SCRAM.

SCRAM

The Salted Challenge Response Authentication Mechanism [SCRAM] is the IETF's proposed replacement for DIGEST-MD5. The mechanism provides quite strong protection against numerous security threats when it is used in conjunction with Transport Layer Security. Because SCRAM is a new technology (in fact, it had not yet been published as an RFC at the time of this writing), it will probably take some time before all XMPP servers support it.

EXTERNAL

The EXTERNAL mechanism [RFC 4422] enables the initiating entity (whether a client or a server) to present a digital certificate during TLS negotiation and then refer to that certificate during authentication, thus obviating the need for passwords altogether. However, very few end users outside of certain specialized environments have digital certificates, so in practice the EXTERNAL mechanism is used more for server-to-server connections than for client-to-server connections.

GSSAPI

The GSSAPI mechanism [RFC 4121] was conceived as a general SASL mechanism (pluggability within pluggability!), but to date has been employed only for use with Kerberos V. The GSSAPI mechanism is deployed even less widely than the EXTERNAL mechanism, but is quite powerful within organizations that use Kerberos for "single sign-on."

ANONYMOUS

The ANONYMOUS mechanism [RFC 4505] enables users to authenticate without having registered accounts on the server. This mechanism is most useful for customer-facing applications, such as call centers and online help systems, where it doesn't make sense to require registration for a one-time use of the XMPP application.

Some of these authentication methods can also result in a mutually authenticated session that invokes a security layer, thus providing integrity protection and encryption. However, this aspect of SASL is not as widely used as its authentication capabilities. Instead, as described in the next section, Transport Layer Security is used for encryption.

Encrypting the Connection

Connecting to an XMPP server using a normal TCP connection (as you saw in the previous section) has the disadvantage of not being secure. Indeed, eavesdroppers who are able to monitor the traffic on your network can intercept everything you send to your server, including personal messages, and even the password you send in the authentication step. Clearly this is not good!

The authentication phase can be made more secure by using an authentication mechanism that, unlike PLAIN, does not send your password in a way that it can be reconstructed from the traffic you send (e.g., DIGEST-MD5). Nevertheless, this still leaves the rest of your communication going over the wire in an unsecured fashion (if, say, DIGEST-MD5 was not used to negotiate a security layer). Another problem is that you have no assurance that the server you are connecting to is indeed the server you think it is. For example, a malicious person can find ways to redirect your connection to his own host, resulting in you sending your credentials to a server without even noticing this. However, these problems are not specific to XMPP: the same issues arise when entering your credit card number on a website, when sending an email with sensitive company information, and so on. This is why smart security professionals have designed a general solution for securing connections. This solution was originally called Secure Sockets Layer (SSL) and is now called *Transport Layer Security* [RFC 5246]. Just like all the other widely used Internet protocols that employ either SSL or TLS, XMPP uses TLS for securing its connections as well. This section describes the XMPP profile of TLS for client-to-server connections.

TLS and SSL

Transport Layer Security is the IETF's evolution of Secure Sockets Layer. SSL was originally developed by Netscape in the early years of the Web to encrypt TCP connections between web browsers and web servers, usually on port 443 ("https") instead of port 80 ("http"). Originally the Jabber community followed the same convention by encrypting client-to-server TCP connections on port 5223 instead of 5222. With the publication of [RFC 3920] in 2004, XMPP adopted the more modern practice of upgrading an unencrypted connection to encrypted using the `<starttls/>` command. This means that an ordinary (unsecured) connection is set up first, after which a `<starttls/>` command is sent to negotiate an encrypted connection.

Let's say that the `wonderland.lit` server has instituted a new security policy. When Alice opens a session, the server greets her with the following stream features announcement:

```
<stream:stream from="wonderland.lit"
               id="d1r3ht0n4"
               version="1.0"
               xmlns="jabber:client"
               xmlns:stream="http://etherx.jabber.org/streams">
  <stream:features>
    <starttls xmlns="urn:ietf:params:xml:ns:xmpp-tls">
      <required/>
    </starttls>
  </stream:features>
```

Not only does the `wonderland.lit` server announce support for secure connections using TLS, it even *requires* encrypted connections. Indeed, in addition to the `<required/>` tag within the `<starttls/>` element, the server doesn't announce support for any authentication mechanisms, so Alice has no choice but to switch to an encrypted connection:

```
<starttls xmlns="urn:ietf:params:xml:ns:xmpp-tls"/>
```

This request is promptly followed by an acknowledgment from the server:

```
<proceed xmlns="urn:ietf:params:xml:ns:xmpp-tls"/>
```

From the point where the `<proceed/>` happened, the regular XMPP stream ends, and the TLS handshake starts happening over the TCP connection itself. This handshake step involves the server sending a certificate to the client, and the client validating the certificate to ensure that the server is indeed the one it claims to be. This handshake occurs directly over the TCP connection using standard TLS messages (not an XML encapsulation of TLS), as defined in the TLS specification. After the handshake has successfully completed, the client restarts its XMPP session, only now encrypting everything it sends using the key received from the server during the TLS handshake:

```
<stream:stream to="wonderland.lit"
                version="1.0"
                xmlns="jabber:client"
                xmlns:stream="http://etherx.jabber.org/streams">
```

Because the connection is now secure, the server responds with more stream features, including authentication mechanisms, allowing the client to start authenticating its XMPP session, as we discussed in the last section:

```
<stream:stream from="wonderland.lit"
                id="c8b7rn6p6"
                version="1.0"
                xmlns="jabber:client"
                xmlns:stream="http://etherx.jabber.org/streams">
  <stream:features>
    <mechanisms xmlns="urn:ietf:params:xml:ns:xmpp-sasl">
      <mechanism>PLAIN</mechanism>
      <mechanism>DIGEST-MD5</mechanism>
    </mechanisms>
  </stream:features>
```

Server Federation

So far, the focus of this chapter has been on creating a connection between a client and a server. However, if you want to send a message to a contact on another server, your server needs to connect to the other server before it can send the message through. This kind of server-to-server connectivity is commonly called *federation*. In this section, we talk about how federated connections are made, what the security considerations are, and how these security problems are solved.

c2s and s2s

Client-to-server connections are often abbreviated as *c2s* in the networking world, whereas server-to-server connections are (not surprisingly) referred to as *s2s* connections.

Server-to-server (s2s) connections basically follow the same pattern as client-to-server connections: after opening a connection to the host serving XMPP for the target JID, the sending server needs to authenticate itself before it is allowed to send a message. Without authentication, any server would be able to pretend that it is responsible for a given domain, and could send messages in the name of any user in that domain (this is called *domain spoofing*).

Just as in the case of clients connecting to a server, servers can also use SASL to authenticate themselves. The SASL mechanisms most commonly used by clients require the user to register in some way with the server and then reference the registered credentials when authenticating. This is impractical for server-to-server connections because XMPP promotes a distributed network where servers don't need to have prior knowledge about each other (this dynamic federation model is similar to email but different from the formal "peering" model public telecommunication networks use).

You might therefore think that SASL cannot be used for inter-domain federation. However, one SASL mechanism comes in handy here: the EXTERNAL mechanism. For server-to-server connections, SASL EXTERNAL is used in conjunction with Transport Layer Security. During the TLS negotiation, the servers exchange certificates in both directions. After the negotiation completes, the servers can then simply refer to the certificates provided via TLS for mutual authentication. Unfortunately, the use of TLS and SASL EXTERNAL is not yet widespread, even though it provides strong server-to-server authentication.

In the case where certificate-based verification is not possible, XMPP servers fall back on the less secure approach of checking the validity of a sending server, called *server dialback*. This approach can be illustrated by the story of a representative from your electric company coming to your house and asking whether he can enter to work on your electric system. Before letting him into your house, you ask for his employee ID number. You then call the number of the electric company's service department (which you looked up in your own phone book), and ask them whether the employee with the given ID is allowed to come and work on your house. After having checked their records, the service department confirms that the person at your door is indeed one of their employees and is authorized to visit you now, so you let him enter. In XMPP, the equivalent of the homeowner is the *receiving server* (to which an s2s connection is being made), the equivalent of the worker is the *originating server* (which is attempting to connect), the equivalent of the phone book is the Domain Name System (DNS), and the equivalent of the service department is the *authoritative server* for the originating domain.

The basic flow of events is as follows:

1. The originating server performs a DNS lookup on the hostname of the receiving server, opens a TCP connection to the discovered IP address and port, and establishes an XML stream with the receiving server.

2. The originating server generates a dialback key and sends that value over its XML stream with the receiving server.

3. The Receiving Server does not immediately accept the connection but instead performs a DNS lookup on the hostname of the authoritative server, opens a TCP connection to the discovered IP address and port, and establishes an XML stream with the authoritative server.

4. The receiving server sends the same dialback key over its XML stream with the authoritative server for verification.

5. The authoritative server replies that the key is valid or invalid.

6. The receiving server informs the originating server whether its identity has been verified or not.

This flow is illustrated in Figure 12-1.

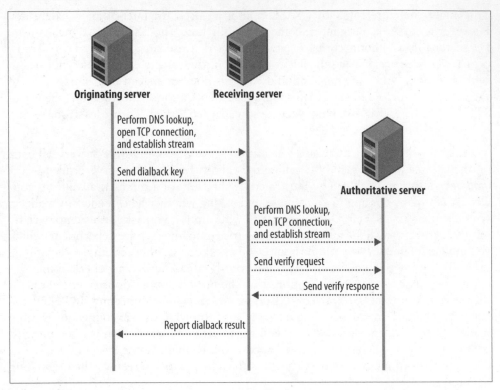

Figure 12-1. Server dialback defines a DNS-based "callback" method that provides weak identity verification

Let's walk through the case where Alice wants to send a message to her sister in the real world. In order to get the message delivered, Alice's server `wonderland.lit` needs to open a connection to `realworld.lit`. A DNS lookup for SRV records for the XMPP server service at `realworld.lit` yields the following result:

```
_xmpp-server._tcp.xmpp.realworld.lit. 86400 IN SRV 10 0 5269 xmpp.realworld.lit
```

Alice's server therefore performs a standard "A" or "AAAA" lookup on `xmpp.real world.lit` to discover that machine's IP address, opens a TCP connection on port 5269 at that IP address, and starts an XML stream:

```
<stream:stream from="wonderland.lit"
               to="realworld.lit"
               version="1.0"
               xmlns="jabber:server"
               xmlns:db="jabber:server:dialback"❶
               xmlns:stream="http://etherx.jabber.org/streams">
```

❶ Inclusion of the `jabber:server:dialback` namespace declaration indicates to the receiving server that the originating server supports the server dialback protocol.

The realworld server sends a response stream header and the stream features:

```
<stream:stream from="realworld.lit" to="wonderland.lit" id="D60000229F" version="1.0"
        xmlns="jabber:server"
        xmlns:db="jabber:server:dialback"
        xmlns:stream="http://etherx.jabber.org/streams">
  <stream:features>
    <dialback xmlns="urn:xmpp:features:dialback">
      <required/>
    </dialback>
  </stream:features>
```

The receiving server apparently requires the originating server to provide some verification of its identity using the dialback protocol. To start this verification process, the wonderland server generates a *dialback key*, which will be used by the receiving server and the authoritative server to verify the originating server. This key is then sent to the realworld server:

```
<db:result from="wonderland.lit" to="realworld.lit">
37c69b1cf07a3f67c04a5ef5902fa5114f2c76fe4a2686482ba5b89323075643
</db:result>
```

To verify whether the server that opened a connection is really the wonderland server, the realworld server now "dials back" to the wonderland server. To do that, it looks up the host serving XMPP for that domain using a DNS SRV query, resulting in the following reply:

```
_xmpp-server._tcp.wonderland.lit. 86400 IN SRV 10 0 5269 cm.wonderland.lit
```

This is the *authoritative server* for `wonderland.lit`. The realworld server now performs a standard "A" or "AAAA" lookup on `cm.wonderland.lit` to discover that machine's IP address, opens a TCP connection on port 5269 at that IP address, and starts an XML stream:

```
<stream:stream from="realworld.lit"
               to="wonderland.lit"
               version="1.0"
               xmlns="jabber:server"
               xmlns:db="jabber:server:dialback"
               xmlns:stream="http://etherx.jabber.org/streams">
```

The `cm.wonderland.lit` machine in turn replies with the normal stream header:

```
<stream:stream from="wonderland.lit"
               id="D60000229F"
               to="realworld.lit"
               version="1.0"
               xmlns="jabber:server"
               xmlns:db="jabber:server:dialback"
               xmlns:stream="http://etherx.jabber.org/streams"
  <stream:features>
    <dialback xmlns="urn:xmpp:features:dialback">
```

```
      <optional/>
    </dialback>
  </stream:features>
```

Now that the realworld server has a reverse connection to the wonderland server, it can ask the latter whether it is trying to connect a stream with the given ID and the given key:

```
<db:verify from="realworld.lit" to="wonderland.lit" id="D60000229F">
  37c69b1cf07a3f67c04a5ef5902fa5114f2c76fe4a2686482ba5b89323075643
</db:verify>
```

The wonderland server confirms that it is indeed trying to connect and that the key given is valid:

```
<db:verify from="wonderland.lit"
           id="D60000229F"
           to="realworld.lit"
           type="valid">
  37c69b1cf07a3f67c04a5ef5902fa5114f2c76fe4a2686482ba5b89323075643
</db:verify>
```

The realworld server is now confident that the stream opened by the originating server is indeed from a server in the wonderland network, and therefore sends a response on its initial stream with the originating server, informing the wonderland.lit server that it may proceed with sending stanzas:

```
<db:result from="realworld.lit" to="wonderland.lit" type="valid">
  37c69b1cf07a3f67c04a5ef5902fa5114f2c76fe4a2686482ba5b89323075643
</db:result>
```

Verification complete!

In the foregoing example, we assumed that the *initiating server* (the server opening the connection) was the same as the *authoritative server* (the server used by the *receiving server* to verify the validity of the key). However, this doesn't always have to be the case. You can compare this to a self-employed electrician picking up the phone when you dial his company's number from the phone book, as opposed to the administration office of the company answering the phone and validating employees.

Although the server dialback protocol provides a relatively good authenticity check, it is still weaker than using TLS plus SASL EXTERNAL for this job. The main weakness of this approach is that it relies on the initiating host being registered through DNS, which means that DNS poisoning attacks can still result in domain spoofing if the DNS security extensions (DNSSEC) are not used. This is the major reason why it is preferable to use certificate-based validation with TLS.

Got Certs?

One of the challenges related to TLS is not support for it in software but the availability of certificates. In the early days, many server administrators installed "self-signed" certificates that were not issued by a recognized *Certification Authority* (CA). But such "homegrown" certificates cause security warnings to pop up in XMPP clients—and security warnings are scary to most end users. Unfortunately, acquiring a certificate that is signed by one of best-known CA's can cost quite a bit of money. To remedy this situation, the XMPP Standards Foundation offers free certificates to administrators of XMPP servers, currently by running an Intermediate CA that uses StartCom (a widely recognized certification authority) as the root CA. For more information or to obtain a free certificate for your XMPP server, visit *http://xmpp.org/ca/*.

Server Components

A third class of entities that can connect to an XMPP server, besides clients and other XMPP servers, is made up of server components. Server components, like MUC components (see Chapter 7), connect to a server and get a specific subdomain of the server assigned to them (e.g., `conference.wonderland.lit`). Whenever the XMPP server receives a stanza addressed to a JID within this domain, it directly routes the stanza to the component over the component's connection with the server.

Setting up a stream between a component and the server is done using a simple handshake protocol, defined in *Jabber Component Protocol* [XEP-0114]. After having opened a connection to the `wonderland.lit` server, our MUC component starts the stream, using the requested subdomain of the component as the `to` target of the stream:

```
<stream:stream xmlns="jabber:component:accept"
               xmlns:stream="http://etherx.jabber.org/streams"
               to="conference.wonderland.lit">
```

The server replies by starting a stream as well:

```
<stream:stream xmlns:stream="http://etherx.jabber.org/streams"
               xmlns="jabber:component:accept"
               from="conference.wonderland.lit"
               id="3BF96D32">
```

At this point, the component needs to authenticate itself with the server. This authentication is done by taking a shared secret known by both the server and the component, and applying a transformation on it. More specifically, the shared secret is appended to the stream ID of the server stream, after which the value is hashed (using SHA-1) and then Base64-encoded. The component then sends the resulting string in a `<handshake/>` element:

```
<handshake>aaee83c26aeeafcbabeabfcbcd50df997e0a2a1e</handshake>
```

After the server has verified that our key is indeed what the server expects it to be, it sends back a successful result:

```
<handshake/>
```

After this handshake has completed, the server will send all stanzas addressed to the `conference.wonderland.lit` domain over this stream to the component, and the component can send stanzas originating from the same domain over the stream.

Because the existing component protocol lacks some flexibility and does not enable a component to upgrade the stream to an encrypted connection using Transport Layer Security, a number of XMPP developers have shown an interest in building a more modern component protocol. The beginnings of such a protocol are documented in a proposal called *Component Connections* [XEP-0225], but further work remains to be done before that protocol will be ready for widespread implementation and deployment.

BOSH: XMPP over HTTP

So far, all of the client-to-server and server-to-server connections we've looked at happen over long-lived TCP connections, where the parties keep that connection open as long as the session is needed. However, in certain situations, it can be difficult or inconvenient to maintain a long-lived TCP connection. The following are some examples:

- Networks with intermittent connectivity can repeatedly interrupt the TCP connection, forcing the client to expend a large number of round trips to frequently re-establish an XMPP session by negotiating stream headers, encryption, authentication, resource binding, roster retrieval, and initial presence.

- On a mobile phone or other portable devices, constantly maintaining a long-lived TCP connection can quickly drain the battery.

- Some web-based applications do not carry any state and as such can't keep a connection open.

- Restrictive firewall settings can prevent even a standard XMPP client from opening a regular TCP connection to an XMPP server.

The solution is to use a connection method that does not require the client to maintain a long-lived TCP connection. The standard way to do so emulates the bidirectional streams that are familiar from the TCP binding, but by efficiently using multiple, synchronous HTTP request/response pairs. This creative re-use of HTTP (similar to, but subtly different from the methodology known as "Comet") is called *Bidirectionalstreams Over Synchronous HTTP*, or BOSH for short. BOSH is defined in two specifications: [XEP-0124] describes the core approach, and [XEP-0206] describes some additional rules and considerations for using BOSH with XMPP systems.

BOSH-based systems are usually deployed with a special *connection manager* that acts as a kind of proxy between the client and the XMPP server, as illustrated in Figure 12-2. In this case, the server is a standard XMPP daemon, the connection manager (or CM) sends XMPP to the server but HTTP to the client, and the client is a hybrid XMPP+HTTP user agent that functions as an XMPP client from the user's perspective but wraps the XMPP traffic in a special <body/> element for sending to the connection manager over HTTP.

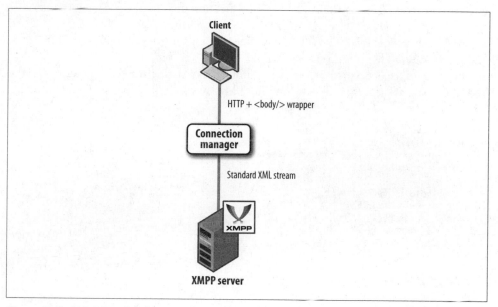

Figure 12-2. In BOSH, the client speaks HTTP to the connection manager, which speaks XMPP to the server

It's Convenient, but Is It Secure?

BOSH is convenient, but because it introduces a connection manager into the traditional XMPP architecture, it also introduces the possibility of new attack vectors on XMPP traffic. These threats are mitigated in several ways: the use of SSL/TLS between the client and the connection manager, as well as between the connection manager and the XMPP server; the large random value for the initial Request ID as described next, inclusion of the Session ID as described below, and optional use of a keying mechanism (not described in this chapter).

Let's suppose that Alice finds herself behind a restrictive firewall after she falls down the rabbit hole. She can't access any XMPP servers on the standard port 5222, but maybe she can use a web client to access a BOSH connection manager being served on port 80 or 443.

First, however, she needs to find the BOSH CM. She could manually configure her client, but it is more efficient and less error-prone to use automated discovery processes. Therefore, her client sends a DNS query for the TXT records associated with the `wonderland.lit` domain. In the DNS answer, her client finds the following record, which matches the format defined in *Discovering Alternative XMPP Connection Methods* [XEP-0156]:

```
_xmppconnect IN TXT "_xmpp-client-xbosh="https://bosh.wonderland.lit/webclient"
```

Now that Alice's client has found a BOSH connection manager, she can start an XMPP session with the `wonderland.lit` XMPP server by sending an initial HTTP request to `https://bosh.wonderland.lit/webclient`. The request consists of an HTTP POST containing a `<body/>` element; in this case, the element is empty, but includes a number of attributes used to set up the BOSH session (line breaks are included for readability only, and the `Content-Length` is based on the XML without line breaks or extraneous whitespace):

```
POST /webclient HTTP/1.1
Host: bosh.wonderland.lit
Content-Type: text/xml; charset=utf-8
Content-Length: 181

<body hold="1"❶
      secure="true"❷
      rid="90029201"❸
      to="wonderland.lit"
      wait="60"❹
      xmpp:version="1.0"
      xml:lang="en"
      xmlns="http://jabber.org/protocol/httpbind"
      xmlns:xmpp="urn:xmpp:xbosh"/>
```

❶ The `hold` attribute sets the maximum number of HTTP requests that the BOSH CM is allowed to queue up for delivery to the client at any one time. Typically, the `hold` attribute is set to a value of `1`, as explained later in this section.

❷ The client includes the `secure` attribute with a value of `true` to tell the BOSH CM that its connection to the XMPP server needs to be secure (i.e., either encrypted via SSL/TLS or hosted on the same machine as the connection manager).

❸ When starting a BOSH session, the client must generate a large, random number that will function as the initial Request ID. The `rid` attribute is then incremented by one with each request the client sends to the BOSH CM.

❹ The `wait` attribute sets the maximum time (in seconds) that the BOSH CM is allowed to wait before responding to a pending request; effectively this sets the timeout period for an HTTP/TCP connection.

The BOSH CM then opens a regular XMPP connection to `wonderland.lit` and receives an XMPP reply (i.e., a response stream header and stream features), which it forwards to Alice in an HTTP response:

```
HTTP/1.1 200 OK
Content-Type: text/xml; charset=utf-8
Content-Length: 390

<body hold="1"
      requests="2"❶
      secure="true"
      sid="3m1ts1htd1s"❷
      wait="60"
      xmpp:version="1.0"
      xmlns="http://jabber.org/protocol/httpbind"
      xmlns:stream="http://etherx.jabber.org/streams"
      xmlns:xmpp="urn:xmpp:xbosh">
  <stream:features>
    <mechanisms xmlns="urn:ietf:params:xml:ns:xmpp-sasl">
      <mechanism>DIGEST-MD5</mechanism>
      <mechanism>PLAIN</mechanism>
      <required/>
    </mechanisms>
  </stream:features>
</body>
```

❶ The requests attribute sets the maximum number of HTTP requests that the client is allowed to have open with the BOSH CM at any one time. Typically the requests attribute is set to a value of 2 (or, more generally, one more than the value of the hold attribute), as explained later.

❷ When it replies to the session creation request, the BOSH CM generates a unique Session ID, which is different from the Stream ID generated by the XMPP server. Each subsequent request and response must then include the sid attribute.

Alice can then authenticate with the server by sending another HTTP request whose <body/> element contains the first step of the SASL authentication handshake (as described earlier in this chapter):

```
POST /webclient HTTP/1.1
Host: bosh.wonderland.lit
Content-Type: text/xml; charset=utf-8
Content-Length: 187

<body rid="90029202" sid="3m1ts1htd1s" xmlns="http://jabber.org/protocol/httpbind">
  <auth xmlns="urn:ietf:params:xml:ns:xmpp-sasl" mechanism="PLAIN">
    AGFsaWNlAHBhc3N3b3JkCg==
  </auth>
</body>
```

The server notifies Alice of success in the HTTP response:

```
HTTP/1.1 200 OK
Content-Type: text/xml; charset=utf-8
Content-Length: 127

<body sid="3m1ts1htd1s" xmlns="http://jabber.org/protocol/httpbind">
  <success xmlns="urn:ietf:params:xml:ns:xmpp-sasl"/>
</body>
```

Now that Alice has successfully authenticated with the server, she needs to restart the stream; this is done by sending a special restart request:

```
POST /webclient HTTP/1.1
Content-Type: text/xml; charset=utf-8
Content-Length: 153

<body rid="90029203"
      sid="3m1ts1htd1s"
      to="wonderland.lit"
      xmpp:restart="true"❶
      xmlns="http://jabber.org/protocol/httpbind"
      xmlns:xmpp="urn:xmpp:xbosh"/>
```

❶ The `xmpp:restart` attribute tells the BOSH CM to restart the XML stream it has opened with the XMPP server on the client's behalf.

The connection manager restarts the stream with the XMPP server and returns a new set of stream features:

```
HTTP/1.1 200 OK
Content-Type: text/xml; charset=utf-8
Content-Length: 345

<body sid="3m1ts1htd1s"
      xmpp:version="1.0"
      xmlns="http://jabber.org/protocol/httpbind"
      xmlns:stream="http://etherx.jabber.org/streams"
      xmlns:xmpp="urn:xmpp:xbosh">
  <stream:features>
    <bind xmlns="urn:ietf:params:xml:ns:xmpp-bind">
      <required/>
    </bind>
    <session xmlns="urn:ietf:params:xml:ns:xmpp-session">
      <optional/>
    </session>
  </stream:features>
</body>
```

Alice now requests a resource:

```
POST /webclient HTTP/1.1
Host: bosh.wonderland.lit
Content-Type: text/xml; charset=utf-8
Content-Length: 233

<body rid="90029204" sid="3m1ts1htd1s" xmlns="http://jabber.org/protocol/httpbind">
  <iq id="vc18f4hj7"
      type="set"
      xmlns="jabber:client">❶
    <bind xmlns="urn:ietf:params:xml:ns:xmpp-bind">
      <resource>rabbithole</resource>
    </bind>
  </iq>
</body>
```

❶ The IQ stanza includes a namespace declaration because the default namespace for BOSH is `http://jabber.org/protocol/httpbind` instead of the default namespace for a client-to-server XMPP stream (i.e., `jabber:client`).

In response, the connection manager returns the binding result it has received from the XMPP server:

```
HTTP/1.1 200 OK
Content-Type: text/xml; charset=utf-8
Content-Length: 232

<body sid="3m1ts1htd1s" xmlns="http://jabber.org/protocol/httpbind">
  <iq id="vc18f4hj7" type="result" xmlns="jabber:client">
    <bind xmlns="urn:ietf:params:xml:ns:xmpp-bind">
      <jid>alice@wonderland.lit/rabbithole</jid>
    </bind>
  </iq>
</body>
```

At this point, Alice has successfully negotiated an XML stream with the XMPP server through the BOSH CM. We assume that she also retrieves her roster and sends initial presence (not shown here), so that she's finally ready to communicate with people on the network.

During the stream negotiation process, the special properties of BOSH have not yet been revealed, because each HTTP POST sent by the client to the connection manager has been answered almost immediately with an HTTP 200 OK containing information that the BOSH CM has received from the XMPP server (stream features, authentication mechanisms and challenge/response combinations, IQ-set and IQ result stanzas related to resource binding and roster retrieval, and initial presence). These interactions all happen within the timeout period that is set by the value of the `wait` attribute (in this case, 60 seconds).

The real usefulness of BOSH comes into the picture when Alice does not send or receive a stanza for longer than the timeout period. When that happens, the connection manager will send keepalives to Alice if the timeout period is about to expire, or will return an empty body element to her if she has more than one HTTP request pending at a time. For instance, in our scenario, Alice has told the BOSH CM that she wants it to hold onto at most one HTTP request at a time (`hold=1`), and the CM has replied that it will let Alice have at most two HTTP requests in play at a time (`requests=2`). Because the timeout period is one minute (`wait=60`), if Alice has not received an HTTP response to her first request within 60 seconds (usually because the BOSH CM has not received any incoming stanzas for her), then the CM will return an HTTP 200 OK response containing an empty `<body/>` element. This response functions as a keepalive. If Alice does not have any outbound stanzas to send at this point, then her client sends an HTTP request that also contains an empty `<body/>` element.

Alice and the CM can keep sending these keepalives every 60 seconds until one of the following happens:

- The BOSH CM receives an incoming stanza for Alice, at which point, the CM will return an HTTP 200 OK response to her with a nonempty <body/> element that contains the incoming stanza.
- Alice sends another outbound stanza, at which point, she will have two HTTP requests in play, thus forcing the connection manager to respond to her *first* HTTP request with an HTTP 200 OK response containing an empty <body/> element.

This approach is illustrated in Figure 12-3.

Let's see how these interactions happen in protocol.

First, Alice sends a message to her sister:

```
POST /webclient HTTP/1.1
Host: bosh.wonderland.lit
Content-Type: text/xml; charset=utf-8
Content-Length: 205

<body rid="90029205" sid="3m1ts1htd1s" xmlns="http://jabber.org/protocol/httpbind">
  <message to="sister@realworld.lit" xmlns="jabber:client">
    <body>Help, I fell down the rabbit hole!</body>
  </message>
</body>
```

Here we assume that Alice does not yet receive an immediate HTTP response from the connection manager because it takes half a minute for Alice's sister to notice the message and then reply. The connection manager therefore *delays* sending an HTTP response until it receives data intended for delivery to Alice. Because this delay does not quite approach the timeout period, the BOSH CM returns a nonempty <body/> element that contains the reply from her sister:

```
HTTP/1.1 200 OK
Content-Type: text/xml; charset=utf-8
Content-Length: 163

<body sid="3m1ts1htd1s" xmlns="http://jabber.org/protocol/httpbind">
  <message from="sister@realworld.lit/home">
    <body>Oh my! How can I help?</body>
  </message>
</body>
```

Alice quickly replies by sending a new HTTP POST to the CM (thus she once again has one HTTP request in play):

```
POST /webclient HTTP/1.1
Host: bosh.wonderland.lit
Content-Type: text/xml; charset=utf-8
Content-Length: 206

<body rid="90029206" sid="3m1ts1htd1s" xmlns="http://jabber.org/protocol/httpbind">
  <message to="sister@realworld.lit/home">
    <body>I don't know yet, it's all very confusing!</body>
  </message>
</body>
```

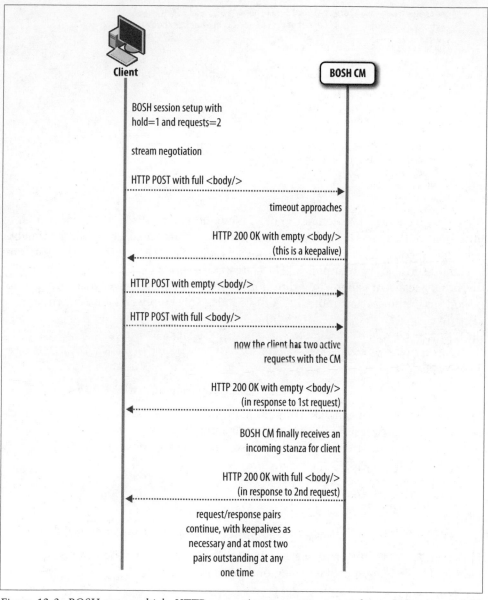

Figure 12-3. BOSH uses multiple HTTP request/response pairs to emulate a bidirectional TCP connection

And Alice's sister just as quickly replies:

```
HTTP/1.1 200 OK
Content-Type: text/xml; charset=utf-8
Content-Length: 194

<body sid="3m1ts1htd1s" xmlns="http://jabber.org/protocol/httpbind">
```

```
          <message from="sister@realworld.lit/home">
            <body>I'm going to find mother, but I'll be back!</body>
          </message>
      </body>
```

Alice thanks her sister and anxiously awaits a reply:

```
POST /webclient HTTP/1.1
Content-Type: text/xml; charset=utf-8
Content-Length: 161

<body rid="90029207" sid="3m1ts1htd1s" xmlns="http://jabber.org/protocol/httpbind">
    <message to="sister@realworld.lit/home">
      <body>Thanks!</body>
    </message>
</body>
```

Alice now has one HTTP request in play. Now, however, Alice's sister has run off to find their mother, so Alice does not receive a reply from her sister within the timeout period. The connection manager therefore tells Alice that it hasn't received any incoming stanzas for her, by returning an HTTP response with an empty **<body/>** element. It does this because it is not allowed to hold on to the request longer than the timeout period set in the **wait** attribute, i.e., 60 seconds. This empty response functions as a keepalive:

```
HTTP/1.1 200 OK
Content-Type: text/xml; charset=utf-8
Content-Length: 70

<body sid="3m1ts1htd1s" xmlns="http://jabber.org/protocol/httpbind"/>
```

Because Alice has not generated any more outbound stanzas, her client immediately sends an HTTP request that also contains an empty **<body/>** element, thus putting the BOSH CM on notice that she is still interested in receiving incoming stanzas:

```
POST /webclient HTTP/1.1
Host: bosh.wonderland.lit
Content-Type: text/xml; charset=utf-8
Content-Length: 85

<body rid="90029208" sid="3m1ts1htd1s" xmlns="http://jabber.org/protocol/httpbind"/>
```

However, Alice is getting nervous, so before the next timeout period expires, she sends another HTTP request containing an outbound stanza:

```
POST /webclient HTTP/1.1
Content-Type: text/xml; charset=utf-8
Content-Length: 167

<body rid="90029209" sid="3m1ts1htd1s" xmlns="http://jabber.org/protocol/httpbind">
    <message to="sister@realworld.lit/home">
      <body>Please hurry!</body>
    </message>
</body>
```

Alice now has two HTTP requests in play, so she has hit the limit set by the `requests` attribute. The BOSH CM therefore sends a reply to her *first* HTTP POST (the empty one). In this case, the response also contains an empty `<body/>` element, because the connection manager has not yet received any incoming stanzas for Alice:

```
HTTP/1.1 200 OK
Content-Type: text/xml; charset=utf-8
Content-Length: 70

<body sid="3m1ts1hld1s" xmlns="http://jabber.org/protocol/httpbind"/>
```

After a short while (less than the timeout period related to the *second* request), Alice's sister finally responds. As a result, the connection manager sends an HTTP response to the last (nonempty) HTTP POST:

```
POST /webclient HTTP/1.1
Host: bosh.wonderland.lit
Content-Type: text/xml; charset=utf-8
Content-Length: 163

<body sid="3m1ts1hld1s" xmlns="http://jabber.org/protocol/httpbind">
  <message from="sister@realworld.lit/home">
    <body>She's on her way!</body>
  </message>
</body>
```

As you can see, by having only two request-response pairs outstanding at any one time, and embedding incoming XMPP stanzas in responses to outgoing HTTP requests sent from the client, BOSH can neatly map XMPP's bidirectional streams to HTTP semantics. Best of all, it achieves this efficiency without forcing the client to constantly poll the connection manager. Exactly how efficient BOSH turns out to be depends on the values of the `hold`, `requests`, and `wait` attributes.

BOSH and Constrained Clients

In constrained clients that cannot maintain two request-response pairs, the client can ask the connection manager to have only one request-response pair outstanding at a time. However, this method means that the connection manager always responds immediately to every request and that it is the responsibility of the client to check for incoming XMPP stanzas at regular intervals (by sending empty `<body/>` elements). As a result, this message is much less efficient, although still a viable alternative to long-lived TCP connections.

Serverless Messaging

XMPP is based on a client-server architecture, which means that you always need a server if you want to communicate between two people. Thanks to the widespread deployment of Internet connectivity in many parts of the world, connecting to a server to communicate via XMPP rarely is a problem. However, in some less fortunate situations, connecting to an XMPP server *can* pose a problem. The following are some examples:

- You might be in a remote location that has no Internet connectivity (say, a rural school), but you still want to use XMPP to communicate with other people in the area.

- You might be at an international conference where you want to discuss the topic of the current talk with the people in the room, but you don't know their JabberIDs.

- You might have fallen down a rabbit hole, and the authorities there block all outbound connections to the Internet!

Indeed, this problem is not limited to XMPP. For example, you might want to find local devices such as printers without any central coordination. However, the problem is more acute in XMPP because it is almost always deployed using a client-server architecture. To solve the more general problem, a team of people at Apple Computer defined a set of technologies known as "zero-configuration networking." These technologies in turn have been applied to real-time communication using XMPP, and this usage has been standardized by the XSF under the name *Serverless Messaging* [XEP-0174].

Picture poor Alice and her friends down the rabbit hole when the queen exclaims, "Off with their net!" and blocks connections to the broader Internet. How will they communicate? It turns out that there's still a local network in Wonderland, so maybe they can use that for communication. To do so, Alice needs to discover who is on the local network and to ensure that the others can find her there.

The basic approach is that each person will multicast special DNS entries to everyone on the local network; as a result, they will collectively manage a reserved top-level domain called .local. For the sake of serverless messaging, we are not interested in all of the services that might exist on the .local domain (printers and the like), but only in entities that advertise support for the presence service using defined DNS PTR, A, and SRV records. (For all the details, refer to the *Multicast DNS* [mDNS] and *DNS-based service discovery* [DNS-SD] specifications.)

To find her friends on the local network, Alice would first broadcast a multicast DNS query for all PTR records that match the _presence._tcp.local. service. Anyone on the local network can answer this query; down the rabbit hole, this query will result in answers like the following:

```
_presence._tcp.local. PTR hatter@mercury._presence._tcp.local.
_presence._tcp.local. PTR rabbit@ivory._presence._tcp.local.
```

Here, Alice finds two people on the local network: the Mad Hatter (who is the user hatter on a machine named mercury) and the White Rabbit (who is the user rabbit on a machine named ivory). Let's say that she wants to chat with the Mad Hatter. She has a pointer to his machine, but she needs to find out the hostname and port number of this machine (mercury). So, she broadcasts another mDNS query, requesting the SRV record of the hatter@mercury presence service. This returns the following information:

```
hatter@mercury._presence._tcp.local. SRV 5562 mercury.local.
```

Now Alice knows that the XMPP client for hatter@mercury is listening on port 5562 of the host mercury.local. The final piece of the puzzle is finding out the actual IP address of mercury.local. This is done by broadcasting an mDNS query for the A (or, for IPv6, the AAAA) DNS record of that hostname; the answer is as follows:

```
mercury.local. A 10.2.1.187
```

At this point, Alice knows exactly where to connect for starting her XMPP conversation with the Mad Hatter. All of this DNS magic has simply been a precursor to XMPP communications! To chat with the Mad Hatter, Alice opens a TCP connection to 10.2.1.187 on port 5562 and starts an XMPP stream:

```
<stream:stream from="alice@odyssey"
               to="hatter@mercury"
               version="1.0"
               xmlns="jabber:client"
               xmlns:stream="http://etherx.jabber.org/streams">
```

The Mad Hatter responds by opening an XMPP stream back to Alice at the IP address and port she has advertised:

```
<stream:stream from="hatter@mercury"
               to="alice@odyssey"
               version="1.0"
               xmlns="jabber:client"
               xmlns:stream="http://etherx.jabber.org/streams">
```

After this handshake, Alice can send <message/> and <iq/> stanzas back and forth to start her conversation, just as she would over a normal XMPP connection. (There is no TLS encryption or SASL authentication for these serverless streams, although methods for doing so are in the works to improve the security of ad-hoc meshes.)

```
<message from="alice@odyssey" to="hatter@mercury">
  <body>I didn't know it was YOUR table; it's laid for a great many more than
  three.</body>
</message>
```

Besides knowing the machines on the network, Alice would also like to find out more detailed information about the people (or fictional characters) behind those machines. This information is also stored in mDNS records, specifically in DNS TXT records that contain a variety of key-value pairs. For example, a request for the Mad Hatter's TXT record might result in the following response:

```
hatter@mercury._presence._tcp.local. IN TXT "
  txtvers=1❶
  status=avail❷
  msg=Having a spot of tea❸
  1st=Mad
  last=Hatter
```

```
nick=thehatter
node=http://psi-im.org/caps❹
ver=QgayPKawpkPSDYmwT/WM94uAluO=❺
hash=sha-1❻
```

❶ This version number is always 1, and the `txtvers` field must always come first in the TXT record value.

❷ This is equivalent to the `<show/>` element from standard XMPP presence, except that mere available presence is mapped to a TXT `show` of `avail`.

❸ This is equivalent to the `<status/>` element from standard XMPP presence.

❹ This is equivalent to the `node` attribute from the XMPP Entity Capabilities extension.

❺ This is equivalent to the `ver` attribute from the XMPP Entity Capabilities extension.

❻ This is equivalent to the `hash` attribute from the XMPP Entity Capabilities extension.

Besides presence information, Alice also received some basic information about the Mad Hatter's identity and the capabilities of his client (as described in Chapter 5). Whenever the Mad Hatter updates his presence information (by publishing a new TXT record), it will be broadcast on the network, notifying everybody of the change.

So far, Alice has discovered and connected to other clients on the network. Of course, she also needs to announce her own XMPP client to the other clients, so that they can contact her as well. She does this by publishing the same types of mDNS and DNS-SD records that she used to discover the other clients:

```
odyssey.local. A 10.2.1.188
_presence._tcp.local. PTR alice@odyssey._presence._tcp.local.
alice@odyssey._presence._tcp.local. SRV 5562 odyssey.local.
alice@odyssey._presence._tcp.local. IN TXT "txtvers=1
  status=avail
  1st=Alice"
```

Serverless messaging provides yet another way to use the same XMPP "primitives" in ways that expand the ability to communicate (even when there is no server in the mix). Future topics in the area of serverless messaging include encryption and authentication using TLS and SASL, as well as the ability to seamlessly bridge between the serverless mode and the traditional client-server mode for improved connections between local meshes and the broader network.

XMPP Security

Everyone says that they like to use secure technologies, but few people rigorously define security—and even fewer do the hard work necessary to make communication systems both secure and usable. Security can mean different things to different people, but there is general agreement among security professionals that the most common threats to communication systems include the following:

- Eavesdropping on communication channels
- Unauthenticated or weakly authenticated users
- Rogue servers
- Address spoofing
- Denial of service attacks
- Viruses, worms, and other malware
- Unwanted communications ("spam")
- Impersonation attacks ("phishing")
- Leaks of personal or privileged information
- Inappropriate logging or archiving
- Buffer overflows and other code security issues

Before you deploy an XMPP application, it's important to understand the track record of XMPP technologies on these critical issues. The good news is that the attacks we discuss here are, so far, mostly theoretical. Even the open XMPP network running on the public Internet since 1999 has experienced very few security issues: no significant denial of service attacks; very little spam; no known instances of phishing, viruses, worms, or other malware; no rogue servers; and only a few code security reports related to particular clients and servers (which were quickly fixed in most cases).

However, the lack of successful attacks is no reason to be complacent. Because information security is a bit of an "arms race" between the bad guys and the good guys, the XMPP community continues to work on ways to prevent these attacks (and others that might arise in the future). So let's look at what XMPP technologies have to offer in the area of security. We can't discuss every possible threat in this book, but the following topics should give you a feeling for the approaches taken by both developers and operators in the XMPP community. (If you have a strong interest in security issues, be sure to join the *security@xmpp.org* discussion list.)

Encryption

Earlier in this chapter, we discussed the use of Transport Layer Security (TLS) for channel encryption. This technology is mandatory to implement for XMPP servers and clients. It is also widely (but not yet universally) deployed by operators of XMPP-based services. The use of TLS overcomes many concerns about the identity of servers on the network and makes it straightforward to encrypt traffic on client-to-server and server-to-server links.

Channel encryption is good, but it leaves a few vulnerable points. Even if you encrypt your connection to your server, your contact encrypts her connection to her server, and the link between the two servers is also encrypted, the messages that you exchange with your friend are still unencrypted inside the servers themselves. This means that the server admins could be logging all of your messages as they pass through. Not good!

The solution is called end-to-end encryption, whereby you and your friend negotiate a method for encrypting your messages so that no one in the middle can read them.

However, end-to-end encryption is a hard problem. The approach taken by the early open source developers was to use the open flavor of Pretty Good Privacy (PGP), called OpenPGP. Unfortunately, typical end users don't have PGP keys. The approach recommended by various IETF security experts during formalization of XMPP was to use Secure/Multipurpose Internet Mail Extensions (S/MIME), but this approach has never taken off in the XMPP community (partly because the resulting technology was not very "Jabberish" and partly because it required users to have digital certificates, which are probably even less common than PGP keys). Another interim technology, Encrypted Sessions, is supported in one open source XMPP client, but its security properties have not been fully validated, and it too is seen as difficult to implement by most developers. The community is currently working on an adaptation of Transport Layer Security that can be exchanged between clients over XMPP, but work on it is not complete as of this writing. Visit *http://xmpp.org* for up-to-date information about end-to-end encryption.

Authentication and Identity

Perhaps the most basic form of trust on a communications network is knowing that the sender of a message is who he says he is. If addresses can be faked or users can be impersonated, trust quickly breaks down and people migrate to a different communications technology.

XMPP includes a number of methods for ensuring relatively strong identity on the network. One such method is authentication: a server will not allow users onto the network unless they first provide proper credentials during the login process. Unless a user's password or other credential information is leaked, the authentication requirement almost guarantees that the person you added to your contact list yesterday or last year is the same person today. In addition, XMPP servers do not allow end users to assert just any "from" address on the stanzas they send; instead, the "from" address is always stamped by the user's server, further strengthening trust in the messages you receive.

Another aspect of identity and authentication relates to domain names. As we discussed earlier in this chapter, XMPP server instances are also checked in inter-domain communication, either via the server dialback protocol or TLS plus SASL (which provide weak and strong identity verification, respectively). Servers are also required to verify incoming stanzas from other domains, so that, say, the `wonderland.lit` server can't masquerade as `looking-glass.lit`. These rules help to prevent faked addresses on the network. These relatively strong identities can also be bootstrapped into trust islands by means of blacklisting and whitelisting other domains, either at the firewall or in XMPP server software.

That said, the use of the full Unicode character set for JabberIDs introduces the possibility of some impersonation attacks, because characters in different scripts can look very much alike. A very simple method that can be implemented even in plain ASCII addresses is to replace the letter "l" with the number "1", as in `paypa1.com` (which has been known to fool end users). When an address can include different characters that are effectively indistinguishable—such as "a" (Latin Small Letter A) and "а" (Cyrillic Small Letter A)— the potential for abuse is significant. For this reason, XMPP clients are encouraged to handle mixed-character addresses carefully.

Spam and Abuse

Every communication system can be a breeding ground for unsolicited bulk messages ("spam") and other forms of abuse. It is currently estimated that 90% or more of the email messages sent over the Internet are spam. What has the XMPP community done to prevent spam from taking over its network?

On the face of it, the fact that XMPP is a distributed technology (just like email) and not a centralized service (like most legacy instant messaging systems) might make you think that the XMPP network would be open to the same kinds of spam threats as the email network. However, there are some important differences:

- Most people assume that you must be able to send an email to any random person on the Internet. Techniques that require you to be authorized before you can send someone an email message are viewed with suspicion. Yet the very same system exists in IM—we call it a roster—without offending anyone. In XMPP, we can leverage presence subscriptions to block messages from anyone who is not in your roster, cutting down on spam quite a bit.

- Spam is not just an annoyance: it's a business. If it is more expensive for spammers to operate on the XMPP network than on, say, the email network, they will tend to stay on the email network. XMPP developers and operators continue to raise the bar for participation; for example, they might require digital certificates from trusted CA's at some point in the next few years, and those certificates could be easily revoked from domains that behave badly on the network.

- Spammers send a lot of messages. However, all XMPP server daemons include built-in rate limiting, which prevents users from sending a large volume of messages in a short period of time. True, a spammer could get around this restriction by creating a large number of accounts on a particular server, but servers could restrict registration by requiring CAPTCHAs or other techniques for account registration (as described in Chapter 6) and by limiting the number of registration attempts per IP address. Yet XMPP is a distributed technology, so spammers could create accounts on multiple servers, thus forcing administrators of legitimate XMPP servers to work together on blocking techniques (e.g., maintaining a repository of blacklisted domains or IP addresses). And so the arms race continues. For some related recommendations for server administrators, see *Best Practices to Discourage Denial of Service Attacks* [XEP-0205].

Summary

Whereas in previous chapters, we explored higher-level XMPP extensions, in this chapter, we delved into the fundamentals: XML streams, TCP and HTTP connection methods, channel encryption via Transport Layer Security (TLS), the authentication framework provided through the Simple Authentication and Security Layer (SASL), dynamic federation of XMPP servers using the Server Dialback protocol, serverless messaging, and key considerations related to the security of XMPP systems. Depending on the type of application you want to build, you may not need to worry about these lower layers of the XMPP stack. However, it is good to know that you have flexibility here, too.

PART III

Putting It All Together

CHAPTER 13

Design Decisions

Now that you've become familiar with the various tools in the XMPP toolkit, let's start to think about how you can use those tools to build an XMPP application (or XMPP-enable an existing application). In this chapter, we explore some of the thought processes underlying successful application development with XMPP. Then in Chapter 14, we illustrate these principles by building an application from the ground up.

Is XMPP the Right Choice?

Like any technology, XMPP has strengths and weaknesses. As legendary Internet protocol designer Marshall Rose once put it, you can build a good helicopter or you can build a good submarine, but you can't build something that is both a good helicopter and a good submarine. Trying to use the same tool to solve every problem usually ends in disaster.

As we mentioned before, XMPP was designed to transmit numerous small snippets of XML data over a decentralized network in close to real time, with built-in presence and straightforward federation. This means that XMPP is not a panacea for all Internet usages and, thankfully, the Internet already has time-tested technologies you can use instead for other tasks: HTTP/HTML, BitTorrent, Real-time Transport Protocol, SMTP/POP/IMAP, Usenet, etc.

So when is XMPP a good choice? Here are some guidelines:

- When you need information about network availability, i.e., presence
- When you need to deliver "just-in-time" alerts and notifications instead of continually polling for updates
- When you need channel encryption, strong authentication, and trusted identities
- When you need communication among a distributed network of entities or servers
- When you need a relatively simple signaling channel to set up multimedia interactions

- When you need the extensibility of XML for custom payloads
- When you want to tap into the large user base on the XMPP network

These considerations have led many cutting-edge software developers to incorporate XMPP into their applications. As of this writing, XMPP technologies seem to be especially popular in the following domains:

Social networking

The main attraction here is that XMPP overcomes the serious scaling problems associated with constantly polling for updated information. As we discussed in Chapter 8, it's much more efficient to treat microblogging, location sharing, and social music services as forms of on-demand micromessaging than as dynamic websites that must be continually polled for updates.

Cloud computing and machine-to-machine communication

In the emerging "Internet of Things," it makes a lot of sense to use real-time messaging to coordinate activities between a distributed network of entities, especially because presence information and service discovery can reveal which entities are both available on the network and capable of handling particular tasks.

Voice, video, and other multimedia sessions

XMPP is not optimized for transferring bandwidth-heavy data such as voice and video, but it is nearly ideal for *managing* such transfers. Existing session management technologies do not natively incorporate three key features of XMPP: presence information, trusted identities, and straightforward federation between domains. Presence enables the same kind of fluid communication that is familiar from instant messaging (no more voicemail!), trusted identities significantly reduce the possibility of spam, and federation makes it possible to finally connect a large number of separate silos and thus increase the power of the Internet's real-time communications network.

How do you implement these and other application types? Usually you won't build your entire application from scratch; instead, you'll mix and match existing code with your own custom code. That means you will install, download, embed, or otherwise employ one or more of the servers, libraries, clients, and other codebases released by various participants in the XMPP developer community. Then you'll build on that foundation to add your own special features. For example, you might write a client plug-in, a bot, a server module, or an external component that will integrate with the infrastructure you've installed. If you get really serious, you might even write your own custom client or server, although that's a bigger task. In any case, no matter how you proceed, you'll need to know how the XMPP developer community works, and how to work with that community, so let's delve into that topic next.

How the XMPP Community Works

In order to build XMPP applications, it helps to understand how the XMPP developer community is structured so that you can get the most out of community-generated software, build your own software, and define XMPP extensions.

Perhaps the most important lesson to learn about the XMPP developer community is that it is extremely diverse, and it has become more and more diverse over the years.

In the beginning, there was one Jabber project: the open source jabberd server created by Jeremie Miller. Immediately, other open source developers contributed to Jeremie's server project, but they also wrote clients for Windows and Mac and Linux that would connect to jabberd, server modules (generically called *components*) that would work with jabberd, and code libraries for Perl and Java and many other languages that would enable other people to create additional code projects. So, right from the start, the community was focused not on a single codebase (as with, say, the Apache web server), but on a technology ecosystem.

Since 1999, that ecosystem has continued to grow and change. Developers have come and gone, early projects disappeared, new projects emerged to take their place, commercial companies and service providers built their own implementations, additional open source server projects came into being, and deployment of all this software became almost commonplace on the Internet. As a result, the XMPP community contains many participants:

- Open source projects and individual developers
- Small consultancies that support particular codebases or offer XMPP expertise in certain domains (e.g., for mobile devices)
- Midsize software development shops
- Large hardware and software companies such as Apple, Cisco, Nokia, and Sun
- Service providers such as Google, LiveJournal, DreamHost, and GMX
- Businesses, universities, and other operators of XMPP services
- The XMPP Standards Foundation (XSF), which loosely coordinates all of this activity but primarily focuses on standardization of the XMPP protocols

Just as XMPP itself is a decentralized technology, so too is the community decentralized. There is no one central location where all of these projects, companies, and other parties host their code, manage their projects, help their users, or share operational experience. Instead, each project has its own website, code repository, and communication channels.

Paradoxically, this decentralized approach has not prevented the community from remaining relatively coherent in its priorities and direction. Given its focus on rough consensus and running code, the various entities in the XMPP community have two primary connection points: the standardization of the XMPP protocols, and the day-to-day operation of the XMPP communications network. If a new server joins the network but it doesn't quite interoperate with existing software and services, you can be sure that the developers of that server will quickly receive bug reports from interested coders in the community. Likewise, the busiest discussion venue run by the XSF is the *standards@xmpp.org* mailing list, where hundreds of developers define new protocol extensions and work to clarify the subtleties of older protocols. (The XSF also runs specialized discussion lists and chat rooms for PubSub, Jingle, BOSH, MUC, social networking, mobile applications, operational challenges, and other such topics; consult *http://xmpp.org* for a full list.)

The fact that the XMPP community is so decentralized can be a bit disorienting at first. For example, you may need to hunt around for a while to find a codebase that meets your needs or a software developer who can solve your problem. On the other hand, this decentralization means that it is quite easy to contribute new code, create new projects, and join the developer community (it also means that problems in one XMPP-related project don't infect all the others, leading to an almost Darwinian survival of the fittest over time).

In the following sections, we talk about how to make use of the many existing software codebases, design and implement new code, and define new XMPP extensions if needed.

Writing XMPP Software

Whether you want to extend an existing application or service to use XMPP, or you want to build an XMPP-based application from the ground up, your adventure will always begin with finding the right ingredients to make your XMPP recipe. You will be able to use some of these ingredients directly off-the-shelf, others will require making some extensions or modifications, and some other parts will have to be created from scratch, either with or without the use of commonly available libraries and SDKs. In this section, we delve deeper into the various aspects involved in building your own XMPP application.

Mixing, Matching, and Extending Existing XMPP Software

In order to build an XMPP application, you will need a few moving parts. Some of these you will be able to use as-is, and others may require tailoring to meet your needs. However, most XMPP applications consist of the following parts:

An XMPP server
> Many open source and commercial XMPP server codebases exist, of which a few are described briefly in "Servers" on page 253. If you want to deploy a serious XMPP application, you'll need to install one of these codebases and run it at your own domain. (The alternative is to run a lightweight bot at one of the public XMPP services, such as Google Talk or jabber.org, but if you do so, you run the risk of

being rate-limited or otherwise restricted by the policies in force at that service.) Existing server projects can typically be extended with extra, custom functionality through server-side modules or add-on components (we talk about these a bit more later in this chapter). Although not very common, it could even happen that your requirements cannot be met by using components or server-side modules. In that case, you may choose to modify the server software (if the license allows it), or even developer your own server implementation. Examples of organizations that chose to build their own XMPP servers are LiveJournal (which released its software as the djabberd codebase) and the Google Talk service.

An XMPP client
Some XMPP-based applications are built around a particular XMPP client. The association between a client and a service can take the form of an existing IM client that has been extended to suit your needs using plug-ins or adaptations to the original codebase. However, it is not uncommon that your application will require a dedicated, new client for what you want to achieve. For example, when building a networked chess game application, you will not start from an IM client; instead, you will create your own application and add XMPP client functionality to it. In that case, you will need to write your own client, possibly making use of one of the many available XMPP client libraries.

Integration with existing infrastructure
In some cases, your application will not be a strict client-server application. Rather, you will integrate with existing infrastructure, such as a database, a content management system, or a distributed computing platform. In this case, XMPP technologies will form the "communications glue" among various entities within your infrastructure, and you may not even need a single server (e.g., each entity could run its own lightweight mini-server and then federate with the other entities).

Because of the decentralized nature of XMPP technologies and the modular approach taken by many XMPP developers, you can mix and match implementations of all your parts. For example, you might use one of the open source XMPP servers, but write your own custom XMPP client. In the next section, we explore what is needed to develop your own XMPP software.

Client Extension, Bot, Component, or Server Module?

When it comes to writing your own XMPP software, there are several approaches that may fit your needs. Often, there is more than one way to reach your goal, so which is best? This section addresses some of the design trade-offs you may face.

A first question that may arise is: Should I put most of my extensions on the server, or should I put the code in the client? The Jabber philosophy has always been to take as much burden as possible from the client and put it in the server. This approach has a number of advantages:

- By keeping the clients as simple as possible, you are making it very easy for another client to be extended or even make use of your application, as the changes that need to be done on the client side are minimal.

- The server often has easy access to information that is hard to retrieve from the client. Moreover, it is a lot easier, safer, and more robust to adapt server-side information from the server software, which has direct access to the data.

Because of this philosophy, XMPP server implementations tend to be architected in a more modular fashion than XMPP clients. You will find that you can much more easily extend XMPP servers using components and plug-ins than you can extend most existing XMPP clients.

When moving the functionality out of the client, you are still left with several options to provide your services from the server side. The easiest way to provide services over XMPP is to create a bot. A bot is a program that logs into a server like a normal client, with a regular JabberID. Other clients typically add this bot to their roster, and a user can then send it messages, to which the bot responds. Such a bot can also react to the presence changes of the people in its roster. For example, there might be a bot called `mapbot@wonderland.lit` that subscribes to all PEP geolocation changes (see Chapter 8) of all clients in its roster. Whenever it receives geolocation information about one of its contacts, it draws a marker on a map, served on some web page. Thanks to the availability of XMPP libraries for a variety of high-level languages, creating a bot can be a very easy way to do interesting things with XMPP in very little time (and code). The fact that bots can connect to any deployed XMPP server makes them very flexible, and allows virtually anyone to run a bot without having to set up a server themselves.

Although bots can yield some interesting XMPP applications, sometimes their capabilities can be restricting because they are bound to one specific JID on a server. This is where components come into play. As discussed in Chapter 12, when a component connects to a server, it is assigned a subdomain of the server. Every stanza that is destined for that subdomain is then delivered to the component, which can act upon it. For example, in Chapter 7, we talked about multiuser chat components getting assigned a subdomain (e.g., `conference.wonderland.lit`); when there is an incoming message for `trial@conference.wonderland.lit`, the server directly routes it to the MUC component without looking at the node part (in this case, `trial`) of the JID. The MUC component treats the node part of the JID as a room name, and posts the message to the `trial` room.

Because the server leaves all internal processing of the subdomain to the component, it also does not keep track of any roster for a component. Since it routes all stanzas to the component directly, including presence stanzas, it is the component's responsibility to maintain a roster based on incoming presence subscription stanzas (if it chooses to). This technique increases the complexity of your implementation, but it also increases the scalability of your implementation because you are no longer limited by a particular server codebase (which typically is architected to handle thousands of concurrent sessions for entities with relatively small rosters, not one session for an entity with an extremely large roster). Some applications that started out with a bot approach have found it necessary to switch to a server component approach when their bot became very popular.

The extra control of a component comes with a price, though. In order for a component to connect to a server, the server needs to be specially configured to allow this component to connect as the handler for a specific subdomain of the server. Because a component needs explicit permissions from the server, not everyone can just run a component on every server. This makes components less flexible than bots. However, because components use a standardized protocol to connect to a server, as we discussed in Chapter 12, one component can be used in combination with many different XMPP server codebases, thus reducing the risk of being "locked in" to a particular server project or product.

Although server components give you more control than bots, at the far end of the scale, there are applications for which they also can be too limiting for your application. For example, your application may need direct access to server internals (such as direct access to the rosters from all users), or you may be dealing with performance-critical applications where a network connection between the server and your component would become a bottleneck. In this case, your application will need to directly tap into the server implementation. The most common approach if you need this much control is to write a server module that is loaded into the server and that gives you direct access to the information you need. However, having full control over the server means that your application will be tied to a particular server implementation. This means that you will have much less flexibility in changing servers later, and that the possibilities for reuse will be significantly reduced.

Rolling Your Own Client or Server

In some cases, extending an existing software codebase might not be enough for your needs. For example, existing clients that could otherwise help solve your problem might be focused on one use of XMPP (for example, instant messaging), whereas your application targets a completely different use case. In this case, you will need to design your own client, tailored to your needs. Aside from purely functional reasons, other considerations may apply, such as license costs.

If you want to build your own software, you are still left with the choice to build it on top of one of the many existing XMPP libraries (see "Libraries" on page 258) or to build your solution from the ground up.

Building your own XMPP client or server from scratch requires a considerable amount of low-level functionality. In many cases, this functionality is supported by external libraries, or in some cases provided by the standard library of the programming language you are targeting. If you are considering building your own solution, you should look for the following low-level functionality:

XML parsing

Because XMPP is an XML-based protocol, an XMPP client or server will obviously need to do some XML parsing. Since XMPP uses a strict subset of the full XML specification, some of the complexity involved in parsing XML can be avoided. Many off-the-shelf XML libraries exist, and many languages even come with XMPP support in their built-in libraries. The most important part to keep in mind is that the XML parser needs to be incremental, and needs to be able to handle incomplete data. An XMPP stream becomes a full XML document only after the XMPP session is over, and the actual XML elements (i.e., the XMPP stanzas) can be delivered in chunks due to network constraints. This functionality is typically available in most stream-based XML parsers (e.g., SAX).

DNS SRV lookups

Many libraries provide an easy interface for doing lookups of host addresses by domain name. However, in order to make deployment as flexible as possible, XMPP allows server administrators to host an XMPP service for a certain domain on a different host than the main domain host. Chapter 12 describes how both clients and servers use DNS SRV lookups to find out the hosts serving XMPP for a specific domain. This advanced DNS query functionality is often omitted in DNS libraries (although it is becoming more common all the time).

Secure TLS connections

Although secure connections often are not very crucial in many protocols, they play a very important role in the XMPP world. At the time of this writing, some key XMPP deployments have explicitly disabled support for nonsecured connections, and we expect many (if not all) services to follow suit at some point. As a result, supporting secure connections using Transport Layer Security (as described in Chapter 12) is practically a hard requirement when building an XMPP application.

Support for channel encryption can be implemented using external dedicated libraries such as OpenSSL and GnuTLS, or by using higher-level toolkit libraries. Many higher-level languages even provide support for TLS (or, equivalently, SSL) in their standard networking libraries. However, keep in mind that many of the higher-level libraries only provide TLS in the form of "secure sockets," i.e., sockets that securely connect to a target host using channel encryption at a specified port (e.g., 443 for HTTPS). By contrast, XMPP starts with an unencrypted connection, and then dynamically upgrades that connection to an encrypted connection using the "STARTTLS" feature of Transport Layer Security. If your library supports only sockets that are encrypted from the initial connection, you may need to write your own TLS support.

SASL authentication

As discussed in Chapter 12, XMPP uses the Simple Authentication and Security Layer (SASL) framework for standards-based authentication between clients and servers. By implementing only the most basic SASL authentication mechanisms (e.g., PLAIN and DIGEST-MD5) in your software, you can support authentication for any XMPP-compliant entity. These basic mechanisms are simple enough that they can be implemented without the need for external libraries. However, for more advanced authentication mechanisms (such as Kerberos using the GSSAPI mechanism), it is probably more convenient to use dedicated SASL libraries (such as Cyrus SASL or GNU SASL).

Internationalization

In order to support non-ASCII characters, the XMPP protocol requires UTF-8 encoding for XMPP streams (see [RFC 3629]). As a result, typically there is no need for special text handling or conversions within an XMPP application. The only part that might be affected is the user interface, which obviously needs to be able to handle international character input and output, as well as encode it accordingly.

Besides the actual XMPP stream, international characters can also appear in JabberIDs. Since JIDs are used to address entities on the XMPP network, they need special treatment with respect to international characters. More specifically, they need to be normalized according to a set of well-defined *string preparation* rules called "stringprep," as defined in [RFC 3454]. These rules handle, amongst other things, case-folding (which is the Unicode equivalent of case-insensitivity for ASCII characters), as well as transforming the domain part of the JID into standard resolvable domains. This is typically done using the GNU Internationalized Domain Names (IDN) Library.

Extending XMPP

XMPP was designed to be extended—after all, the "X" in both XMPP and XML stands for "extensible"! Over the years, the XMPP developer community has built a long "runway" of XMPP extensions, making it possible for you to create lots of interesting applications with XMPP. Usually you can just mix and match existing extensions to build the functionality you need. However, sometimes the feature you need in your application is not yet defined in any of the existing extensions. In this section, we delve into XMPP extensibility by showing you how to define your own custom XMPP extensions, and even publish them as freely available specifications for use by the entire community.

How to Design Custom Extensions

Extensibility is really quite easy: just create your own XML data structure and associated namespace, and then place it into an XMPP message, presence, or IQ stanza.

For example, let's say that you have built an online reading club and you want to exchange information about books so that users of your service can do things like share recommendations. Scanning the existing XMPP extensions, you don't find anything that meets your needs, so you decide to define a new XML format that looks something like this:

```
<message>
  <bookinfo xmlns="http://example.com/schemas/bookinfo">
    <title>XMPP: The Definitive Guide</title>
    <subtitle>Building Real-Time Applications with Jabber Technologies</subtitle>
    <isbn>9780596521264</isbn>
    <note>One of my favorite books!</note>
  </bookinfo>
</message>
```

A custom format like this is very much preferable to overloading of existing XMPP data structures, such as in the negative example shown here:

```
<message>
  <body>One of my favorite books!</body>
  <subject>XMPP: The Definitive Guide;
           Building Real-Time Applications with Jabber Technologies</subject>
  <thread>9780596521264</thread>
</message>
```

The contrast between these two examples illustrates one of the key principles of protocol design in the Jabber community: the core XMPP specifications are sacred. Any feature you might need can probably be defined farther up the XMPP protocol stack than in the core streaming, messaging, and presence layer (and if you think that you need to modify the core layer, think again). Instead, focus higher up the stack by defining new namespaces that can be included in message or IQ stanzas (and, rarely, presence stanzas).

Another key principle is to keep presence as small and focused as possible. It's easy to think that presence is a good model for sending notifications each time someone's music player loads a new tune, including complete information about the title, performer, running time, track number, lyrics, or even associated artwork. If the listener has 100 online friends in his roster, though, your application will result in 100 large presence notifications every 3 or 4 minutes, which is not very network-friendly. In fact, presence is the primary bottleneck in any messaging and presence technology, being responsible for as much as 90% of the traffic, so it's important to use presence only for information that determines whether someone is online and available for communication.

A third key principle is to keep XMPP clients as simple as possible (without putting undue strain on XMPP servers). This is often a delicate balancing act. Sometimes clients really do know best (e.g., about user preferences or local network conditions), and therefore need to include more complexity. Usually it is inefficient to ask servers to complete too many tasks related to a given stanza or to perform deep packet inspection in order to route a message. Clients cannot be trusted to properly enforce security policies, and therefore the server must take charge in such matters. And so on.

Finally, it is important to reuse existing protocols where possible. Just as you would not write your own TCP or TLS implementation to create an XMPP client (if at all possible), it doesn't make sense to define a new transport binding for XMPP or rip out lower layers of the XMPP protocol stack when creating a new XMPP application. Similarly, try to embed existing data formats into XMPP rather than defining new formats. In this sense, the "bookinfo" example we just showed you is wrongheaded because it could have easily reused data formats from the Dublin Core Initiative or DocBook instead of defining a new XML namespace.

For more detailed recommendations about protocol design, consult the *Protocol Design Guidelines* [XEP-0134], informally known as "The Tao of XMPP."

Standardizing New Extensions

So you've created a custom XMPP extension, and it's really useful in your application. In fact, it's so useful that you think other developers might want to add support for it, too. How can you advertise it to the world and receive feedback on it so that it gets even better?

Naturally, you could just post it on your project or company website, but that won't necessarily result in feedback from other developers. The solution is to publish your protocol to a centralized location where everyone who cares about XMPP technologies can read, review, and comment on your extension: the *http://xmpp.org* website, run by the XSF.

The XSF was founded in the summer of 2001 to document the core Jabber protocols and to define new extensions to those protocols. It does this through a developer-friendly standards process focused on a series of documents called XMPP Extension Protocols, or XEPs. The basic idea is simple (for all the details, refer to [XEP-0001]):

1. Anyone can submit a proposal for an XMPP extension by sending an email to *editor@xmpp.org* (see [XEP-0143] for further instructions).

2. The XMPP Council, elected by the members of the XSF, determines whether to publish a given proposal as an official XEP.

3. When an XEP is first published, it has a status of Experimental.

4. After the XEP has been discussed, improved, and hopefully implemented, it can advance to a status of Draft.

5. Eventually, after the XEP has been implemented, deployed, and improved even further, it can advance to a status of Final.

XEPs are discussed mainly on the *standards@xmpp.org* list, a high-traffic mailing list that is the primary venue for XMPP developers to clarify existing protocols and define new ones. If you are interested in XMPP technologies, this "standards list" is the place to be.

Unlike for-pay industry consortia, the XSF does not require monetary contributions in order to participate in its standards process. Furthermore, the XSF's "intellectual property rights" policy ensures that XMPP extensions are patent-free and that anyone can implement XMPP technologies under any license they care to use for their software. These policies maintain the legacy of XMPP's roots in the open source Jabber community.

What does public standardization give you that just defining a private extension does not? Aside from the fame of authoring an official XEP and the warm glow of having contributed something back to the community, working through the XSF's standards process usually results in a stronger technology, because many smart people will review your proposal, suggest improvements, point out potential security concerns, and implement it more widely (leading to better interoperability and therefore a more powerful network effect).

Even so, it doesn't always make sense to standardize your custom XMPP extensions. Perhaps they define "one-off" features that are not of general interest. Perhaps they are part of the "special sauce" in your product and you don't want the world to find out about your trade secrets. Perhaps you simply don't have the time to document how your extension works in the rigorous way that's usually required of protocol specifications (although the friendly folks at the XSF are always happy to help with the writing of specifications). However, many organizations and projects that define custom extensions have found it quite beneficial to submit their extensions to the XSF for more formal standardization (including big companies like Apple and Google), and you might too.

Summary

In this chapter, we covered many of the high-level issues you may face when you set out to build an XMPP application, including how to work with the XMPP developer community, how to use existing code developed by that community, how to write your own XMPP-based software, and how to define protocol extensions to XMPP. Now let's apply those insights by building an XMPP application from the ground up.

CHAPTER 14

Building an XMPP Application

In this chapter, we start with an existing application and look at different ways of XMPP-enabling it with techniques you've learned earlier in the book.

The CheshiR Microblogging Platform

Meet "CheshiR," our very own "microblogging" service. From the CheshiR website, you can post short pieces of text about what you are currently doing, reading, or thinking. Other people can then subscribe to (or "follow") your postings, which means that they will receive a notification any time you post a new update. Figure 14-1 shows the home page of a CheshiR user with three contacts.

The CheshiR service is implemented in Python, using a very simple design. On one side, there is the HTTP frontend, which serves the web pages of the service. Whenever a user posts a message, it is sent to the CheshiR backend, which stores all the messages and subscriptions in a database. To display the homepage of a user, the frontend asks the backend for all messages sent by that user's contacts.

To extend the reach of our service and improve the experience of our users, we are going to investigate different ways of integrating XMPP into our platform. Because we like the principles of agile software development, we'll take an iterative approach, with focused code sprints to add a few well-defined features during each sprint.

First Sprint: The CheshiR XMPP IM Bot

Analysis

Having a web interface to post messages on CheshiR is convenient for our users, because it avoids the need to install a special application to read or post messages to their microblog. However, the downside of a web interface is that our users constantly need to switch to their web browser and hit the "Reload" button to find out whether new messages have arrived. Not only is such a *polling* system inconvenient for the user, but

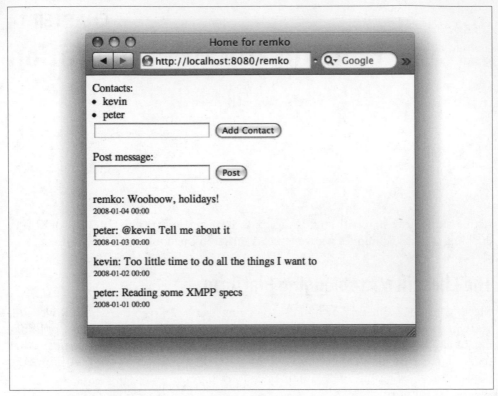

Figure 14-1. Posting and receiving microblogs via the CheshiR web interface

it also puts a high load on the service itself (see Chapter 8). Each time a user reloads the web page to see if new messages are waiting, the HTTP frontend of our service needs to query the backend database to render the "messages page" for that user. Since this page doesn't change that often (at best, a few new messages have arrived, which still leaves the rest of the page unchanged), this means a lot of data is needlessly requested over and over again. Moreover, this approach won't scale over the long term: the more users our service attracts, the more requests for new messages our service will need to process. We're already starting to worry that our web server will eventually succumb to the high load of requests, so we do some research about technologies that might help us send a notification whenever a user posts to her microblog.

Design

Our research indicates that a technology called XMPP might help to solve the user's inconvenience and the server's scalability problem. We decide that a simple XMPP "frontend" might enable our users to interact with their microblogs from within the comfort of their IM clients (or specialized microblogging clients). What's more, the service will automatically *push* new messages to the connected XMPP clients. Whenever a notification arrives at the IM client, the user will be notified of the new message, removing the need for the user to regularly poll for new messages. And with users no longer constantly polling for new messages, the heavy load of handling the page requests in the HTTP frontend will also be lifted.

Our small team of developers gathers around the whiteboard to sketch out the architecture shown in Figure 14-2. Whereas the web-based approach always sends requests from the browser to the HTTP frontend through to the backend, the XMPP approach also has events going in the other direction. Besides being able to interact with the web service from a standard IM client, XMPP also provides a standard interface for communicating with dedicated, custom CheshiR applications, tailored specifically toward microblogging.

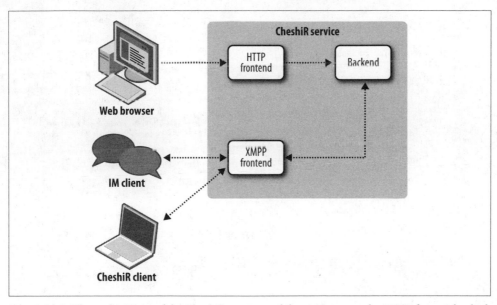

Figure 14-2. The architecture of the CheshiR service: web browsers query the HTTP frontend, which in turn queries the backend; IM and custom clients post messages to the backend through the XMPP interface, while the backend notifies the XMPP clients of incoming messages when they arrive

For our first sprint we decide to design the CheshiR frontend as a simple bot (similar to the basic "echo" XMPP service discussed in Chapter 2). Users can add the bot as a contact to their existing rosters, and interact with it the same way they interact with regular contacts. Whenever a user sends a message to the bot, the message is forwarded to the microblog of the user in question. Conversely, if someone that the user is following posts a message, the bot sends this message to the user's IM client. Besides allowing our users to post to the microblog by sending a message to the bot, we also want the bot to automatically post all the <status/> text that users post in their presence updates (e.g., "in a meeting" or "stepped out for lunch"). This gives users of our XMPP service the extra convenience of sharing their status on their microblog and on their IM network with only one operation.

We quickly sketch out what the user's interaction will look like—pretty much standard IM conversations, as shown in Figure 14-3.

Figure 14-3. Posting and receiving microblogs via the CheshiR IM bot

Coding

Now that we have the basic design set, we do a bit of research into off-the-shelf XMPP libraries. Because we find that the Python language is great for fast prototyping as well as high-scale application development (as mentioned, our backend is written in Python), we check out several of the available Python libraries. After looking at APIs and developer support, we select SleekXMPP (the same library used for the echo bot in Chapter 2).

Once we settle on the library to use, getting the bot implemented is rather straightforward. The basic code for our implementation is encapsulated in a Bot class, as you can see in Example 14-1.

Example 14-1. CheshiR IM bot implementation

```
class Bot :
  def __init__(self, jid, password, backend, url) :
    self.url = url
    self.xmpp = sleekxmpp.ClientXMPP(jid, password)
    self.xmpp.add_event_handler("session_start", self.handleXMPPConnected)
    for event in ["message", "got_online", "got_offline", "changed_status"] :
      self.xmpp.add_event_handler(event, self.handleIncomingXMPPEvent)
    self.backend = backend
    self.backend.addMessageHandler(self.handleMessageAddedToBackend)

  def handleXMPPConnected(self, event):
    self.xmpp.sendPresence()

  def handleIncomingXMPPEvent(self, event) :
    message = event["message"]
    user = self.backend.getUserFromJID(event["jid"])
    self.backend.addMessageFromUser(message, user)

  def handleMessageAddedToBackend(self, message) :
    body = message.user + ": " + message.text
    htmlBody = "<a href=\"%(uri)s\">%(user)s</a>: %(message)s" % {
      "uri": self.url + "/" + message.user,
      "user" : message.user, "message" : message.text }
    for subscriberJID in self.backend.getSubscriberJIDs(message.user) :
      self.xmpp.sendMessage(subscriberJID, body, mhtml=htmlBody)

  def start(self) :
    self.xmpp.connect()
    self.xmpp.process()
```

The functions are as follows:

- In the constructor of Bot, add_event_handler is called to register the bot to handle several XMPP events: incoming XMPP messages, users changing their XMPP presence, and the start of the XMPP session (right after the authentication process has finished).

- addMessageHandler registers our bot to be notified of messages added to the backend. These messages could have been added through the web interface or the XMPP interface.

- In the handleXMPPConnected function, the bot will send initial presence whenever it logs in (e.g., after being disconnected if the server goes down); this will make the bot pop up in the roster of all our subscribers.

- In the `handleIncomingXMPPEvent` function, any incoming XMPP message will be mapped to a user of the blog platform, and the new message will be submitted to the backend for storage.

- In the `handleMessageAddedToBackend` function, the bot will generate an outbound XMPP message to all of the user's followers. This message contains two main child elements: the plain text of the notification is included in the XMPP `<body/>` child of the message stanza, and a formatted version of the notification is included using XHTML-IM. The formatted version includes auto-generated links to the CheshiR homepage of the person who posted the message.

To add the bot to CheshiR, we simply instantiate it at the start of our application, as shown in Example 14-2. The bot needs an XMPP account at a server, which it logs into on startup. CheshiR users can then add this bot as a contact in their contact list, and send messages to it.

Example 14-2. Instantiating the CheshiR IM bot upon application start

```
def main() :
  backend = SimpleBackend()
  bot = Bot("bot@cheshir.lit", "mypass", backend, "http://cheshir.lit")
  bot.start()
  httpFrontend = HTTPFrontend(8080, backend)
  httpFrontend.start()
```

With less than 30 lines of code, we were able to create a simple, generic interface to our microblogging platform!

Second Sprint: Configuring the CheshiR XMPP IM Bot

Analysis

We now have a bot that monitors both incoming messages and users' status changes, and then posts these to the CheshiR service. After a few weeks, some users complain that their feeds get filled with "Auto Status (idle)" messages, just because their IM client automatically changes the status message after long periods of inactivity. A bit of brainstorming in the developer room leads us to think that could let users disable the automatic posting of presence changes to their microblog. Either way, account configuration methods are in order, so we head back to the whiteboard for a design session.

Design

We envision several possibilities:

- Enable users to configure their accounts via the website.

- Force users to send a magic message to the CheshiR bot, such as `disable_sta tus_monitoring`.
- Use a native XMPP configuration method, such as ad-hoc commands (see Chapter 11).

Because we're really starting to get into this XMPP stuff, we decide to experiment with the ad-hoc commands approach.

Coding

Fortunately, the library we're using makes it easy to add support for ad-hoc commands. With only a few more lines of code, we're able to provide an interface to the users' settings. There are five notable changes:

- In the constructor, `registerPlugin` is called to load support for the three XEPs we need: *Data Forms* [XEP-0004], *Service Discovery* [XEP-0030], and *Ad-Hoc Commands* [XEP-0050].
- Also in the constructor, there are now separate handlers for incoming messages and incoming presence changes, namely `handleIncomingXMPPEvent` and `handleIncomingXMPPPresence`, respectively.
- The last change to the constructor is that a form is created with the Data Forms plug-in and then registered with the Ad-Hoc Commands plug-in, to allow the users to query the command and run it.
- In the new presence change handler `handleIncomingXMPPPresence`, the bot now calls the backend implementation to check whether a user's presence should be monitored for changes before it creates a new post from it.
- The last change is the new handler for the configuration command, `handleConfigurationCommand`, which reads the new value out of the submitted form and updates the configuration in the backend.

These changes are highlighted in Example 14-3.

Example 14-3. Configurable CheshiR IM bot implementation, with the differences from the basic IM bot shown in Example 14-1

```
class ConfigurableBot :
  def __init__(self, jid, password, backend, url) :
    self.url = url
    self.xmpp = sleekxmpp.ClientXMPP(jid, password)
    for plugin in ["xep_0004", "xep_0030", "xep_0050"] :
      self.xmpp.registerPlugin(plugin)
    self.xmpp.add_event_handler("session_start", self.handleXMPPConnected)
    self.xmpp.add_event_handler("message", self.handleIncomingXMPPEvent)
    for event in ["got_online", "got_offline", "changed_status"] :
      self.xmpp.add_event_handler(event, self.handleIncomingXMPPPresence)
    self.backend = backend
    self.backend.addMessageHandler(self.handleMessageAddedToBackend)
```

```
    configurationForm = self.xmpp.plugin["xep_0004"].makeForm("form", "Configure")
    configurationForm.addField(
        var="monitorPresence", label="Use my status messages",
        ftype="boolean", required=True, value=True)
    self.xmpp.plugin["xep_0050"].addCommand("configure", "Configure",
        configurationForm, self.handleConfigurationCommand)

def handleConfigurationCommand(self, form, sessionId):
    values = form.getValues()
    monitorPresence = True if values["monitorPresence"] == "1" else False
    jid = self.xmpp.plugin["xep_0050"].sessions[sessionId]["jid"]
    user = self.backend.getUserFromJID(jid)
    self.backend.setShouldMonitorPresenceFromUser(user, monitorPresence)

def handleIncomingXMPPPresence(self, event):
    user = self.backend.getUserFromJID(event["jid"])
    if self.backend.getShouldMonitorPresenceFromUser(user):
        self.handleIncomingXMPPEvent(event)

def handleXMPPConnected(self, event):
    self.xmpp.sendPresence()

def handleIncomingXMPPEvent(self, event):
    message = event["message"]
    user = self.backend.getUserFromJID(event["jid"])
    self.backend.addMessageFromUser(message, user)

def handleMessageAddedToBackend(self, message) :
    body = message.user + ": " + message.text
    htmlBody = "<a href=\"%(uri)s\">%(user)s</a>: %(message)s" % {
        "uri": self.url + "/" + message.user,
        "user" : message.user, "message" : message.text }
    for subscriberJID in self.backend.getSubscriberJIDs(message.user) :
        self.xmpp.sendMessage(subscriberJID, body, mhtml=htmlBody)

def start(self) :
    self.xmpp.connect()
    self.xmpp.process()
```

Third Sprint: Scaling the CheshiR XMPP Service Using a Server Component

Analysis

A few more weeks pass by, and we notice that our XMPP service is becoming rather slow. Sometimes it even stops working due to a lack of resources. After some investigation, we discover that it is actually our bot that is causing some havoc. It seems that our XMPP interface has become very popular—in fact, the bot's roster is so large that the server cannot handle it any longer.

The reason for this scenario is that many XMPP server implementations are not optimized to deal with huge rosters like the one from our bot. (All XMPP servers reach such a limit eventually, because they simply are not designed for rosters with 10,000 or 100,000 items!) Because we've run into a limit on the number of CheshiR users who can interact with the bot, we need to find a more scalable way of providing the hot new XMPP interface to our users.

So we ask ourselves: why does our XMPP server need to keep track of the bot's roster in the first place? Our CheshiR backend *knows* who signed up for the XMPP service, so why does this information need to be duplicated in the XMPP server's database? The root cause is presence routing, which is described in detail in Chapter 3. Whenever our bot generates a presence notification, our server needs to distribute that information to every user of the XMPP service. Additionally, whenever one of our users connects to the XMPP network, it will query the presence of our bot (using a presence probe), and our bot's XMPP server will automatically answer to this with the current presence of the bot.

However, if we could offload control of presence-related functionality from the server, maybe we would no longer need the server to keep track of the bot's roster. It's time to head back to the whiteboard and see what we can come up with....

Presence Scaling in Components

In fact, it's not the presence that's the problem, per se, but the roster. When a bot logs into the server and requests the roster, the server must fetch the entire roster and send it as one giant stanza to the bot. Although it's probably vain to believe that we can handle this better than the server can, we can improve matters by not handling it at all. Because, unlike our bot, a component isn't tied to this atomic roster get, the roster can be loaded from disk lazily, or in stages, and as such avoid the load of a (potentially) multi-hundred-megabyte roster stanza. The load saved from not probing the presence of our contacts is also significant, as our component need not know the contacts' status on login and will be happy to see presence stanzas trickle in over time.

Design

To solve our scalability problems, we do a bit more research into XMPP and discover that most XMPP servers are architected in a modular way that enables the server to offload stanza processing onto an external component. This approach seems like it might solve our scalability issues, so we decide to transform our CheshiR bot into an XMPP *server component*. This will require some code changes as well as some configuration changes to our XMPP server so that our server will allow our new component to connect as a trusted part of the system. As described in Chapter 13, this means that our component will be assigned a predefined subdomain of the server, and will directly receive all stanzas addressed to this domain without the server taking any other actions.

This, of course, means that our component will need to handle presence broadcasts and probe responses on its own, which might be just what we need to make the system more scalable.

Coding

Our design decisions lead us to refactor the bot code so that it will run as a component. However, it turns out that we don't need to make too many changes. Handling of incoming presence, message events, and messages added from the web interface behaves exactly the same as before. The main difference is that now everything related to presence broadcasting and presence subscriptions needs to be handled by the component itself. Here's an overview of the modifications:

- Because initial presence broadcasting is no longer handled by the server, the component needs to send out its presence to all its users in handleXMPPConnected.

- Whenever an XMPP user probes for the presence of our XMPP service, handle XMPPPresenceProbe sends back the presence of the component (which in this case, is always "available").

- When an XMPP user subscribes to the component's presence, handleXMPPPresenceSubscription automatically authorizes the subscription request, and sends the current presence of the component to the user. Additionally, because the component wants to listen to presence changes from CheshiR user, it also sends a subscription request to the originating user.

These modifications are shown in Example 14-4, which you can compare to the simple bot code in Example 14-1.

To deploy these changes, we just need to replace our bot with a server component in our application, as shown in Example 14-5.

Example 14-4. CheshiR IM server component implementation (the most important differences with the basic bot implementation from Example 14-1 are highlighted)

```
class SimpleComponent :
  def __init__(self, jid, password, server, port, backend) :
    self.xmpp = sleekxmpp.componentxmpp.ComponentXMPP(jid, password, server, port)
    self.xmpp.add_event_handler("session_start", self.handleXMPPConnected)
    self.xmpp.add_event_handler("changed_subscription",
        self.handleXMPPPresenceSubscription)
    self.xmpp.add_event_handler("got_presence_probe",
        self.handleXMPPPresenceProbe)
    for event in ["message", "got_online", "got_offline", "changed_status"] :
      self.xmpp.add_event_handler(event, self.handleIncomingXMPPEvent)
    self.backend = backend
    self.backend.addMessageHandler(self.handleMessageAddedToBackend)

  def handleXMPPConnected(self, event) :
    for user in self.backend.getAllUsers() :
      self.xmpp.sendPresence(pto = self.backend.getJIDForUser(user))
```

```
def handleIncomingXMPPEvent(self, event) :
  message = event["message"]
  user = self.backend.getUserFromJID(event["jid"])
  self.backend.addMessageFromUser(message, user)

def handleXMPPPresenceProbe(self, event) :
  self.xmpp.sendPresence(pto = self.backend.getJIDForUser(user))

def handleXMPPPresenceSubscription(self, subscription) :
  if subscription["type"] == "subscribe" :
    userJID = subscription["from"]
    self.xmpp.sendPresenceSubscription(pto=userJID, ptype="subscribed")
    self.xmpp.sendPresence(pto = userJID)
    self.xmpp.sendPresenceSubscription(pto=userJID, ptype="subscribe")

def handleMessageAddedToBackend(self, message) :
  body = message.user + ": " + message.text
  for subscriberJID in self.backend.getSubscriberJIDs(message.user) :
    self.xmpp.sendMessage(subscriberJID, body)

def start(self) :
  self.xmpp.connect()
  self.xmpp.process()
```

Example 14-5. Instantiating the CheshiR IM server component upon application start

```
def main() :
  backend = SimpleBackend()
  component = SimpleComponent(
    jid = "component.cheshir.lit", password = "mypass",
    server = "cheshir.lit", port = 5060, backend = backend)
  component.start()
  httpFrontend = HTTPFrontend(8080, backend)
  httpFrontend.start()
```

We now have an XMPP service that no longer puts the burden of roster and presence management on the XMPP server. As a result, our service is more scalable. From the perspective of our users, the only thing that has changed is that they now need to add posts.cheshir.lit to their roster instead of bot@cheshir.lit. (Some XMPP servers can redirect traffic for a particular user@domain.tld address to a component, so even this might not be necessary.)

Fourth Sprint: Registering with the CheshiR Server Component

Analysis

So far, we've assumed that our users would sign up for the XMPP service from the CheshiR web page, where they would provide the JID they would use for posting and receiving messages. But we know that some XMPP clients enable you to register with services from within the client itself, using in-band registration as described in "What's in a Nick?" on page 85. Adding this feature sounds like it might make our service even easier to use and further differentiate it from the crowded microblogging field, so we decide to investigate the possibility.

Design

To provide in-band registration, we look for a plug-in in SleekXMPP that provides jabber:iq:register functionality. Unfortunately, after looking through the documentation and source code, we conclude that SleekXMPP does not yet have support for in-band registration (although that might have changed by the time you read this book!). So we will have to write our own custom handling for IQ requests for the jabber:iq:register namespace. Some hacking is in order....

We envision a registration screen of the kind in Figure 14-4.

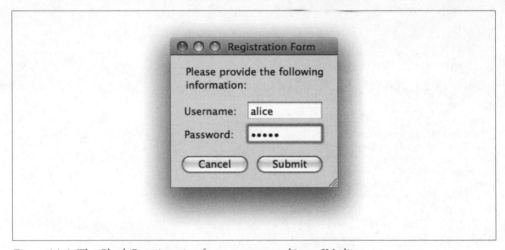

Figure 14-4. The CheshiR registration form, as presented in an IM client

Coding

To make this happen, it seems that we need to add a few new pieces of code to our component:

1. First, we need the xep_0030 plug-in, which allows us to announce support for the jabber:iq:register extension in the service discovery information of our component.

2. Next, we register handlers for both get and set IQ requests for the jabber:iq:register namespace. This way, whenever a user's client wants to register with the service, it will first send an IQ-get request to find out what information it needs to provide to the service. Upon receiving such a request,

handleRegistrationFormRequest sends back a response, adding a username and password element, indicating that it expects this information when the user registers.

3. After the user has entered the requested information, the user's client submits the registration form by embedding the filled form in an IQ-set request to the component, which is processed by handleRegistrationRequest.

4. After having extracted the username and password from the received form, the component checks whether registration with these credential succeeds. If it does, a successful (empty) result is sent back, acknowledging successful registration. If registration fails (for example, because of an incorrect password), the component informs the user of the problem by sending back an IQ reply with an error payload.

These changes are shown in Example 14-6.

Example 14-6. CheshiR IM server component with in-band registration support (only the changed and new methods since Example 14-5 are shown)

```
class RegistrableComponent :
  def __init__(self, jid, password, server, port, backend) :
    self.xmpp = sleekxmpp.componentxmpp.ComponentXMPP(jid, password, server, port)
    self.xmpp.add_event_handler("session_start", self.handleXMPPConnected)
    self.xmpp.add_event_handler("changed_subscription",
        self.handleXMPPPresenceSubscription)
    self.xmpp.add_event_handler("got_presence_probe",
        self.handleXMPPPresenceProbe)
    for event in ["message", "got_online", "got_offline", "changed_status"] :
      self.xmpp.add_event_handler(event, self.handleIncomingXMPPEvent)
    self.backend = backend
    self.backend.addMessageHandler(self.handleMessageAddedToBackend)
    self.xmpp.registerPlugin("xep_0030")
    self.xmpp.plugin["xep_0030"].add_feature("jabber:iq:register")
    self.xmpp.add_handler("<iq type='get' xmlns='jabber:client'>" +
      "<query xmlns='jabber:iq:register'/></iq>", self.handleRegistrationFormRequest)
    self.xmpp.add_handler("<iq type='set' xmlns='jabber:client'>" +
      "<query xmlns='jabber:iq:register'/></iq>", self.handleRegistrationRequest)

  def handleRegistrationFormRequest(self, request) :
    payload = ET.Element("{jabber:iq:register}query")
    payload.append(ET.Element("username"))
    payload.append(ET.Element("password"))
    self.sendRegistrationResponse(request, "result", payload)

  def handleRegistrationRequest(self, request) :
    jid = request.attrib["from"]
    user = request.find("{jabber:iq:register}query/{jabber:iq:register}username")
    password = request.find("{jabber:iq:register}query/{jabber:iq:register}password")
    if self.backend.registerXMPPUser(user, password, jid) :
      self.sendRegistrationResponse(request, "result")
    else :
      error = self.xmpp.makeStanzaError("forbidden", "auth")
      self.sendRegistrationResponse(request, "error", error)
```

```
def sendRegistrationResponse(self, request, type, payload = None) :
  iq = self.xmpp.makeIq(request.get("id"))
  iq.attrib["type"] = type
  iq.attrib["from"] = self.xmpp.fulljid
  iq.attrib["to"] = request.get("from")
  if payload :
    iq.append(payload)
  self.xmpp.send(iq)
```

Fifth Sprint: Extending the Server Component with Rosters

Analysis

Will, the marketing guy, says we need to boost communication among our users. Right now, all messages from a user's contact are delivered to his client in one continuous stream. Whenever a user wants to respond to one of his contact's posts, he starts his message with "@contact", a popular convention on microblogging services. Although this way of communicating works, marketing thinks we should be able to improve the user experience for this, which would increase the "stickiness" of our service (whatever that means). So once again we sketch out some ideas at the whiteboard.

Design

We already mentioned that our server component gets assigned the complete posts.cheshir.lit subdomain. So far, we've only used the domain JID to send and receive messages. However, because we have a whole domain at our disposal, we can create as many arbitrary JIDs as we want. This means that people's posts can come from, say, alice@posts.cheshir.lit or rabbit@posts.cheshir.lit, not just posts.cheshir.lit. Conversely, sending a message to rabbit@posts.cheshir.lit could prefix that message with "@rabbit" before posting it to your microblog, thus simulating a public one-to-one conversation in the microblogging style.

We can extend this feature a bit by associating the user's presence on the XMPP network with his alias on the CheshiR service. In particular, when we receive a presence change from a user's real JID, we will republish it to his CheshiR account as his latest post and as his presence status on CheshiR. The basic idea is shown in Figure 14-5.

Coding

To implement these enhanced features, we need to change the behavior of a few of the methods from our previous version of the component:

- Instead of sending one presence stanza from the XMPP service to every user, handleXMPPConnected needs to send a presence stanza for each follower of every user, containing the last message of the contact as a presence status.

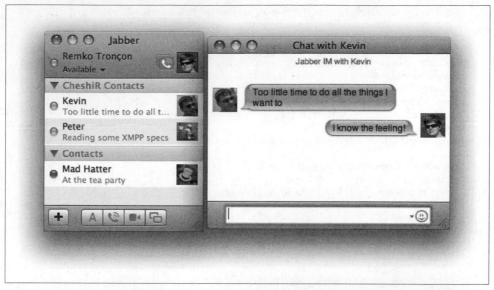

Figure 14-5. Using the CheshiR server component from an XMPP client: CheshiR contacts are mixed with regular XMPP contacts, messages from different contacts get delivered in their own chat dialog, and the message sent to Kevin will result in the message "@kevin I know the feeling!" being posted on Remko's microblog

- Incoming XMPP messages that are directed to a user need to have "@user" pre-pended to them in `handleIncomingXMPPMessage`.

- Since the user's server will send presence to every one of the user's contacts, there will be multiple incoming presence stanzas. Because we don't want to post a presence event more than once, we'll only listen to the presence events directed to the component itself in `handleIncomingXMPPPresence`.

- `handleXMPPPresenceProbe` returns the last message for presence probes directed to contacts.

- Whenever a user subscribes to our service, the component sends a presence subscription request for every contact in the user's contact list, which results in the contacts getting added to the user's XMPP roster.

- Whenever a message is posted using the web interface, we send a message to all subscribed users, and send it from the corresponding JID of the author. This delivers the message to the XMPP clients as a message from the contact.

Example 14-7 shows the updated version of the bot, which uses the helper methods shown in Example 14-8.

Example 14-7. Extended CheshiR IM server component implementation

```
class Component :
  def __init__(self, jid, password, server, port, backend) :
    self.componentDomain = jid
```

```
    self.xmpp = sleekxmpp.componentxmpp.ComponentXMPP(jid, password, server, port)
    self.xmpp.add_event_handler("session_start", self.handleXMPPConnected)
    self.xmpp.add_event_handler("changed_subscription",
        self.handleXMPPPresenceSubscription)
    self.xmpp.add_event_handler("got_presence_probe",
        self.handleXMPPPresenceProbe)
    self.xmpp.add_event_handler("message", self.handleIncomingXMPPMessage)
    for event in ["got_online", "got_offline", "changed_status"] :
        self.xmpp.add_event_handler(event, self.handleIncomingXMPPPresence)
    self.backend = backend
    self.backend.addMessageHandler(self.handleMessageAddedToBackend)

def handleXMPPConnected(self, event) :
    for user in self.backend.getAllUsers() :
        self.sendPresenceOfAllContactsForUser(user)

def handleIncomingXMPPMessage(self, event) :
    message = self.addRecipientToMessage(event["message"], event["to"])
    user = self.backend.getUserFromJID(event["jid"])
    self.backend.addMessageFromUser(message, user)

def handleIncomingXMPPPresence(self, event) :
    if event["to"] == self.componentDomain :
        user = self.backend.getUserFromJID(event["jid"])
        self.backend.addMessageFromUser(event["message"], user)

def handleXMPPPresenceProbe(self, event) :
    self.sendPresenceOfContactToUser(contactJID=event["to"], userJID=event["from"])

def handleXMPPPresenceSubscription(self, subscription) :
    if subscription["type"] == "subscribe" :
        userJID = subscription["from"]
        user = self.backend.getUserFromJID(userJID)
        contactJID = subscription["to"]
        self.xmpp.sendPresenceSubscription(
            pfrom=contactJID, pto=userJID, ptype="subscribed", pnick=user)
        self.sendPresenceOfContactToUser(contactJID=contactJID, userJID=userJID)
        if contactJID == self.componentDomain :
            self.sendAllContactSubscriptionRequestsToUser(userJID)

def handleMessageAddedToBackend(self, message) :
    userJID = self.getComponentJIDFromUser(message.user)
    for subscriberJID in self.backend.getSubscriberJIDs(message.user) :
        self.xmpp.sendMessage(mfrom=userJID, mto=subscriberJID, mbody=message.text)
        self.xmpp.sendPresence(pfrom=userJID, pto=subscriberJID, pstatus=message.text)
```

Example 14-8. CheshiR IM server component helper methods

```
def sendPresenceOfAllContactsForUser(self, user) :
    userJID = self.backend.getJIDForUser(user)
    for contact in self.backend.getContacts(user) :
        contactJID = self.getComponentJIDFromUser(contact)
        self.sendPresenceOfContactToUser(contactJID = contactJID, userJID = userJID)

def sendPresenceOfContactToUser(self, contactJID, userJID) :
    message = self.backend.getLastMessage(contactJID).text
```

```
    self.xmpp.sendPresence(pto = userJID, pfrom = contactJID, pshow = message)

def sendAllContactSubscriptionRequestsToUser(self, userJID) :
  user = self.backend.getUserFromJID(userJID)
  for contact in self.backend.getContacts(user) :
    contactJID = self.getComponentJIDFromUser(contact)
    self.xmpp.sendPresenceSubscription(
        pfrom=contactJID, pto=userJID, ptype="subscribe", pnick=contact)

def addRecipientToMessage(self, message, recipientJID) :
  contact = self.getUserFromComponentJID(recipientJID)
  return ("@" + contact if contact else "") + " " + message

def getUserFromComponentJID(self, jid) :
  return jid.split("@",1)[0] if "@" in jid else None

def getComponentJIDFromUser(self, user) :
  return user + "@" + self.componentDomain

def start(self) :
  self.xmpp.connect()
  self.xmpp.process()
```

Future Sprints

A living service like CheshiR doesn't stand still. We're already thinking about additional enhancements. Here are two intriguing possibilities:

- We've heard a lot about the XMPP PubSub technology and how it can overcome scalability issues. Perhaps it would make sense to re-architect the XMPP frontend as a PubSub service, providing a PubSub interface for custom clients out there. In fact, we could probably even replace the CheshiR backend with a PubSub service, storing all posts and subscription information in PubSub nodes and their subscriptions.

- The micromessaging model behind CheshiR and other microblogging services has some intriguing similarities to groupchat. What if we created a personalized Multi-User Chat room for each user, where they could interact with their subscribers in a familiar groupchat interface? The room occupants could even be aliases because we don't want to force everyone to park in multiple groupchat rooms.

Unfortunately we don't have space to explore these potential sprints in detail, so we leave them as an exercise for the reader.

A CheshiR Server Module or Dedicated Server?

So far, we have seen how to integrate XMPP into an application by building either a bot or a server component. Both approaches yield a solution that is independent from the server you are using to deploy your application. This is mostly an advantage, but the downside of having an external XMPP integration is that you don't have access to the server internals, and this can limit both the functionality and the performance of your application. In fact, our CheshiR server component has started to take on the same kind of presence features that are usually the responsibility of an XMPP server, and it's likely that the server developers will do a better job of this than component developers will!

In the case of CheshiR, we could make use of a tight integration with an XMPP server by directly manipulating the rosters of our contacts. As a result, we wouldn't have to send subscription requests back and forth whenever a user registers with the service, or whenever a user subscribes to one of his contact's notifications.

However, building a CheshiR server module would be very specific to a given server codebase. In particular, this level of integration would require us to code directly to the server's internal API, rather than using a wire protocol to communicate, so exploring this solution will take us outside the realm of XMPP itself and into the world of a particular codebase. Similarly, we could go even further and build our own dedicated XMPP server implementation.

Before deciding to build a server module or a dedicated server, we would need to weigh the costs and benefits. Is the XMPP interface really core to the CheshiR service? Can we justify the vendor lock-in associated with writing a module for a specific server, or the investment in building and maintaining an entirely new server codebase? Sometimes the benefits of these paths do outweigh the costs, but only if messaging and presence are core to your business.

Summary

In this chapter, we explored how to build an XMPP application through the example of a microblogging system. Clearly you could make many different kinds of applications using XMPP, and we cannot describe them all here. The thought processes and design decisions involved might differ somewhat if you want to create, say, a voice and video chat service, a whiteboarding client, a location tracker, a network monitoring system, or an online gaming application. For any given type of application, you will need to focus more carefully on certain parts of the system (e.g., the server rather than the client), write more code instead of reusing existing code, integrate more completely with non-XMPP systems, design more XMPP extensions, or work more closely with XMPP community. However, our intent in this book has been to give you the tools you need to build any kind of XMPP application. If we succeeded, you should be able to take the tools we have described and apply them in a wide range of projects, products, and services. We wish you success in using XMPP technologies and invite you to join the ongoing conversation in the XMPP community as more and more developers collaborate to build out the real-time Internet.

PART IV

Appendixes

A Guide to XMPP Specifications

XMPP is defined in a number of documents called specifications. These documents define the precise XML that is sent back and forth to complete all the use cases we've discussed in this book (and many more). The XMPP specifications contain many examples to help developers understand exactly how XMPP works, and would fill several books as long as this one if published all together. Here we provide a brief guide to these specifications, which are published in two series: several documents in the IETF's Request for Comments (RFC) series, and a large and growing number of XMPP Extension Protocols in the XMPP Standards Foundation's XEP series.

XMPP RFCs

The IETF's RFC series contains specifications that define most of the core technologies of the Internet, including the Internet Protocol (IP) itself, Transmission Control Protocol (TCP), User Datagram Protocol (UDP), Simple Mail Transfer Protocol (SMTP), Hypertext Transfer Protocol (HTTP), Session Initiation Protocol (SIP), and many others. In 2004, the IETF published two RFCs that define the basis for all XMPP technologies.

RFC 3920 defines XML streams along with all of the stream-level features required to build XMPP applications, including:

- The basic XMPP architecture and address format
- The use of Transmission Control Protocol (TCP) as the underlying transport for XMPP communications
- The use of Transport Layer Security (TLS) for stream encryption
- The use of Simple Authentication and Security Layer (SASL) for stream authentication
- The use of Unicode, UTF-8, and stringprep for fully internationalized addresses and text

- The use of XML in XMPP, including prohibited features of XML and the inclusion of XML namespaces
- The basic semantics of the message, presence, and IQ stanzas
- Error conditions that can be communicated at the XML stream, SASL, and XMPP stanza levels

RFC 3921 defines the instant messaging and presence features required to build XMPP applications, including:

- Management of rosters (contact lists)
- Handling of presence subscriptions
- Handling of presence notifications, whether broadcast or directed

RFC Revisions

As of this writing, RFC 3920 and RFC 3921 are under active revision to incorporate errata, clarify ambiguities, improve their readability, define additional error codes, etc. These documents, called [rfc3920bis] and [rfc3921bis] in the terminology of the IETF, provide the most accurate definition of XMPP and might have been published as replacement RFCs (with new numbers) by the time you read this book. For the latest versions of the revised specifications, visit *http://xmpp.org*.

XMPP Extension Protocols

The XMPP Extension Protocol (XEP) series specifies extensions to the core of XMPP as defined in the RFCs. The XEP series is produced by the XMPP Standards Foundation and published at *http://xmpp.org*. There are five types of XEP documents:

Standards Track
    The mainstay of the XEP series, Standards Track XEPs describe XMPP protocol extensions in the various stages of the XSF's standards process.

Informational
    Informational XEPs do not define new protocols, but act as support documents for the XEP series, providing best practices and usage profiles.

Historical
    Used to document XMPP protocol extensions developed outside the XSF's standards process that have gained widespread usage within the XMPP developer community, several of these predate the XMPP RFCs and even the XSF itself (which was founded in 2001).

Humorous
    Usually published on April 1st, these provide tongue-in-cheek protocol extensions or other light-hearted XMPP-related documentation. They *may* provide amusement but *should not* be taken seriously.

Procedural
> These XEPs do not define XMPP extensions, but describe the processes of the XMPP Standards Foundation itself.

In addition to the five types of XEPs, there are also several states that XEPs can be in:

Experimental
> XEPs of any type start off in the Experimental state after their acceptance by the XMPP Council. Implementing Experimental protocol XEPs isn't an inherently bad idea if they solve a problem you have, but the protocol might change—usually in the details, but sometimes radically—so it's not recommended to make primary software releases using these XEPs.

Proposed
> XEPs that are under consideration for advancement from Experimental to Active or Draft have a temporary state of Proposed.

Deferred
> Experimental XEPs change status to Deferred if no progress (either advancement in the XEP process, or modifications) is made on them in 12 months. Deferring an XEP doesn't imply that the XEP is on the path to rejection, but the same implementation warnings apply as to Experimental XEPs.

Retracted
> Retracted XEPs have been removed from the standards process at their authors' request.

Deprecated
> An older XEP may be Deprecated when a newer XEP is released that supersedes it. It's recommended that you do not implement these, except for the sake of backward compatibility with older software.

Obsolete
> When the XMPP Council determines that a previously accepted XEP should no longer be used, it enters the Obsolete stage. It's recommended that you do not implement these.

Rejected
> If the XMPP Council determines that an XEP is unsuitable for use within the XMPP community, it is Rejected.

When a non-Standards Track XEP is ready for advancement from Experimental, it can enter the Active stage:

Active
> This catch-all state for non-Standards Track XEPs is used for all documents currently in use.

Standards Track XEPs have a well-defined "track" that they proceed along; after the Experimental state, they advance as follows:

Draft
> A Standards Track XEP enters the Draft state after it has undergone extensive community review (and preferably implementation) and has been voted for advancement from Experimental by the XMPP Council. Once an XEP advances to Draft, it typically is implemented in multiple codebases and deployed in production XMPP services. This experience can lead to clarifications and revisions, which are incorporated into the specification while it is in the Draft state.

Final
> After an XEP has been in the Draft state for a while (sometimes years), the XMPP Council can choose to issue a "Call for Experience" regarding the protocol. At that time, the XEP undergoes a thorough review by the developer community, which evaluates the specification for accuracy and completeness, formulates a list of implementations, and determines whether those implementations are interoperable. The XMPP Council can then vote for the XEP to be advanced to Final status. Although modifications can still be made to the XEP in Final, these must essentially be clarifications or tweaks: no backward-incompatible changes can be made. Relatively few XEPs have advanced to the Final state, although this is caused more by a focus on new work than a lack of maturity in existing protocols.

The following pages describe many of the XEPs that were published at the time of this writing. However, some XEPs are not described here, in particular those with status of Retracted, Rejected, Deprecated, or Obsolete. A list of all XEPs, including those not mentioned here, is maintained at *http://xmpp.org*. Unless otherwise noted, the specifications described here are Standards Track XEPs:

XEP-0001: XMPP Extension Protocols
> This Procedural XEP defines the XEP publishing process, detailing the XEP types and states listed earlier, and the procedures for advancing and expiring XEPs. Reading this XEP can provide some interesting insight into the work of the XMPP Standards Foundation.

XEP-0004: Data Forms
> The Data Forms extension defines a data exchange format using forms with typed fields (similar to HTML forms). By embedding Data Forms in other protocols, it is possible to offer customized options to a user without defining them in the outer protocol. We discussed Data Forms in Chapter 6.

XEP-0009: Jabber-RPC
> This XEP describes how to use XMPP as a transport for remote procedure calls using the format defined in [XML-RPC].

XEP-0012: Last Activity
> The Last Activity protocol is used for querying a client or server to find out when the user was last active on the network.

XEP-0013: Flexible Offline Message Retrieval

Flexible Offline Message Retrieval provides a method for a finer control of the delivery of offline messages during a client's login. It allows a client to check the quantity of offline messages, and fetch and remove specific or all messages. There is some support for it in servers, but it is not widely implemented in clients, perhaps because few users need to manage a large number of offline messages.

XEP-0016: Privacy Lists

The protocol described in Privacy Lists was originally defined in XEP-0016 and then published in RFC 3921, but it has since been moved back to XEP-0016 because the protocol is not needed in rfc3921bis. The Privacy Lists protocol provides a server-side method for blocking incoming and outgoing stanzas to other entities based full or partial JID, subscription state, or roster group. [XEP-0191] provides a simplified interface to the same kind of information.

XEP-0020: Feature Negotiation

This is a building-block XEP for negotiating the parameters used in communication between two entities. It is used mainly in XEP-0096 for negotiating file transfer stream details.

XEP-0027: Current Jabber OpenPGP Usage

This Historical specification describes the usage of OpenPGP for improving the end-to-end security of XMPP exchanges between clients. The protocol is implemented in several clients, but the lack of OpenPGP usage among end users has limited its deployment. This XEP is likely to be replaced in time by a more user-friendly end-to-end encryption technique.

XEP-0030: Service Discovery

The Service Discovery protocol is used extensively throughout the XMPP protocol stack. As we saw in Chapter 5, Service Discovery provides a mechanism for discovering both the capabilities of an entity (its identity, and the features and protocols it supports) and the items associated with the entity (such as the rooms hosted by an MUC service or the nodes on a PubSub service).

XEP-0033: Extended Stanza Addressing

Extended Stanza Addressing enables stanzas to be addressed to multiple recipients in a manner close to that of SMTP, such as `cc`, `bcc`, and `replyto` directives.

XEP-0045: Multi-User Chat

Multi-User Chat is a chat room/chat channel/text conference protocol with administration functions such as kicking, banning, and room configuration. We discussed the "MUC" protocol in Chapter 7.

XEP-0047: In-Band Bytestreams

In-Band Bytestreams or "IBB" is a Standards Track XEP defining a transport mechanism for binary data within a standard XMPP stream. It covers chunking the data to allow normal traffic to continue while a data transfer proceeds. We discussed IBB in Chapter 10.

XEP-0048: Bookmarks

The Bookmarks specification provides a format for server-side storage of bookmarks to web pages and chat rooms (including a hint to clients to auto-join selected chat rooms at login time).

XEP-0049: Private XML Storage

This is a description of the Historical protocol for storing arbitrary private user data on the user's server (such as XEP-0048's bookmarks). This protocol might be superseded at some point by a profile of the Publish-Subscribe protocol (see XEP-0222).

XEP-0050: Ad-Hoc Commands

This XEP defines a method for discovering and executing commands on remote entities, where the commands and their parameters are not known in advance. We discussed this protocol in Chapter 11.

XEP-0053: XMPP Registrar Function

This is a Procedural document describing the workings of the XMPP Registrar, which maintains registries of XML namespaces, application parameters, and other dynamic information used throughout the XMPP protocol stack. The Registrar is located at *http://xmpp.org/registrar/*.

XEP-0054: vcard-temp

The vcard-temp XEP provides documentation of the Historical protocol the Jabber community uses for storage and retrieval of XML-formatted vCards. We discussed this protocol in Chapter 4.

XEP-0055: Jabber Search

This is a Historical protocol that is primarily used for querying directories of users. Through Data Forms, a service may define additional search methods beyond the standard fields included in the XEP.

XEP-0059: Result Set Management

Result Set Management is used to deal with large results of queries to services such as Jabber Search, Service Discovery, Publish-Subscribe, and Message Archiving. It provides methods for paging through a result set as well as direct access to arbitrary subsets, allowing access to data sets that would be infeasible to transfer in their entirety.

XEP-0060: Publish-Subscribe

PubSub, discussed at some length in Chapter 8, provides a rich protocol for push-based notifications of content on presubscribed data nodes, as well as mechanisms for dynamically creating subscriptions based on interests defined in entity capabilities data (see XEP-0115). The "Personal Eventing Protocol" (XEP-0163) is a subset of PubSub.

XEP-0065: SOCKS5 Bytestreams

SOCKS5 Bytestreams is a method of establishing out-of-band binary streams. Such bytestreams are primarily used for file transfer, as described in XEP-0096. Although mainly aimed at peer-to-peer streams, mediated transfers (through a specialized proxy) are also supported. We discussed this protocol in Chapter 10.

XEP-0066: Out-of-Band Data

Out of Band Data provides a mechanism for exchanging a reference to data stored outside XMPP, such as a file at an HTTP URL.

XEP-0068: Field Standardization for Data Forms

This is an Informational XEP describing the process of formalizing the field variables used in Data Forms by various XMPP extensions. The XMPP Registrar maintains a registry of such fields.

XEP-0070: Verifying HTTP Requests via XMPP

This XEP defines a method for verifying identity in an HTTP request with a call-back message over XMPP. This allows you to have a system that can authenticate on HTTP using Jabber identity.

XEP-0071: XHTML-IM

XHTML-IM is a profile of XHTML used for markup of XMPP messages, particularly for instant messaging. Cutting out large amounts of XHTML, this provides semantic markup and formatting for chat text, while attempting to avoid the security issues inherent in some XHTML tags. We discussed XHTML-IM in Chapter 4.

XEP-0072: SOAP Over XMPP

This XEP defines a SOAP Protocol Binding, which allows XMPP to be used as a transport for SOAP payloads. It also describes provision of a WSDL definition for discovering the service.

XEP-0077: In-Band Registration

In-Band Registration may be offered by an XMPP service to allow account creation and/or user registration from within an XMPP stream. This can be used in several ways, including account creation on XMPP servers and registration with services such as Multi-User Chat rooms, as discussed in Chapter 7.

XEP-0078: Non-SASL Authentication

This document is Obsolete, but it defines the original Jabber protocol for authentication (and resource binding) by clients. The protocol defined here was superseded by the use of SASL as defined by the IETF's XMPP Working Group, but is still supported by many clients, servers, and libraries for the sake of backward compatibility and interoperability testing.

XEP-0079: Advanced Message Processing

The Advanced Message Processing (AMP) protocol defines an approach for changing the handling of message stanzas. It provides features such as short-lived messages (which are not delivered after they expire) and automatic message receipts. This protocol hasn't become very popular, but would be quite useful in scenarios that require reliable delivery of messages.

XEP-0080: User Location

    User location is an XEP describing a payload format for representing information about the geographical location of a user, primarily for transport over PubSub and PEP.

XEP-0082: XMPP Date and Time Profiles

    This simple Informational XEP describes best practices for representation of dates and times in XMPP, reusing certain profiles of the ISO 8601 format.

XEP-0083: Nested Roster Groups

    This is a very short Informational XEP describing a common format for naming roster groups to denote a hierarchy. Mostly this just means putting the string `::` between each layer of the hierarchy in the roster group name (e.g., `Top level::Mid level::Lowest level`).

XEP-0084: User Avatar

    This is a Standards Track XEP describing a format for storing user avatars in PEP or PubSub. As avatars are much larger than typical PEP payloads, it uses two nodes: one with metadata (primarily a hash of the avatar), which notifications are sent from, and a data node containing the avatar itself, which users' clients query when they need an avatar that matches a previously unseen hash in the metadata. This format is expected to supplant vCard-based avatars (XEP-0153) over time.

XEP-0085: Chat State Notifications

    Chat State Notifications is an extension documenting a protocol for sending notifications during a chat, such as when one user is typing, has stopped typing, or has left a chat. It supersedes the older "message events" protocol described in XEP-0022. We discussed this protocol in Chapter 4.

XEP-0086: Error Condition Mappings

    This Informational specification is Deprecated but remains useful because it describes a mapping of the modern XML-formatted error conditions to the older error code numbers, which are still supported in a number of implementations.

XEP-0092: Software Version

    This XEP provides a very simple mechanism for requesting version information about another entity. Eventually this protocol will probably be superseded by the service discovery extension method described in XEP-0232 (which can be automated using Entity Capabilities).

XEP-0095: Stream Initiation

    Stream Initiation is a method for negotiating a data stream between two entities. In principle, this protocol can be used to negotiate any stream type, but in practice it is used only for file transfers in XEP-0096. The Jingle extensions now informally supersede Stream Initiation as a session initiation protocol, and once implementations catch up, this fact will probably be formalized.

XEP-0096: File Transfer

This protocol uses XEP-0095's Stream Initiation protocol for initiating file transfers, as discussed in Chapter 10. It is expected that Jingle file transfers will eventually supersede the SI approach.

XEP-0100: Gateway Interaction

This Informational XEP provides best practices for workflows between XMPP clients and gateway (or "transport") services to other networks (such as proprietary chat networks). It discusses registering and unregistering, logging into, and logging out of the gateways, as well as adding and deleting contacts and message sending to contacts on the other side of the gateway. Because gateways have become less important over time as XMPP has emerged as a standalone technology, we do not cover gateways in this book.

XEP-0106: JID Escaping

This protocol is used for encoding the characters into the node part (the part before the @) of a JID that would normally be disallowed (space, ", &, ', /, :, <, >, and @). This is useful when translating addresses from other systems, such as in gateways to other messaging networks or when a new IM system needs to create XMPP addresses from existing email credentials.

XEP-0107: User Mood

User Mood defines a format for information about a user's mood, used as a payload sent over PEP. The XEP contains a list of predefined mood values, which are sent together with an optional mood message; this is a very similar approach to user presence in XMPP itself.

XEP-0108: User Activity

Similar to User Mood, User Activity defines a PEP payload. User Activity defines a set of activity values, such as doing_chores and eating, and specific activities to complement these, such as cleaning, cooking, having_a_snack, and having_lunch.

XEP-0114: Jabber Component Protocol

This is a record of the Historical protocol used for communication between XMPP servers and external components, such as transports to other messaging networks or MUC services. Although XEP-0114 is widely used, it might be supplanted at some point by a component protocol that provides stronger security and greater flexibility (see XEP-0225).

XEP-0115: Entity Capabilities

Entity Capabilities is used extensively in other specifications for passive discovery of the capabilities of remote entities. This XEP obviates the need for explicit Disco requests in most cases by transmitting a hash of an entity's capabilities inside their presence stanza. As long as you've seen this hash before, and queried an entity to discover the features it corresponds to, there's no need to "disco" an entity with this hash. We discussed this technology in Chapter 5.

XEP-0118: User Tune

User Tune is another XEP defining a PEP payload. This one describes the music that a user is listening to.

XEP-0122: Data Forms Validation

This XEP defines extensions to Data Forms that allow the submitting entity to validate the contents of a form before submission. It includes further specification of data types, such as dates and other XML types, and includes validation methods both by range and by matching regular expressions.

XEP-0124: Bidirectional-streams Over Synchronous HTTP (BOSH)

Not directly an XMPP extension, BOSH defines an alternative stream transport so that real-time traffic can be sent over HTTP instead of TCP. BOSH is quite useful in constrained environments where long-lived TCP connections are not feasible, such as browser-based clients and mobile telephony networks. Together with XEP-0206, XEP-0124 defines an alternative transport for XMPP. We discussed BOSH in Chapter 12.

XEP-0126: Invisibility

This is an Informational XEP listing best practices for using XMPP privacy lists to allow an entity to be "invisible" to the majority of the network, while allowing the entity to continue to communicate with entities as they wish.

XEP-0127: Common Alerting Protocol (CAP) Over XMPP

This is an Informational XEP providing methods for sending CAP data over XMPP, either as a PubSub payload or using direct messages. The CAP format is used for emergency notifications, weather alerts, and the like.

XEP-0128: Service Discovery Extensions

Service Discovery Extensions is an Informational best practices XEP describing the inclusion of extended information in Disco results. This is particularly useful for MUC and PubSub services.

XEP-0130: Waiting Lists

This Historical XEP defines a rarely seen protocol for adding a user without an XMPP account to a waiting list, so you can be notified when they create an account.

XEP-0131: Stanza Headers and Internet Metadata (SHIM)

SHIM defines header information for XMPP stanzas, allowing XMPP stanzas to include things such as keywords, stanza creation dates, and in-reply-to data.

XEP-0133: Service Administration

This specification provides an informational list of useful Ad-Hoc Commands for server administrators. The list includes, amongst others, adding and deleting users on the service, changing passwords, sending messages to all users, and setting welcome messages.

XEP-0134: Protocol Design Guidelines

Also known as "The Tao of XMPP," this Informational XEP was written to help designers of XMPP extensions in creating protocols that fit well with the existing infrastructure, and make the best use of the available XMPP resources. It includes guidelines such as not attempting to modify core behavior, keeping complexity in the server so clients can be simple, and reusing existing protocols where possible.

XEP-0136: Message Archiving

Message Archiving provides a method for the server-side storage of message history. As well as describing automatic archiving by the server, it also defines a method for uploading existing history from a client and retrieving history data.

XEP-0137: Publishing SI Requests

This protocol is used for announcing the availability of a file for file transfer, either through direct messaging or PubSub.

XEP-0138: Stream Compression

Stream Compression defines a mechanism for application-level negotiation of (typically ZLIB) compression for an XMPP stream. TLS also provides compression mechanisms, but these are not always available; in these cases, Stream Compression is useful.

XEP-0141: Data Forms Layout

This XEP defines extensions for Data Forms to specify the layout of fields when rendered in a client. These include the relative layout of fields, and splitting forms into pages and section hierarchies.

XEP-0143: Guidelines for Authors of XMPP Extension Protocols

A spiritual partner to Protocol Design Guidelines (XEP-0134), this Procedural document describes the process of writing an XEP document, covering the submission process, the file formats, the sections of an XEP, and a style guide. Read this if you are thinking of submitting a proposal for publication as an XEP.

XEP-0144: Roster Item Exchange

This protocol is used for transferring information on roster items between entities (e.g., to tell someone about another person they might want to chat with). It includes formats for suggesting addition, deletion, and modification of records.

XEP-0145: Annotations

This Historical XEP documents a protocol in use in the community for storing (annotating) information, primarily about roster items.

XEP-0146: Remote Controlling Clients

This is an Informational XEP listing five ad-hoc commands for controlling XMPP clients: changing status, forwarding unread messages, changing settings, accepting pending subscription requests, and leaving groupchats. We discussed these commands in Chapter 11.

XEP-0147: XMPP URI Scheme Query Components

This Informational XEP provides a list of query parts for XMPP URIs. These query parts specify actions such as sending messages, subscribing to entities, service registration, and joining MUC rooms.

XEP-0149: Time Periods

This Informational XEP describes a common format for transmitting time periods in XMPP stanzas, conforming to the XMPP Date and Time Profiles XEP. The protocol could be used, for example, to mark up a presence notification to specify that you will be do-not-disturb in a meeting for the next two hours.

XEP-0153: vCard-Based Avatars

This is a Historical XEP documenting a protocol for avatar exchange. In this protocol, the avatar is stored in the photo field of a user's vCard, and the hash of the current avatar is announced in a user's presence packets. Annotating presence packets for data like these is generally ill-thought-of in XMPP, and it is now preferable to support the standards track XEP-0084 User Avatar. However, the vCard-Based Avatars approach is still widely deployed, and many clients support it for backward compatibility with existing software.

XEP-0155: Stanza Session Negotiation

This rarely used specification defines a method for negotiating parameters for a communication session between two entities that do not share presence information, such as encryption, chat state notifications, formatting, and archiving. It is quite possible that this XEP will be deprecated or obsolete at some point.

XEP-0156: Discovering Alternative XMPP Connection Methods

This XEP defines a way to use DNS records in discovering multiple methods for connecting to an XMPP server (e.g., a BOSH URL).

XEP-0157: Contact Addresses for XMPP Services

This is an Informational definition of methods for supplying contact addresses for an XMPP service over email and XMPP. It defines contact addresses such as those for reporting abuse, security issues, and contacting a system administrator.

XEP-0158: CAPTCHA Forms

This defines defines a method for querying a user with CAPTCHA forms to attempt to verify that a user is a human and not an automated process. This can be used in situations such as when joining an MUC room or registering an account on a server, in an attempt to limit abuse, particularly automated spam. The XEP lists several types of possible CAPTCHAs, including the common image-based ones, as well as audio identification and text challenges. We discussed this approach in Chapter 6.

XEP-0160: Best Practices for Handling Offline Messages

This is an Informational XEP defining best practices for handling messages sent to JabberIDs that do not have any online resources when the message is sent. As well as discussing general issues, it provides specific advice for each of the `<message/>` stanza types: `normal`, `chat`, `groupchat`, `headline`, and `error`.

XEP-0163: Personal Eventing Protocol

The Personal Eventing Protocol or PEP specification is used in several other XEPs, and defines a profile of PubSub that is useful for broadcasting information relating to a user's state, such as the User Tune, User Mood, and User Activity XEPs. Originally defining several new features, these were deemed valuable enough to be moved into the core PubSub XEP, and PEP is now simply a profile of PubSub, with an emphasis on sane defaults. We discussed PEP in Chapter 8.

XEP-0166: Jingle

Jingle is a method for initiating streams between two entities. Currently used in several XEPs related to voice and video calling, it's currently considered that Jingle will become increasingly relevant to the XMPP community as more XEPs are written that rely upon it (such as file transfers and screen sharing). Chapter 9 covered Jingle technologies in detail.

XEP-0167: Jingle RTP Sessions

One of the series of Jingle XEPs, this specification defines an application type for the negotiation of streams using RTP (the Real-time Transport Protocol), such as voice and video.

XEP-0170: Recommended Order of Stream Feature Negotiation

This Informational XEP defines best practices for the ordering of XMPP stream feature negotiation. These recommendations have been incorporated into rfc3920bis.

XEP-0171: Language Translation

Language Translation is a protocol that defines the use of language translation services over XMPP. Including both automatic and manual translation, it provides methods for the discovery of translation services, as well as the methods for requesting and receiving translations. It allows both direct translation and translation through one or more intermediate ("pivot") languages.

XEP-0172: User Nickname

This XEP defines a method for transmission of a user nickname for a user over several transport methods, including presence, PubSub and direct messaging. It allows a user to know the consistent nicknames by which other users identify themselves, even when they do not share presence information, or when inside an MUC.

XEP-0174: Serverless Messaging

This XEP defines methods for discovery of, and communication with, other Serverless Messaging entities on a network. As we discussed in Chapter 12, serverless messaging is founded on DNS-based Service Discovery and Multicast DNS, thereby enabling entities to locate each other and chat without a common server. Using this method, entities communicate using peer-to-peer XMPP streams. It is useful when multiple entities do not have connectivity to the broader Internet (e.g., remote locations, trains, etc.) and for ad-hoc situations, such as conferences and conventions.

XEP-0175: Best Practices for Use of SASL ANONYMOUS

This Informational XEP specifies best practices for use of the SASL ANONYMOUS mechanism in the authentication process of clients with XMPP servers. Using this mechanism, it is possible (where allowed) for a client to obtain a temporary server-provided JID without user authentication, which is destroyed when the client's session ends. Some services currently use this to provide simple web access to MUC rooms, where a user can join an MUC room without an XMPP account simply by visiting a web page.

XEP-0176: Jingle ICE-UDP Transport Method
Another XEP in the Jingle series, this defines an XMPP profile of Interactive Connectivity Establishment (ICE). The ICE methodology (defined by the IETF) provides effective traversal of environments hostile to peer-to-peer sessions, such as Network Address Translation (NAT) systems that otherwise make establishing media traffic streams difficult.

XEP-0177: Jingle Raw UDP Transport Method
This XEP defines a transport method for UDP data transmission, but without the sophisticated NAT traversal methodology of the Jingle ICE-UDP Transport Method. It is mainly useful to intermediate servers or call managers that host an "always-on" media relay.

XEP-0178: Best Practices for Use of SASL EXTERNAL with Certificates
As the name suggests, this Informational XEP defines best practices for the use of certificates with the SASL EXTERNAL mechanism, both in client-to-server and server-to-server authentication.

XEP-0181: Jingle DTMF
Jingle DTMF defines a format for encoding DTMF (Dual Tone Multi-Frequency) events in an XMPP stream when they cannot be encoded directly into the corresponding stream (such as RTP). DTMF is used mainly for interaction with older telephony networks, especially Interactive Voice Response (IVR) systems.

XEP-0182: Application-Specific Error Conditions
This Procedural document defines the use of a registry of error conditions, maintained by the XMPP Registrar at *http://xmpp.org/registrar/errors.html*.

XEP-0184: Message Receipts
This is a method for a sender to request notification when a message has reached the recipient. It is similar to the Read Receipts that email provides.

XEP-0185: Dialback Key Generation and Validation
This Informational XEP discusses the generation of the keys used in the dialback between servers that is used for identity verification during stream initiation.

XEP-0186: Invisible Command
This specification provides an alternative invisibility protocol to XEP-0126. Where XEP-0126 uses Privacy Lists to make an entity appear invisible, Invisible Command uses an explicit command sent to a supporting server.

XEP-0189: Public Key Publishing
This XEP defines methods for sharing an entity's public keys used in cryptography, with transport methods both over PEP/PubSub and direct querying of entities.

XEP-0190: Best Practice for Closing Idle Streams

This Informational XEP describes the best practices for handling the closing of a stream due to inactivity. This mostly amounts to sending a closing `</stream:stream>`, sending no stanzas after this, and waiting for the other entity to also send a stream-closing element before terminating the stream. This recommendation is included in rfc3920bis.

XEP-0191: Simple Communications Blocking

This is an alternative to Privacy Lists, providing a simpler interface when the more complete control offered by Privacy Lists isn't required. Simple Communications Blocking provides only two commands: either "block this contact" or "unblock this contact."

XEP-0192: Proposed Stream Feature Improvements

This XEP defines improvements to feature negotiation and advertisement during establishment of an XML stream between two entities. The recommendations have been included in rfc3920bis.

XEP-0193: Proposed Resource Binding Improvements

Along with XEP-0192, this is another XEP defining improvements for the next version of the XMPP RFCs, this time the binding to a resource by a client.

XEP-0194: User Chatting

User Chatting (Standards Track) defines a method for revealing (via PEP/PubSub) which chat rooms a user is in.

XEP-0195: User Browsing

Similar to XEP-0194, User Browsing is an XEP for announcing the web pages that a user visits.

XEP-0196: User Gaming

The third in this series of personal eventing payload XEPs, User Gaming publishes events detailing the games a user plays.

XEP-0197: User Viewing

The last of the four XEPs in this series, User Viewing is an XEP for publishing information about the video that a user is watching.

XEP-0198: Stream Management

This defines a set of improvements to XMPP stream handling relating to reliable delivery, disconnection detection, and session resumption. Defining stanza acknowledgments and pings, it allows an entity to know which stanzas are delivered before a disconnection, and allows a session to resume after a disconnection by providing the identity of the last received stanza. Because these features are defined at the stream level, they provide reliable XMPP sessions for an individual hop.

XEP-0199: XMPP Ping

A complement to Stream Management, XMPP Ping defines entity to entity pings, allowing disconnects to be tested at any hop between two XMPP entities, or end-to-end.

XEP-0201: Best Practices for Message Threads
> Because message threads or conversations are traditionally an under-specified area of XMPP, this Informational XEP attempts to provide best practices for handling the `<thread/>` element in message stanzas. It covers handling of threads with different message types, and the creation and termination of threads.

XEP-0202: Entity Time
> This defines a protocol for querying an XMPP Entity's local time, including the time-zone offset from UTC.

XEP-0203: Delayed Delivery
> This XEP defines a protocol for stamping the time in an XMPP stanza, so that if delivery is delayed, the original send-time can be determined. Examples are given for receiving presence on login, offline messages, and messages sent in a chat room before one joins it.

XEP-0205: Best Practices to Discourage Denial of Service Attacks
> This is an Informational XEP defining a series of practices for alleviating the effects of denial of service attacks. These include approaches such as rate limiting connections, limiting the number of concurrent connections, the number of allowed resources for one user, and the size of stanzas.

XEP-0206: XMPP Over BOSH
> Partner to the BOSH protocol (XEP-0124), this XEP defines the use of BOSH as a transport layer for XMPP streams.

XEP-0209: Metacontacts
> Metacontacts is a term coined for the merging of several accounts belonging to one user into a single logical contact. This XEP defines methods for doing this in XMPP, including metacontacts that span several accounts, in a way that allows the metacontacts to persist when any of the accounts are missing or offline.

XEP-0220: Server Dialback
> Originally defined in the XMPP RFCs but since moved to an XEP, Server Dialback is the process of (weakly but usually effectively) verifying the initiator of an XMPP S2S stream by attempting a return connection to the service the initiator claims to be (looked up over DNS). We discussed the server dialback protocol in Chapter 12.

XEP-0221: Data Forms Media Element
> This XEP defines a `<media/>` element for data forms that can reference media types such as audio and video. Currently this is used only in CAPTCHA Forms (XEP-0158) for spam prevention.

XEP-0222: Best Practices for Persistent Storage of Public Data via Publish-Subscribe
> This Informational XEP simply describes how PubSub can be used to store persistent data relating to an entity, such as its public cryptographic keys.

XEP-0223: Best Practices for Persistent Storage of Private Data via Publish-Subscribe
Partner to XEP-0222, this Informational XEP discusses how PubSub can be used to store private data for an entity. Over time, this is expected to replace the iq:private mechanism defined in XEP-0049.

XEP-0224: Attention
This simple XEP defines a stanza that can be sent to request the attention of a conversation partner or other contact. This typically results in a buzz, nudge, or other attention-getting action on the contact's machine.

XEP-0225: Component Connections
A possible replacement for the Jabber Component Protocol (XEP-0114), this XEP provides methods for components to connect to servers using the now-standard mechanisms in XMPP, such as TLS and SASL; it also allows multiple hostnames to bind on a single connection.

XEP-0226: Message Stanza Profiles
In XMPP, `<message />` stanzas can have many types of payload, some of which are confusing and some nonsensical when presented together. This Informational XEP attempts to list profiles for the many payload types, providing best practices for the combination of these payloads.

XEP-0229: Stream Compression with LZW
This XEP describes how the LZW compression algorithm may be used with Stream Compression (XEP-0138), as an alternative to the ZLIB algorithm used in that specification.

XEP-0231: Bits of Binary
Bits of Binary is a protocol for exchanging small amounts of binary data within an XMPP stream. The data can be referenced with a `cid` identifier, allowing entities to request the data only the first time they need it, and subsequently cache the binary data and receive only references to it. We discussed this extension in Chapter 10.

XEP-0232: Software Information
This is an alternative to the Software Version protocol (XEP-0092). Software Information allows the transmission of information about a software deployment, such as the version, within a service discovery result. As a consequence of embedding this inside `disco#info` payloads, Entity Capabilities will be able to cache the result, reducing the need for polling across the network.

XEP-0234: Jingle File Transfer
This Standards Track XEP defines a Jingle application for file transfer between entities. While not currently widely deployed, it is expected to slowly replace the established SI File Transfer protocol (XEP-0096) as more XMPP clients converge on the use of Jingle.

XEP-0235: OAuth Over XMPP

Predictably, this XEP defines a mechanism for using the OAuth protocol over XMPP to gain access to resources. This allows external entities to access protected resources of a user through the sharing of tokens, obviating the need for providing third-party services with either your authentication details or unmitigated access to your account. For example, you may allow a third-party service to modify your vCard or publish PEP data on your behalf, but not access your roster or communicate with your contacts.

XEP-0237: Roster Versioning

This XEP provides a solution to the problem of retrieving roster information anew for each session, which slows down the client login process, especially on mobile devices. The Roster Versioning modification enables the server to assign a sequence number to each revision of the roster information so that when a client logs in, it can specify the most recent version it has cached. If the version has not changed, the server will inform the client that it is up-to-date; if it has changed, the server will send roster pushes for the changed roster items.

XEP-0244: IO Data

IO Data provides a richer alternative to Data Forms and Ad-Hoc Commands, including more heavily structured data. The IO Data protocol is heavily biased toward control of computational systems, with transaction semantics and inclusion of job duration tracking.

XEP-0245: The /me Command

This XEP documents the Historical practice of transforming the text `/me does something` in the recipient's client to be rendered in some way that denotes the user "doing something." It is often rendered so that if a user Alice sends `/me heads down the rabbit hole`, it is displayed to the recipient user as `* Alice heads down the rabbit hole`.

XEP-0249: Direct MUC Invitations

Although the MUC protocol includes a mechanism for requesting that an MUC room in which you are a participant send an invitation to a contact, privacy lists or local policy may prevent the invitee from receiving the invite (since it doesn't know or hasn't whitelisted the MUC room). This XEP simply allows sending an MUC invite directly from one user to another, solving the problem because contacts will already be able to send messages to each other.

XEP-0251: Jingle Session Transfer

This specification defines methods for transferring a Jingle session (usually a voice chat session) from one party to another. Both attended transfer and unattended transfer are handled by this protocol.

XEP-0253: PubSub Chaining

Sometimes it is desirable to subscribe one publish-subscribe node to another for the purpose of lightweight data aggregation; this XEP specifies several useful techniques for such "chaining" functionality.

XEP-0254: PubSub Queueing

The full potential of the XMPP publish-subscribe extension is only just beginning to be explored. XEP-0060, the base pubsub specification, defines protocols that implement the "Observer" design pattern. By contrast, XEP-0254 defines several small extensions that enable XMPP pubsub systems to support another major design pattern, usually called the "Queueing" or "Point-to-Point" pattern.

XEP-0255: Location Query

The XMPP geolocation payload format defined in XEP-0080 provides useful information about an entity's physical location. However, many devices cannot directly produce data such as GPS coordinates; therefore, XEP-0255 provides a way for such devices to use data they have (such as cellular phone beacons) to query a location service to discover data in a format that can be communicated via XEP-0080.

XEP-0256: Last Activity in Presence

This specification defines a way to notate a presence update with information that is formatted according to the Last Activity specification (XEP-0012). As a result, a user can know when a contact was last active when first receiving availability data during a presence session.

XEP-0258: Security Labels in XMPP

The concept of a security label is commonly understood from government and military applications (for example, "Top Secret"), but applies to many kinds of information systems. XEP-0258 defines methods for including security label data in XMPP communications.

XEP-0259: Message Mine-ing

In some XMPP systems, a message sent to an address that has multiple online resources can be delivered to more than one of those resources. This specification provides a way for a given resource to claim the message so that the other resources will not show it to the user.

XEP-0260: Jingle SOCKS5 Bytestreams Transport Method

In order to reuse the SOCKS5 Bytestreams protocol (XEP-0065) in Jingle for file transfer, end-to-end encryption, and other streaming data exchanges, this specification defines a Jingle-specific method for setting up a SOCKS5 bytestream.

XEP-0261: Jingle In-Band Bytestreams Transport Method

Just as XEP-0260 defines a Jingle-specific method for reusing the SOCKS5 Bytestreams protocol, XEP-0261 defines a similar method for reusing the In-Band Bytestreams protocol (XEP-0047).

XEP-0262: Use of ZRTP in Jingle RTP Sessions

XEP-0167, the specification for Jingle voice calls, recommends using Secure Real-time Transport Protocol (SRTP) for encryption of audio data. An alternative encryption technology is ZRTP, developed by Phil Zimmerman, the inventor of Pretty Good Privacy (PGP). XEP-0262 defines a way to use ZRTP in Jingle for secure voice calls.

Humorous XEPs

As well as the genuine protocol extensions and guideline documents listed in the previous section, the XSF publishes a range of humorous XEPs, usually on April 1st of each year, showing that even protocol geeks have a sense of humor:

XEP-0076: Malicious Stanzas
> Malicious Stanzas defines an `<evil/>` element, which can be added to XMPP stanzas to indicate that they are sent with malicious intent. This is in tandem with a similar IETF April Fool's day protocol for specifying an "evil bit" in IPv4.

XEP-0132: Presence Obtained via Kinesthetic Excitation (POKE)
> POKE defines a method of requesting that a remote client physically interacts with a user to determine their presence.

XEP-0148: Instant Messaging Intelligence Quotient (IM IQ)
> This April Fool's XEP describes the `jabber:iq:iq` namespace, used for server-side calculation of a user's intelligence, and the inclusion of the result in outbound stanzas.

XEP-0169: Twas The Night Before Christmas (Jabber Version)
> This is a rendering of the classic Christmas poem in XMPP stanzas, using mechanisms such as requests for the time revealing that it was the night before Christmas, presence revealing the mouse asleep, and User Location revealing that the children were in bed.

XEP-0183: Jingle Telepathy Transport Method
> This XEP defines a transport definition for Jingle that initiates a telepathic communication stream.

XEP-0207: XMPP Eventing via Pubsub
> It was once a long-standing joke in the XMPP community that all other specifications could be rewritten to use PubSub as the transport layer. This XEP was an April Fool's attempt to do this.

XEP-0239: Binary XMPP
> More bandwidth-efficient transmission of XMPP has long been of interest among some members of the community, and one possible approach is a binary representation of the XML. This XEP is a humorous approach to binary XMPP: converting all stanza text directly into the binary representation of the stanza strings, and then encoding this in `<zero/>` and `<one/>` XML elements.

XMPP Compliance Suites

Each year the XSF releases Standards Track recommendations that describe reasonable sets of XEPs to support interoperability in the XMPP sphere. The compliance suites for 2009 are (or, depending on when you read this, were) XEP-0242 and XEP-0243. Refer to *http://xmpp.org* for more up-to-date compliance suites.

XEP-0242: XMPP Client Compliance 2009

Client Compliance 2009 recommendation is split into Core Client and Advanced Client suites. The Core Client list consists of only the XMPP RFCs, Service Discovery, and Entity Capabilities. The Advanced Client lists the Core Client features, Server-Based Privacy Rules, Simple Communications Blocking, Multi-User Chat, vcard-temp, and Chat State Notifications.

XEP-0243: XMPP Server Compliance 2009

The Server Compliance 2009 is similarly split into Core Server and Advanced Server suites. The Core Server compliance requires compliance to the XMPP RFCs and to Service Discovery. The Advanced Server list includes Core Server, Server-Based Privacy Rules, Simple Communications Blocking, Multi-User Chat, and vcard-temp, similar to the Advanced Client list. Advanced Server additionally lists BOSH, XMPP Over BOSH, and Personal Eventing Protocol; this difference reflects the fact that clients do not need these features to interact, but that enough clients require them of their servers to make them worthy of inclusion.

Popular Servers, Clients, and Libraries

In this book, we focused primarily on XMPP protocols and the thought processes and design decisions involved in building XMPP applications. There's a good reason for this: so many XMPP-based software codebases exist that describing XMPP only in terms of a particular server, library, or API might limit your ability to translate what you've learned into other codebases. However, we would be remiss if we didn't describe some of the more popular software projects in the XMPP community. This list is only a snapshot of the (mostly free and open source) software projects that are relatively active at the time of this writing. By the time you read this, it's possible that some of these projects will have disappeared or at least become obsolete, while new projects will have emerged, so visit *http://xmpp.org* for up-to-date links to the wealth of XMPP-based software applications.

Servers

The following list describes the most popular open source XMPP servers:

djabberd
> This is the server created by SixApart for its LiveJournal deployment, known as LJ Talk. The djabberd codebase is designed to be extremely modular. It is something of a bare-bones implementation without a lot of polish or packaging, so if you use it, be prepared to get your hands dirty. The original developers still contribute to the project, and patches come in on a fairly regular basis. Language: Perl. License: GPL. Website: *http://www.danga.com/djabberd/*.

ejabberd
> The ejabberd project was started by several developers in Russia. The primary focus of development has since shifted to Process-one, a company in France that also provides support for the codebase. The server is well-known for its scalability, and it can be clustered across multiple instances. However, the code is written in Erlang (a functional programming language), which could scare off some potential users and contributors (to be fair, the project receives a large number of code contributions, perhaps because there are not many prominent Erlang projects).

Language: Erlang. License: GPL. Website: *http://www.process-one.net/en/ejab berd/*.

jabberd

The jabberd codebase is the direct descendant of the original server created by Jeremie Miller, the inventor of Jabber/XMPP technologies (who learned the C programming language by developing the server!). For many years, jabberd was the reference implementation of the Jabber protocols (even before they were named XMPP), and some of the oddities in the XMPP RFCs are there for backward compatibility with the jabberd server. The project has become less active over the years, but the code is very stable and is still maintained by Matthias Wimmer. Language: C. License: GPL. Website: *http://jabberd.org/*.

jabberd2

The jabberd2 project sounds like an upgraded version of the jabberd project, but in fact it is a totally separate codebase. This is another highly modular server, with separable routers, connection mangers, and the like. Some of the early design ideas were provided by Jeremie Miller, but the server was essentially created by Rob Norris, who then moved on to other pursuits; the project was effectively abandoned for a while, then resurrected by Tomasz Sterna. Language: C. License: GPL. Website: *http://jabberd2.xiaoka.com/*.

Openfire

Openfire was originally a commercial product ("Jive Messenger") developed by Jive Software. The company decided to open source the code in 2004, first under the name Wildfire and then (after trademark issues arose) as Openfire. The server is very easy to install, runs on both Windows and Unix systems, and is especially popular with small to midsize businesses and universities. Language: Java. License: GPL. Website: *http://www.igniterealtime.org/projects/openfire/*.

Prosody

Prosody is a relatively new codebase written in the Lua programming language. The Prosody team is focusing on simplicity for server administrators (e.g., ease of installation, minimal hardware requirements) and flexibility for developers (e.g., the ability to rapidly protocol new features). Language: Lua. License: MIT. Website: *http://prosody.im/*.

Tigase

The Tigase server, primary developed by Artur Hefczyc, is becoming very popular with companies that want a scalable but accessible codebase. The server is quite feature-complete, including support for PubSub and other advanced XMPP extensions. Language: Java. License: GPL. Website: *http://www.tigase.org/*.

In addition to the foregoing, there are a number of less popular open source servers, as well as commercial servers sold by the likes of Cisco, Isode, and Sun Microsystems. Because the XMPP community has less direct experience with these servers, it is difficult to review them here. However, that doesn't mean they won't meet your needs, so be sure to check the complete list of servers at *http://xmpp.org*.

Clients

There are dozens and dozens of XMPP clients in existence—this section describes only a small sample. For ease of reference, we list code clients by computing platform, not the name of the client. Except where noted, these clients are open source, and in all cases, they can be freely downloaded or come bundled with an existing operating system.

Cross-Platform (Linux, Mac OS X, Windows)

Coccinella

The Coccinella client initially started out as a dedicated XMPP client with built-in whiteboarding; the developers have also added support for voice communication via integration with the open source Asterisk system. License: GPL. Website: *http://coccinella.im/*.

Jeti

Jeti is a Java applet that provides XMPP support on a wide variety of computing platforms. The codebase is quite mature and well-supported. License: GPL. Website: *http://jeti.sourceforge.net/*.

Psi

The Psi client traditionally targeted "power users," but these days tries to provide a usable interface for everyone. It has implementations of many of the XMPP extensions, and it provides tools for service administration and exploration of the XMPP network. License: GPL. Website: *http://psi-im.org/*.

Spark

Spark is a business-oriented client, and is closely related to the Openfire server. Besides integration with the Openfire server, it also provides semi-proprietary audio and video communication capabilities. License: LGPL. Website: *http://www.igniterealtime.org/projects/spark/*.

Swift

Swift is a young client developed by two of the authors of this book (Remko and Kevin). The project aim is to build a client entirely driven by user needs, providing an intuitive interface to the most commonly required tasks. Website: *http://swift.im/*.

Tkabber

Few people would say that Tkabber is the prettiest client in the world, but it supports many XMPP extensions and runs on a large number of computing platforms. License: GPL. Website: *http://tkabber.jabber.ru/*.

Linux

Empathy

Empathy reuses the user interface from the Gossip client on top of a flexible framework for desktop integration. The client supports many IM protocols, as well as voice and video chat. License: GPL. Website: *http://live.gnome.org/Empathy*.

Gajim

Gajim is a full-featured, dedicated XMPP client written in Python. It is available in a large number of languages and supports many advanced XMPP features, with a special focus on strong security. License: GPL. Website: *http://gajim.org/*.

Gossip

Gossip is a dedicated XMPP client for the GNOME desktop that puts a premium on being user-friendly for normal users. License: GPL. Website: *http://developer .imendio.com/projects/gossip/*.

Kopete

Kopete is a multiprotocol client for the KDE desktop, which includes good support for XMPP. License: GPL. Website: *http://kopete.kde.org/*.

Pidgin

Pidgin, formerly known as Gaim, is a very popular multiprotocol client for Linux (it can also be built on Windows). Its underlying library, libpurple, is shared with the Adium client for Mac OS X. License: GPL. Website: *http://pidgin.im/*.

Mac OS X

Adium X

Adium X is the most popular multiprotocol IM client for Mac OS. It shares the libpurple library with the Pidgin client, which has good support for most basic (and some advanced) XMPP features. License: GPL. Website: *http://adiumx.com/*.

iChat

iChat is a proprietary IM client that comes free with the Macintosh operating system. It has supported Jabber functionality for several years, originally in serverless messaging mode and then in client-server mode. The client is very user-friendly but deliberately does not support more advanced features, such as chat room configuration or ad-hoc commands. License: Proprietary. Website: *http://www.apple .com/macosx/features/ichat.html*.

Windows

Exodus

Exodus was developed by Peter Millard, one of the early contributors to the Jabber open source community. Since Peter's death in 2006, there have been no new releases of Exodus, but it is still a solid XMPP client. License: GPL. Website: *http://code.google.com/p/exodus/*.

JAJC

JAJC is an ICQ-like client designed to run on any 32-bit Windows machine. License: Proprietary. Website: *http://jajc.jrudevels.org/*.

Miranda IM

Miranda IM is a multiprotocol client designed to be very light on system resources, extremely fast, and customizable. It provides an extensible plug-in architecture, including a plug-in for XMPP functionality. License: GPL. Website: *http://www.miranda-im.org/*.

Pandion

Pandion (formerly RhymBox) is a user-friendly, dedicated XMPP client that is quite popular with end users. License: Proprietary. Website: *http://www.pandion.be/*.

Web Browsers

Claros Chat

Claros Chat is a full-featured Jabber client for the Web, built using Java Server Pages and standard Ajax connectivity. License: GPL. Website: *http://www.claros.org/web/showProduct.do?id=2*.

iJab

The iJab client is completely written in JavaScript, based on the JSJaC library and Google Web Toolkit. License: GPL. Website: *http://code.google.com/p/ijab/*.

Jabbear

Jabbear is a no-download client that works in any web browser and supports a number of XMPP features, including file transfer. License: Proprietary. Website: *http://www.jabbear.com/en/*.

JWChat

JWChat is the longest-running XMPP web client project and is built by the same developers as the JSJaC library. It supports instant messaging, rosters, and multiuser chat via JavaScript and HTML on the client side. License: GPL. Website: *http://blog.jwchat.org/jwchat/*.

SamePlace

SamePlace is an extension to the popular Firefox web browser. It supports instant messaging as well as more advanced collaboration features. License: GPL. Website: *http://www.sameplace.cc/*.

SparkWeb

SparkWeb follows the example of the Spark client by focusing on the needs of business users. It includes support for multi-user chat and strong security. License: GPL. Website: *http://www.igniterealtime.org/projects/sparkweb/*.

TrophyIM

TrophyIM is built using the Strope library and works in all recent browsers. License: MIT. Website: *http://code.google.com/p/trophyim/*.

Libraries

For ease of reference, we list code libraries by language, not the name of the library.

ActionScript

ActionScript is a scripting language used primarily for the development of websites and software using the Flash environment. The only XMPP library for ActionScript is as3xmpp, created by Daniel Dura for ActionScript 3. License: New BSD License. Website: *http://code.google.com/p/as3xmpp/*.

C

The C programming language is one of the most widely used languages in existence. The following are the three main XMPP libraries for C:

iksemel

The iksemel library is a highly portable, low-footprint codebase that supports all core XMPP functionality. The code is quite modular and can be trimmed as needed, making iksemel a good choice for embedded systems and other platforms that require low memory usage and fast performance. The code is stable but not frequently updated. License: LGPL. Website: *http://code.google.com/p/iksemel/*.

Loudmouth

Loudmouth is intended to be easy to use and highly extensible. It is used in the Gossip client and in several other projects. There are also bindings for Ruby. License: GPL. Website: *http://groups.google.com/group/loudmouth-dev*.

Strophe

Strophe is a well-documented library for developing XMPP clients, including robust TLS and SASL support. Strophe comes in two flavors: C (libstrophe) and JavaScript (strophejs). License: GPL. Website: *http://code.stanziq.com/strophe/*.

C++

C++ is a powerful, general-purpose, object-oriented programming language that has long been quite popular with software developers in a wide variety of domains. There are two main C++ libraries for XMPP development:

gloox
> The gloox library is a very solid, well-documented, full-featured C++ library. It is designed to be easy to use, extensible, and platform independent. License: GPL/Commercial. Website: *http://camaya.net/gloox*.

Iris
> Iris is a Qt/C++ library that includes support for all core XMPP protocols and a number of extensions. License: GPL/Commercial. Website: *http://delta.affinix.com/iris/*.

C#

C# is a simple, modern, general-purpose, object-oriented programming language developed by Microsoft. With a syntax heavily influenced by C++, Delphi, and Java, as well as broad support in Windows tools and the .NET Framework, C# has become a popular choice for many developers. The following are the primary open source libraries:

agsXMPP
> agsXMPP is an SDK that can be used for client, component, and server development. License: GPL/Commercial. Website: *http://www.ag-software.de/*.

jabber-net
> The jabber-net library provides a set of .NET controls for sending and receiving XMPP data. It includes support for client connections, server components, presence, service discovery, and other XMPP primitives. License: LGPL. Website: *http://code.google.com/p/jabber-net/*.

Flash

Flash is a software environment for building rich web interfaces, and its two main libraries are:

TwhiX
> TwhiX is an XMPP library for Flash 9+ using an event-driven style. It supports the core XMPP protocols (including encrypted connections), and additional extensions can be added through its plug-in-based architecture. License: Apache 2.0. Website: *http://code.google.com/p/twhix/*.

XIFF

> XIFF is the longest-established XMPP library for Flash. It supports the core XMPP protocols and a number of extensions. License: LGPL. Website: *http://www.igni terealtime.org/projects/xiff/*.

Java

Java is a general purpose, object-oriented programming language developed by Sun Microsystems. Although originally developed for client-side applications, it is also quite popular in servers and general applications. Its two main libraries are:

JSO

> The Jabber Stream Objects (JSO) library is a solid implementation that is mainly used for component and server development. It includes low-level support for Jabber/XMPP protocol elements, as well as a fully controllable stream connection interface, with the goal of providing a highly customizable and flexible platform for building Jabber-based applications. License: LGPL. Website: *https://jso.dev .java.net/*.

Smack

> Smack is a very popular, full-featured library for writing clients, bots, and other applications. It was produced by the same developers who created the Openfire server and the Spark client. License: Apache. Website: *http://www.igniterealtime .org/projects/smack/*.

JavaScript

JavaScript is the most popular scripting language for client-side web development. Because the integration of Jabber features into websites is of inherent interest, there are many JavaScript libraries for XMPP development, as listed here:

JSJaC

> JSJaC is an object-oriented library that supports client connections to XMPP servers via BOSH or the older HTTP Polling method. It uses the Ajax methodology and is fully compatible with all major Ajax/JavaScript frameworks. License: Mozilla Public License or GPL or LGPL. Website: *http://blog.jwchat.org/jsjac/*.

Strophe

> Strophe is a well-documented library for developing XMPP clients, including robust TLS and SASL support. Strophe comes in two flavors: C (libstrophe) and JavaScript (strophejs). License: GPL. Website: *http://code.stanziq.com/strophe/*.

XMPP4GWT

> The XMPP4GWT library is created by the producers of the Tigase XMPP server and uses the Google Web Toolkit (GWT) framework. License: GPLv3. Website: *http://www.tigase.org/en/project/xmpp4gwt*.

xmpp4js
> The xmpp4js library is used in the Soashable web-based messenger. It has been heavily tested and has a strong emphasis on reusability and extensibility. License: LGPL. Website: *http://xmpp4js.sourceforge.net/*.

Perl

Perl is a high-level, general-purpose, interpreted, dynamic programming language. It is still very popular for scripting and even application development (e.g., the djabberd server is written in Perl). Its two main libraries are:

AnyEvent::XMPP
> AnyEvent::XMPP (formerly Net::XMPP2) is an event-driven Perl library that offers support for the core XMPP RFCs and a significant number of XMPP extensions. Website: *http://www.ta-sa.org/projects/net_xmpp2.html*.

Net::XMPP
> Net::XMPP is an updated version of Net::Jabber, the original Perl library for Jabber written by Ryan Eatmon (one of the earliest developers in the Jabber open source community). Website: *http://www.ta-sa.org/projects/net_xmpp2.html*.

PHP

PHP is a popular scripting language for building dynamic websites. There are two main PHP libraries for XMPP development:

Lightr
> Lightr is an XMPP client that is intended to be run by an Ajax-enabled frontend and therefore functions as a library for Web/Jabber integration. License: BSD. Website: *https://area51.myyearbook.com/trac.cgi/wiki/Lightr*.

XMPPPHP
> XMPPPHP is a successor to the older Class.Jabber.PHP project. It supports all of the core XMPP functionality, including TLS encryption. License: GPL. Website: *http://code.google.com/p/xmpphp/*.

Python

Python is a dynamic, object-oriented programming language that is widely used for scripting and software development. There are many XMPP libraries for Python, but here are the most active projects:

PyXMPP
> PyXMPP is a stable library developed by Jacek Konieczny. The library provides solid support for the core XMPP RFCs and a number of XMPP extensions (service discovery, vCards, data forms, etc.). It can be used to create both clients and server components. License: LGPL. Website: *http://pyxmpp.jajcus.net/*.

SleekXMPP

SleekXMPP is primarily developed by Nathan Fritz and is used in Chapter 14 of this book as the basis for application development. The library is fairly recent but has strong support for the XMPP RFCs, as well as the XEPs that are Draft or Final. License: GPL. Website: *http://code.google.com/p/sleekxmpp/*.

Twisted

Twisted is an event-driven networking engine that has support for just about every network protocol in existence, including XMPP. Although Twisted has been used for some client development, its forte is component development, and it is even being used as the basis for an XMPP server daemon. License: MIT. Website: *http://twistedmatrix.com/*.

xmpppy

The xmpppy library focuses on scripting with XMPP. It inherits some code from the older jabber.py library and has been used to write both bots and server components. License: GPL. Website: *http://xmpppy.sourceforge.net/*.

Ruby

Ruby is a dynamic, reflective, object-oriented programming language that focuses on simplicity and productivity. Its two main libraries are:

XMPP4R

The primary XMPP library for Ruby is XMPP4R, an event-based codebase that aims to be fully XMPP compliant, with support for the XMPP RFCs and a number of XEPs. The code is well-documented and the developers use unit tests to ensure stability. License: Ruby License (GPL-compatible). Website: *http://home.gna.org/xmpp4r/*.

xmpp4r-simple

xmpp4r-simple is a stripped-down version of XMPP4R, which is easier for developers to use in building simple Ruby applications. License: Ruby License (GPL-compatible). Website: *http://code.google.com/p/xmpp4r-simple/*.

Further Practical Considerations

This appendix provides a few tips that can help you along the path of learning about, implementing, and deploying XMPP applications.

Getting Started

A good way to start your experiments with XMPP technologies is to download a client, create an account at one of the public XMPP servers, and explore some of the chat rooms, bots, and other resources available on the network. Here's how:

1. Visit *http://xmpp.org* and follow the links to the client software page, where you can find XMPP clients for just about every computing platform imaginable. Almost all of these clients can be downloaded without charge ("free as in beer"), and many of them are also open source ("free as in speech") so that you can inspect the source code to see how they work.

2. You might already have an XMPP account but you just don't know it (for example, an existing Gmail or Live Journal account also functions as an XMPP account). If not, you can create an account at the jabber.org IM service or any one of the hundreds of public XMPP servers.

3. Once you have logged in to your account, join the primary developer chat room on the XMPP network: `jdev@conference.jabber.org`. The coders in this room can always provide helpful pointers to the latest news and developments related to Jabber/XMPP technologies. They can also help you think through the design processes involved in building your own XMPP applications, so make the jdev room your first port of call on the network.

If you like what you see, you might consider running your own XMPP server, because it's easier to debug your code if you have access to both sides of an XML stream. Your server can start out as a private deployment (not connected to the public XMPP network) while you work out the kinks, but it is also straightforward to federate your server if you so please. Visit the server download page at *http://xmpp.org* to experiment with deploying your own XMPP service.

Finally, if you get more deeply interested in contributing to the XMPP community, you'll want to find a project you can help out with (e.g., one of the open source clients, servers, or libraries) and join one of the busy email discussion lists hosted by the XSF (there is a complete inventory of these lists at *http://xmpp.org*).

Debugging Tools

When you are developing an application, it's handy to have good debugging tools. Some of the most useful tools XMPP developers have are those that observe and manipulate the underlying XML stream. In the olden days before support for TLS and SASL became widespread, one way to work with client-to-server streams was to simply telnet to a server on port 5222, copy and paste in the authorization elements using *Non-SASL Authentication* [XEP-0078], and directly control the stream by typing raw XML. An example of a telnet session is shown in Example C-1, using non-SASL authentication over an unencrypted stream (not recommended except for experimentation!).

Example C-1. Good old-fashioned telnet enables you to experiment with XMPP sessions

```
$ telnet wonderland.lit 5222
Trying 192.0.2.1...
Connected to wonderland.lit.
Escape character is "^]".

<stream:stream to="wonderland.lit" xmlns="jabber:client"
            xmlns:stream="http://etherx.jabber.org/streams">

<stream:stream from="wonderland.lit" id="B7392AAOBX" xmlns="jabber:client"
            xmlns:stream="http://etherx.jabber.org/streams">

<iq id="a1" type="get">
  <query xmlns="jabber:iq:auth">
    <username>alice</username>
  </query>
</iq>

<iq id="a1" type="result">
  <query xmlns="jabber:iq:auth">
    <username/>
    <password/>
    <digest/>
    <resource/>
  </query>
</iq>

<iq id="a2" type="set">
  <query xmlns="jabber:iq:auth">
    <username>alice</username>
    <resource>telnet</resource>
    <password>rabbitsrock</password>
  </query>
```

```
</iq>

<iq id="a2" type="result"/>

<presence/>

<presence from="alice@wonderland.lit/telnet" to="alice@wonderland.lit/telnet"/>

<message from="alice@wonderland.lit/telnet" to="sister@realworld.lit" type="chat">
  <body>Help, I fell down the rabbit hole!</body>
</message>

<presence type="unavailable"/>

<presence from="alice@wonderland.lit/telnet"
          to="alice@wonderland.lit/telnet" type="unavailable"/>
</stream:steam>
```

These days, less primitive methods exist. One approach is to use a command-line script such as sendxmpp, although this does not necessarily show you the complete XML. Another approach is to use one of the many XMPP clients that provide an *XML Console*. A sample is shown in Figure C-1; as you can see, such an XML console enables you to observe the incoming and outgoing stanzas, and to send new stanzas directly. Some clients even keep a ringbuffer of recent stanzas so that you can recover interesting stanzas after the event.

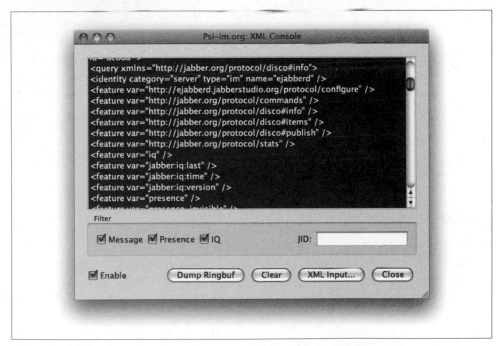

Figure C-1. The Psi client's XML console can be used to view the XML streams

As well as viewing the incoming and outgoing streams, these XML consoles allow you to inject stanzas into the outgoing stream directly, as in Figure C-2. To avoid the server disconnecting you due to typing mistakes, some XML consoles will even warn you of XML errors in your stanza before you send it.

Figure C-2. The Psi client's XML console allows you to send XML stanzas in the stream manually— even XML that will cause you to be disconnected!

The XML console is most useful for developers building client-to-server applications. For server-to-server development, most XMPP daemons can be run in debug mode so that you can view the stanzas that are sent to and from the server (this can also be very helpful for client-to-server development so that you can see both the output of your client and what a given server implementation does with the stanzas you send). For more challenging debugging tasks (e.g., related to UTF-8 encoding of non-ASCII characters, as described in [RFC 3629]), a network protocol analyzer such as Wireshark can also prove quite useful.

Network Setup

When the time comes to deploy an XMPP service on the network, you probably want it to be accessible to as wide an audience as possible. If your service is using standard XMPP ports as registered with the Internet Assigned Numbers Authority (IANA), that means exposing port 5222 if you want to allow client-to-server access and port 5269 if you want to allow server-to-server access. Depending on deployment scenarios and access policies, you might want to host this machine in the "DMZ" of your organization's network, or behind the firewall.

Deployment of an XMPP-based service also requires proper configuration of Domain Name System (DNS) settings. Although standard "A" and "AAAA" lookups are a fallback method for IPv4 and IPv6 respectively, the preferred method is to define DNS Service (SRV) records. SRV records are similar to the MX records used for email servers, except that they can be used by any application type. The SRV records for XMPP enable you to specify exactly which machine or machines a client or server should connect to in order to reach the XMPP service for your domain.

To specify an XMPP service for client-to-server connectivity at the wonderland.lit domain, you would define one or more SRV records for the _xmpp-client._tcp.wonderland.lit service. For example, if you have two different machines (x1 and x2) that handle client-to-server traffic, you would define two SRV records, such as the following:

```
_xmpp-client._tcp.wonderland.lit. 86400 IN SRV 10 10 5222 x1.wonderland.lit
_xmpp-client._tcp.wonderland.lit. 86400 IN SRV 10 5 5222 x2.wonderland.lit
```

To specify an XMPP service that enables server-to-server connectivity, you would define one or more SRV records for the _xmpp-server._tcp.wonderland.lit service. For example, if you have a special machine s2s.wonderland.lit that handles your server-to-server traffic, you would define one SRV record, such as the following:

```
_xmpp-server._tcp.wonderland.lit. 86400 IN SRV 10 5 5269 s2s.wonderland.lit
```

If your XMPP service includes add-on components (e.g., multi-user chat rooms) that need to be accessed by users from other domains, you will also need to define xmpp-server SRV records for those components; this enables SRV lookups for the purpose of server-to-server connectivity (e.g., to be used in a server dialback negotiation). For example, if you host MUC rooms at conference.wonderland.lit, then you would probably define an SRV record for s2s connectivity using the same host you defined for normal server-to-server traffic, as follows:

```
_xmpp-server._tcp.conference.wonderland.lit. 86400 IN SRV 10 5 5269 s2s.wonderland.lit
```

Glossary

Authentication

In computer systems, authentication is the act or process of establishing that someone or something is what they claim to be. In XMPP, authentication most often occurs when a server confirms that a connecting client has the proper credentials to establish a session on behalf of a registered account (these credentials usually take the form of a username and password, but can also be a digital certificate, a shared secret, or a temporary token). Authentication can also occur between two peer servers based on the use of digital certificates issued by a common certification authority. The original authentication method used in the XMPP community [XEP-0078] has been superseded by use of the Simple Authentication and Security Layer (SASL), defined in [RFC 4422].

Bare JID

XMPP developers often use the term "bare JID" to refer to a JabberID of the form `user@domain.tld`, in contrast to a "full JID" of the form `user@domain.tld/resource`.

BOSH

BOSH (Bidrectional-stream Over Synchronous HTTP) is an alternative HTTP binding for XMPP traffic between a client and a server, which uses a paired sequence of HTTP requests and responses to mimic the bidirectional XML streams used over the standard TCP binding. BOSH is used mainly by web clients and mobile devices that cannot maintain long-lived TCP connections.

Bot

A bot is an automated entity that typically connects to a server as a client and then provides services to human users and other bots, either directly or in a chat room.

Client

A client is an entity that authenticates with a server to access the network, typically by providing credentials associated with an account registered on the server. A client need not be controlled by a human user and might be an automated entity, such as a bot.

Component

Most XMPP servers are written in a modular fashion that enables server administrators to provide extended features by adding a server-side component to the XMPP router itself. Such components are typically used to provide multi-user chat rooms, gateways or "transports" to legacy IM systems, and other specialized functionality.

Dialback

The server dialback protocol provides a way for a server that receives a connection from an originating peer to "call back" the authoritative server based on a DNS lookup for the domain name asserted by the originating server. Dialback results in weak identity verification and is commonly used on the XMPP network to help prevent address spoofing.

Encryption

In information security, encryption is the conversion of data into a form that cannot be accessed or understood by unauthorized entities (thus ensuring the *confidentiality* of information but not necessarily its authenticity or integrity). In XMPP, encryption comes in two flavors. Channel encryption provides data confidentiality for an XML stream between a client and a server or between two servers, but does not encrypt the data while it is processed by a server; in XMPP this is accomplished through an XMPP profile of the Transport Layer Security (TLS) protocol that is defined in [RFC 5246]. Several XMPP technologies for end-to-end encryption have been proposed over the years (including OpenPGP, S/MIME, XML Encryption, in-band Diffie-Hellman key exchange, and end-to-end TLS), but as of this writing, none has yet gained overwhelming consensus among XMPP developers.

Federation

XMPP servers connect to each other dynamically based on DNS lookups and either server dialback or domain certificates issued by trusted certification authorities. This ad-hoc connection model is similar to the model used on the email network and does not require the kind of formal peering agreements that are common on traditional telecommunication networks.

Full JID

XMPP developers often use the term "full JID" to refer to a JabberID of the form `user@domain.tld/resource`, in contrast to a "bare JID" of the form `user@domain.tld`.

Gateway

A gateway is a server-side component that provides connectivity and protocol translation between an XMPP system and a non-XMPP system, such as SIP/SIMPLE or Internet Relay Chat (IRC), or a closed communications silo, such as AOL Instant Messenger (AIM), ICQ, Windows Live Messenger, or Yahoo! Instant Messenger.

Gateways (also called "transports") were important in the early days of the Jabber open source community but have become much less important over the years as more organizations have deployed native XMPP systems.

IQ

The IQ stanza is one of the three top-level elements that can be sent over an XML stream. The different IQ types enable structured interaction between XMPP entities; specifically, an IQ stanza of type `get` is similar to the HTTP GET method, and an IQ stanza of type `set` is similar to the HTTP POST and PUT methods.

Jabber Identifier (JID)

An XMPP address as used natively by clients, servers, components, and other entities; it is fully internationalized and is typically of the form `domain.tld` (for a server or service), `node@domain.tld` (for an account, bot, or chat room), or `user@domain.tld/resource` (for a connected client or device).

Message

The IQ stanza is one of the three top-level elements that can be sent over an XML stream. It provides a "fire-and-forget" mechanism for pushing information from one entity to another, similar to an email or SMS message.

Multi-User Chat (MUC)

An XMPP extension (defined in XEP-0045) for multi-party information exchange, similar to Internet Relay Chat (IRC). Typically MUC is used for textual chat, but there are no restrictions on the information that can be passed through an MUC room.

Personal Eventing Protocol (PEP)

A profile of Publish-Subscribe (defined in XEP-0163) that enables a user account to function as a virtual pubsub service by integrating standard XMPP presence and roster semantics into publish-subscribe routing and access decisions.

Presence

Presence is information about the network availability of an entity. In XMPP, presence information is typically shared only with entities that have an explicit subscription to that information. The presence stanza is one of the three top-level elements that can be sent over an XML stream.

Publish-Subscribe (PubSub)

An XMPP extension (defined in XEP-0060) for data syndication, alerts and notifications, rich presence, and other use cases that implement the "observer" design pattern.

Resource

In XMPP, a "resource" is a connected device, client, or application that has authenticated for a particular account. An XMPP server will allow multiple simultaneous resources for a given account, up to some configurable limit. A connected resource has an address of the form `user@domain.tld/resource`.

Roster

A roster is a user's contact list, including the state of the user's presence subscription to each contact. The roster is stored on the server so that a user can access it from any device or client.

Server

An XMPP server is the authoritative entity for a given domain (such as example.com). A server typically manages accounts on behalf of users, authenticates connecting clients, enforces local policies such as channel encryption, connects as necessary to other servers, etc.

Service Discovery ("disco")

A method for determining the identity and features of any entity on the network, defined in XEP-0030.

Stanza

The basic unit of meaning in XMPP, formed by the first-level child element of an XML stream. The three stanza types are message, presence, and IQ.

Stream

An XML stream is the dynamic container for all XMPP communication. A client negotiates a stream with a server to gain access to the network, and a server can negotiate a stream with a peer server to enable federated communication among different domains. Many core features (such as authentication and channel encryption) occur at the level of the stream. Once a stream is negotiated, an entity can send an unbounded number of stanzas over the stream.

Bibliography

[DNS-SD] Cheshire, Stuart. Krochmal, Marc. *DNS-Based Service Discovery (http://tools .ietf.org/html/draft-cheshire-dnsext-dns-sd)*.

[mDNS] Cheshire, Stuart. Krochmal, Marc. *Multicast DNS (http://tools.ietf.org/html/ draft-cheshire-dnsext-multicastdns)*.

[RFC 1928] Leech, Marcus. *SOCKS Protocol Version 5 (http://www.ietf.org/rfc/rfc1928 .txt)*.

[RFC 2111] Levinson, Edward. *Content-ID and Message-ID Uniform Resource Locators (http://www.ietf.org/rfc/rfc2111.txt)*.

[RFC 2426] Dawson, Frank. Howes, Tim. *vCard MIME Directory Profile (http://www .ietf.org/rfc/rfc2426.txt)*.

[RFC 2831] Leach, Paul. Newman, Chris. *Using Digest Authentication as a SASL Mechanism (http://www.ietf.org/rfc/rfc2831.txt)*.

[RFC 3454] Hoffman, P. Blanchet, M. *Preparation of Internationalized Strings ("stringprep") (http://www.ietf.org/rfc/rfc3454.txt)*.

[RFC 3629] Yergeau, F. *UTF-8, a transformation format of ISO 10646 (http://www.ietf .org/rfc/rfc3629.txt)*.

[RFC 3920] Saint-Andre, Peter. *Extensible Messaging and Presence Protocol: Core (http: //www.ietf.org/rfc/rfc3920.txt)*.

[rfc3920bis] Saint-Andre, Peter. *Extensible Messaging and Presence Protocol: Core (http: //tools.ietf.org/html/draft-saintandre-rfc3920bis)*.

[RFC 3921] Saint-Andre, Peter. *Extensible Messaging and Presence Protocol: Instant Messaging and Presence (http://www.ietf.org/rfc/rfc3921.txt)*.

[rfc3921bis] Saint-Andre, Peter. *Extensible Messaging and Presence Protocol: Instant Messaging and Presence (http://tools.ietf.org/html/draft-saintandre-rfc3921bis)*.

[RFC 4121] Zhu, Larry. Jaganathan, Karthik. Hartman, Sam. *The Kerberos Version 5 Generic Security Service Application Program Interface (GSS-API) Mechanism: Version 2 (http://www.ietf.org/rfc/rfc4121.txt)*.

[RFC 4287] Nottingham, Mark. Sayre, Robert. *The Atom Syndication Format (http:// www.ietf.org/rfc/rfc4287.txt)*.

[RFC 4422] Melnikov, Alexey. Zeilenga, Kurt. *Simple Authentication and Security Layer (http://www.ietf.org/rfc/rfc4422.txt)*.

[RFC 4505] Zeilenga, Kurt. *Anonymous Simple Authentication and Security Layer (SASL) Mechanism (http://www.ietf.org/rfc/rfc4505.txt)*.

[RFC 4616] Zeilenga, Kurt. *The PLAIN Simple Authentication and Security Layer (SASL) Mechanism (http://www.ietf.org/rfc/rfc4616.txt)*.

[RFC 5122] Saint-Andre, Peter. *Internationalized Resource Identifiers (IRIs) and Uniform Resource Identifiers (URIs) for the Extensible Messaging and Presence Protocol (XMPP) (http://www.ietf.org/rfc/rfc5122.txt)*.

[RFC 5246] Rescorla, Eric. Dierks, Tim. *The Transport Layer Security (TLS) Protocol Version 1.2 (http://www.ietf.org/rfc/rfc5246.txt)*.

[SCRAM] Menon-Sen, Abhijit. Newman, Chris. Melnikov, Alexey. *Salted Challenge Response (SCRAM) SASL Mechanism (http://tools.ietf.org/html/draft-newman-auth -scram-08)*.

[SOAP] Gudgin, Martin. Hadley, Marc. Mendelsohn, Noah. Moreau, Jean-Jacques. Nielsen, Henrik Frystyk. Karmarkar, Anish. Lafon, Yves. *SOAP Version 1.2 Part 1: Messaging Framework (Second Edition) (http://www.w3.org/TR/soap12-part1/)*.

[XEP-0001] Saint-Andre, Peter. *XMPP Extension Protocols (http://xmpp.org/extensions/ xep-0001.html)*.

[XEP-0004] Eatmon, Ryan. Hildebrand, Joe. Miller, Jeremie. Muldowney, Thomas. Saint-Andre, Peter. *Data Forms (http://xmpp.org/extensions/xep-0004.html)*.

[XEP-0009] Adams, DJ. *Jabber-RPC (http://xmpp.org/extensions/xep-0009.html)*.

[XEP-0016] Millard, Peter. Saint-Andre, Peter. *Privacy Lists (http://xmpp.org/exten sions/xep-0016.html)*.

[XEP-0030] Hildebrand, Joe. Millard, Peter. Eatmon, Ryan. Saint-Andre, Peter. *Service Discovery (http://xmpp.org/extensions/xep-0030.html)*.

[XEP-0033] Hildebrand, Joe. Saint-Andre, Peter. *Extended Stanza Addressing (http:// xmpp.org/extensions/xep-0033.html)*.

[XEP-0045] Saint-Andre, Peter. *Multi-User Chat (http://xmpp.org/extensions/xep-0045 .html)*.

[XEP-0047] Karneges, Justin. *In-Band Bytestreams (IBB) (http://xmpp.org/extensions/ xep-0047.html)*.

[XEP-0050] Miller, Matthew. *Ad-Hoc Commands (http://xmpp.org/extensions/xep -0050.html)*.

[XEP-0054] Saint-Andre, Peter. *vcard-temp (http://xmpp.org/extensions/xep-0054 .html)*.

[XEP-0060] Millard, Peter. Saint-Andre, Peter. Meijer, Ralph. *Publish-Subscribe (http: //xmpp.org/extensions/xep-0060.html)*.

[XEP-0065] Smith, Dave. Miller, Matthew. Saint-Andre, Peter. *SOCKS5 Bytestreams (http://xmpp.org/extensions/xep-0065.html)*.

[XEP-0068] Hildebrand, Joe. Saint-Andre, Peter. *Field Standardization for Data Forms (http://xmpp.org/extensions/xep-0068.html)*.

[XEP-0071] Saint-Andre, Peter. *XHTML-IM (http://xmpp.org/extensions/xep-0071 .html)*.

[XEP-0072] Forno, Fabio. Saint-Andre, Peter. *SOAP Over XMPP (http://xmpp.org/ex tensions/xep-0072.html)*.

[XEP-0077] Saint-Andre, Peter. *In-Band Registration (http://xmpp.org/extensions/xep -0077.html)*.

[XEP-0078] Saint-Andre, Peter. *Non-SASL Authentication (http://xmpp.org/extensions/ xep-0078.html)*.

[XEP-0079] Miller, Matthew. Saint-Andre, Peter. *Advanced Message Processing (http:// xmpp.org/extensions/xep-0079.html)*.

[XEP-0080] Hildebrand, Joe. Saint-Andre, Peter. *User Location (http://xmpp.org/exten sions/xep-0080.html)*.

[XEP-0084] Saint-Andre, Peter. Millard, Peter. Muldowney, Thomas. Missig, Julian. *User Avatar (http://xmpp.org/extensions/xep-0084.html)*.

[XEP-0085] Saint-Andre, Peter. Smith, Dave. *Chat State Notifications (http://xmpp.org/ extensions/xep-0085.html)*.

[XEP-0086] Norris, Robert. Saint-Andre, Peter. *Error Condition Mappings (http://xmpp .org/extensions/xep-0086.html)*.

[XEP-0094] Saint-Andre, Peter. *Agent Information (http://xmpp.org/extensions/xep -0094.html)*.

[XEP-0095] Muldowney, Thomas. Miller, Matthew. Eatmon, Ryan. *Stream Initiation (http://xmpp.org/extensions/xep-0095.html)*.

[XEP-0096] Muldowney, Thomas. Miller, Matthew. Eatmon, Ryan. *SI File Transfer (http://xmpp.org/extensions/xep-0096.html)*.

[XEP-0107] Saint-Andre, Peter. Meijer, Ralph. *User Mood (http://xmpp.org/extensions/ xep-0107.html)*.

[XEP-0108] Meijer, Ralph. Saint-Andre, Peter. *User Activity (http://xmpp.org/exten sions/xep-0108.html)*.

[XEP-0114] Saint-Andre, Peter. *Jabber Component Protocol (http://xmpp.org/exten sions/xep-0114.html)*.

[XEP-0115] Hildebrand, Joe. Saint-Andre, Peter. Tronçon, Remko. Konieczny, Jacek. *Entity Capabilities (http://xmpp.org/extensions/xep-0115.html)*.

[XEP-0118] Saint-Andre, Peter. *User Tune (http://xmpp.org/extensions/xep-0118.html)*.

[XEP-0124] Paterson, Ian. Smith, Dave. Saint-Andre, Peter. *Bidirectional-streams Over Synchronous HTTP (BOSH) (http://xmpp.org/extensions/xep-0124.html)*.

[XEP-0127] Saint-Andre, Peter. Fletcher, Boyd. *Common Alerting Protocol (CAP) Over XMPP (http://xmpp.org/extensions/xep-0127.html)*.

[XEP-0128] Saint-Andre, Peter. *Service Discovery Extensions (http://xmpp.org/exten sions/xep-0128.html)*.

[XEP-0133] Saint-Andre, Peter. *Service Administration (http://xmpp.org/extensions/xep -0133.html)*.

[XEP-0134] Saint-Andre, Peter. *Protocol Design Guidelines (http://xmpp.org/extensions/ xep-0134.html)*.

[XEP-0136] Paterson, Ian. Perlow, Jon. Saint-Andre, Peter. Karneges, Justin. *Message Archiving (http://xmpp.org/extensions/xep-0136.html)*.

[XEP-0138] Hildebrand, Joe. Saint-Andre, Peter. *Stream Compression (http://xmpp.org/ extensions/xep-0138.html)*.

[XEP-0143] Saint-Andre, Peter. *Guidelines for Authors of XMPP Extension Protocols (http://xmpp.org/extensions/xep-0143.html)*.

[XEP-0146] Tronçon, Remko. Saint-Andre, Peter. *Remote Controlling Clients (http:// xmpp.org/extensions/xep-0146.html)*.

[XEP-0147] Saint-Andre, Peter. *XMPP URI Scheme Query Components (http://xmpp .org/extensions/xep-0147.html)*.

[XEP-0156] Hildebrand, Joe. Saint-Andre, Peter. *Discovering Alternative XMPP Con- nection Methods (http://xmpp.org/extensions/xep-0156.html)*.

[XEP-0158] Paterson, Ian. Saint-Andre, Peter. *CAPTCHA Forms (http://xmpp.org/ex tensions/xep-0158.html)*.

[XEP-0163] Saint-Andre, Peter. Smith, Kevin. *Personal Eventing Protocol (http://xmpp .org/extensions/xep-0163.html)*.

[XEP-0166] Ludwig, Scott. Beda, Joe. Saint-Andre, Peter. McQueen, Robert. Egan, Sean. Hildebrand, Joe. *Jingle (http://xmpp.org/extensions/xep-0166.html)*.

[XEP-0167] Ludwig, Scott. Saint-Andre, Peter. Egan, Sean. McQueen, Robert. Cio- noiu, Diana. *Jingle RTP Sessions (http://xmpp.org/extensions/xep-0167.html)*.

[XEP-0172] Saint-Andre, Peter. Mercier, Valerie. *User Nickname (http://xmpp.org/ex tensions/xep-0172.html)*.

[XEP-0174] Saint-Andre, Peter. *Serverless Messaging (http://xmpp.org/extensions/xep -0174.html)*.

[XEP-0176] Beda, Joe. Ludwig, Scott. Saint-Andre, Peter. Hildebrand, Joe. Egan, Sean. *Jingle ICE-UDP Transport Method (http://xmpp.org/extensions/xep-0176.html)*.

[XEP-0177] Beda, Joe. Saint-Andre, Peter. Ludwig, Scott. Hildebrand, Joe. Egan, Sean. *Jingle Raw UDP Transport Method (http://xmpp.org/extensions/xep-0177.html)*.

[XEP-0184] Saint-Andre, Peter. Hildebrand, Joe. *Message Receipts (http://xmpp.org/ extensions/xep-0184.html)*.

[XEP-0191] Saint-Andre, Peter. *Simple Communications Blocking (http://xmpp.org/ex tensions/xep-0191.html)*.

[XEP-0203] Saint-Andre, Peter. *Delayed Delivery (http://xmpp.org/extensions/xep-0203 .html)*.

[XEP-0205] Saint-Andre, Peter. *Best Practices to Discourage Denial of Service Attacks (http://xmpp.org/extensions/xep-0205.html)*.

[XEP-0206] Paterson, Ian. Saint-Andre, Peter. *XMPP Over BOSH (http://xmpp.org/ex tensions/xep-0206.html)*.

[XEP-0207] Saint-Andre, Peter. *XMPP Eventing via Pubsub (http://xmpp.org/extensions/ xep-0207.html)*.

[XEP-0221] Paterson, Ian. Saint-Andre, Peter. *Data Forms Media Element (http://xmpp .org/extensions/xep-0221.html)*.

[XEP-0225] Saint-Andre, Peter. *Component Connections (http://xmpp.org/extensions/ xep-0225.html)*.

[XEP-0231] Saint-Andre, Peter. Šimerda, Pavel. *Bits of Binary (http://xmpp.org/exten sions/xep-0231.html)*.

[XEP-0234] Saint-Andre, Peter. *Jingle File Transfer (http://xmpp.org/extensions/xep -0234.html)*.

[XEP-0244] Wagener, Johannes. Willighagen, Egon. Heusler, Andreas. Markmann, Tobias. Spjuth, Ola. *IO Data (http://xmpp.org/extensions/xep-0244.html)*.

[XEP-0248] Saint-Andre, Peter. Meijer, Ralph. *PubSub Collection Nodes (http://xmpp .org/extensions/xep-0248.html)*.

[XML-RPC] Winer, Dave. *XML-RPC Specification (http://www.xmlrpc.com/spec)*.

Index

Symbols

<starttls/> command, 173

A

"AAAA" lookups, 166, 177, 267
access control, 43
access_model option (PubSub), 111
action attribute
    ad-hoc commands, 155
    Jingle, 125
<active/> element (chat state notifications), 50
Ad-Hoc Commands, 153, 236
<address/> element (extended stanza addressing), 155
address spoofing, 12
addresses, 14–16
    presence priorities and, 36
    XMPP accounts, 15
addressing (PubSub), 98
admin affiliation (MUC), 85
admins (MUC), 81
Advanced Message Processing (see AMP)
affiliations (MUC), 84
"Agent Information", 61
Ajax, 17
allowinvites option (MUC), 89
AMP (Advanced Message Processing), 21, 58, 237
annotations, 241
ANONYMOUS mechanism (SASL), 172
anonymous room type (MUC), 91
application types, 124
Application-Specific Error Conditions, 244

applications, 5–7
    building, 211
architecture, 11–14
ASCII characters in resource identifiers, 15
asynchronicity (stanzas), 24
Atom data, 92
attention, 247
audio, 124, 242, 246
authentication, 4, 12, 194
    SASL, 25, 169, 175
authoritative servers (dialback), 175, 177, 178
authorize access model (PubSub), 112
auto-creation feature (PubSub), 107
"availability status", 35
avatars, 238
away value (<show/> element), 35

B

ban commands (MUC), 82
bans, 81, 84
bare JIDs, 15, 36
Base64-encoded data, 138
Bidirectional-streams Over Synchronous HTTP (see BOSH)
binary data, 137–152
Bits of Binary (see BOB)
<block/> element (communications blocking), 56
blocking communications, 55
    advanced, 57
BOB (Bits of Binary), 137, 247
bookmarks, 236
boolean value, for <field/> type attribute, 70
BOSH (Bidirectional-streams Over Synchronous HTTP), 180–189, 240

We'd like to hear your suggestions for improving our indexes. Send email to *index@oreilly.com*.

XMPP Over BOSH, 246
bots, 25, 203
broadcasts (presence), 37

C

element (entity capabilities), 66
c2s (client-to-server), 166, 174
element (Jingle), 128
CAP (Common Alerting Protocol), 240
capabilities advertisement, 5
CAPTCHA (Completely Automated Public
    Turing Test to Tell Computers and
    Humans Apart), 71, 137, 242
element (data forms), 72
Cascading Style Sheets (CSS), 53
case folding (addresses), 16
case-insensitivity of JIDs, 15
CCS (Cascading Style Sheets), 53
changesubject option (MUC), 89
channels (Jingle), 124
chat sessions, 46, 47
    notifications, 48–52
chat states, 49
chat value (element), 35
cid: URL, 138
client extensions, 203
client sessions, 165
client-server architecture, 11
client-to-server (c2s), 166
clients
    controlling, 153–160
    list of, 255–258
    service discovery, using with, 64–68
cloud computing, 6, 200
CM (connection managers), 181
collection nodes (PubSub), 114
collection option, 111
Comet, 17, 180
element (ad-hoc commands),
    163
commands (remote), 153–164
Common Alerting Protocol (CAP), 240
communication blocking, 55
    advanced, 57
communication primitives, 18–25
Completely Automated Public Turing Test to
    Tell Computers and Humans Apart
    (CAPTCHA), 72, 137, 242
compliance suites, 250

Component Connections, 247
components, 201
    servers, 14
        modules, 78
element (chat state
        notifications), 50
connection managers (CM), 181
connection methods, 165–196
contact lists, 4
    rosters, 32
content-add action (Jingle), 135
content-modify action (Jingle), 135
content-remove action (Jingle), 135
create-and-configure feature (PubSub), 108
crowd control (MUC), 81–85, 91
custom commands, providing, 160–163

D

data forms, 5, 69–75, 86, 153, 234
    commands and, 156–160
    protocol, 87
    using, 71–73
    validation, 240
Data Forms Layout, 241
data storage via Publish-Subscribe, 246, 247
data streams, 139
data syndication, 6
datagram transport method, 127
dates, 238
debugging tools, 264
deferred extensions, 233
element (presence), 35
Delayed Delivery, 246
deliver_notifications option (PubSub), 111
deliver_payloads option (PubSub), 111
denial of service attacks, 246
deprecated extensions, 233
element (Jingle), 125
description-info action (Jingle), 135
descriptions of files, 149
Dialback Key Generation and Validation, 244
DIGEST-MD5 mechanism (SASL), 168
direct federation model, 13
Direct MUC Invitations, 248
directed presence, 37
    going offline and, 38
    groupchat and, 79
"disco" (see service discovery)
disco#info method, 59–61

Jingle ICE-UDP Transport, 132
Jingle Raw UDP Transport, 128

K

kick command (MUC), 82

L

lang option (MUC), 90
Language Translation, 243
Last Activity, 234
Last Activity in Presence, 249
leaf nodes (PubSub), 114
libraries, list of, 258–262
list-multi value, for <field/> type attribute, 71
list-single value, for <field/> type attribute, 71
Location Query, 249
LZW compression, 247

M

machine-to-machine communication, 200
maxusers option (MUC), 90
max_items option (PubSub), 111
max_payload_size option (PubSub), 111
/me command, 248
element (data forms), 75, 246
media sessions, setting up, 132
media, including in data forms, 74
mediated data, 124
member affiliation (MUC), 84
members-only rooms (MUC), 85
membersonly option (MUC), 90
Message Archiving, 241
Message Mine-ing, 249
Message Receipts, 244
stanza, 16, 18–19, 56, 101, 247
message threads, 246
messaging extensions, 58
metacontacts, 246
middleware, 6
Miller, Jeremie, xiii, 7, 9, 201
moderated rooms (MUC), 85
moderatedroom option (MUC), 90
moderator role (MUC), 85
moderators (MUC), 81
MUC (Multi-User Chat), 77–93
    data transports and, 92
    Direct MUC Invitations, 248
    nicknames and, 85–87

multi-party interactions, 77–93
multi-party messaging, 4
Multi-User Chat, 235 (see MUC)
multiple hops (networks), 13

N

NATs (Network Address Translators), 131
negotiation (Jingle), 124
nested avatar, 238
Nested Roster Groups, 238
Network Address Translators (NATs), 131
networks (servers), 12
nicknames (MUC), 85–87
nodes (PubSub)
    discovering, 104–107
    management, 107–117
    managing access, 112–114
    payloads, 102
node_type option (PubSub), 111
non-SASL authentication, 237, 264
normal messages, 46
element (error handling), 56
notification-only nodes (PubSub), 102
notifications service, 4
notify_config option (PubSub), 111
notify_delete option (PubSub), 111
notify_retract option (PubSub), 111
notify_sub option (PubSub), 111

O

OAuth Over XMPP, 248
obsolete extensions, 233
"offline messages", 38, 46
one-to-one messaging, 4
open access model (PubSub), 112
open rooms (MUC), 85
open source, 8
    clients, 255–258
    libraries, 258–262
    servers, 253–254
OpenPGP, 194
element (stream features), 168
out-of-band, 142–145, 237
outcast affiliation (MUC), 84
outcast, changing affiliations to, 83
owner affiliation (MUC), 85

P

participant role (MUC), 84

passwords, 168
    authentication options and, 171
    encryption and, 172

element (chat state notification), 51

payload-included nodes, 102

element (Jingle), 128

payloads (PubSub), 102

peer reflexive candidate type (Jingle), 133

peer-to-peer, 124

peer-to-peer media sessions, 5

"peering" models, 175

PEP (Personal Eventing Protocol), 43, 117, 242

persistent nodes (PubSub), 103

persistentroom option (MUC), 90

persist_items option (PubSub), 111

personal eventing, 117–122

Personal Eventing Protocol (see PEP)

PGP (Pretty Good Privacy), 194, 249

PLAIN mechanism (SASL), 168
    authentication options, 171

"point of presence", 15

POKE (Presence Obtained via Kinesthetic Excitation), 250

polling systems, 95

POP, 11

port 443, 173

port 5222, 166, 264

port 5223, 173

port 80, 173

presence, 4, 11, 31–44
    explicit service discovery and, 64
    instant messaging, 5
    PEP and, 118
    publish-subscribe model, 96
    PubSub extension and, 117
    service discovery, 64
    using, 42–44

presence access model (PubSub), 112

presence leaks, 73

presence notifications, 33

Presence Obtained via Kinesthetic Excitation (POKE), 250

presence priorities, 36

presence probes, 34

presence sessions, 38

stanza, 16, 19, 32

presence subscriptions, 20, 31–33

presence-based routing, 42

presencebroadcast option (MUC), 90

presence_based_delivery option (PubSub), 111

Pretty Good Privacy (PGP), 194, 249

element (ad-hoc commands), 161

primitives, 11
    communication, 18–25

priorities, 36
    presence-based routing and, 42

element (presence), 36, 157

privacy, 91

privacy lists, 55, 57, 235

private messages, 81

Private XML Storage, 236

procedural XEP documents, 233

element (Transport Layer Security), 173

proposed extensions, 233

Proposed Resource Binding Improvements, 245

Proposed Stream Feature Improvements, 245

Protocol Design Guidelines, 42, 240

proxies, sending data through, 143–145

Public Key Publishing, 244

publicroom option (MUC), 90, 92

element, 101

publish-subscribe, 28, 59, 93, 95–122, 236
    PubSub extension and, 98

publish-subscribe method, 14, 20, 39

Publishing SI Requests, 241

publish_model option (PubSub), 112

PubSub extension, 96–122
    access schemes, 112
    node management, 107–117
    personal eventing, 117–122
    publishing/receiving notifications, 100
    PubSub Chaining/Queueing, 248
    subscriptions, 98

Q

queries, 241

element, 23

R

Real-time Transport Protocol (RTP), 124

About the Authors

Peter Saint-Andre has been contributing to the Jabber/XMPP developer community since late 1999, where he has focused on technology standardization as author of the XMPP RFCs and numerous XMPP extension protocols. Since 2002, he has also served as executive director of the XMPP Standards Foundation.

Kevin Smith is currently chair of the XMPP Council, having served as a council member since 2006, and is also the coauthor of several XMPP extensions. He was the project leader on the Psi XMPP client for several years, and is now a developer on the Swift client. He holds a Ph.D. from the School of Engineering, Computer Science, and Mathematics at the University of Exeter.

Remko Tronçon, a member of the XMPP Standards Foundation, coauthor of several XMPP protocol extensions, and former lead developer of Psi, is a developer of the Swift Jabber/XMPP project. He holds a Ph.D. in engineering (computer science) from Katholieke Universiteit Leuven.

Colophon

The animal on the cover of *XMPP: The Definitive Guide* is a kanchil mouse deer. The kanchil (*Tragulus kanchil*) lesser mouse deer of Southeast Asia is the smallest of all ungulates. At a mature size, they can be as little as 45 cm (18 in) and 2 kg (4.4 lb). Another name for this little creature is chevrotain. In Indonesia, they are called kanchil ("KON-chil"), and in Malaysia, pelandok ("puh-LON-do"). There are nine species of chevrotains/mouse deer that make up the Tragulidae family.

Mouse deer are small, secretive creatures, about the size of a cat, that live in the jungles of Africa, Asia, and many Pacific islands. They have the legs and tail of a deer and the face and body of a mouse (but they are neither really a mouse nor a deer).

Mouse deer eat only plants, but lots of animals eat the mouse deer. To stay alive, they must be quick and smart. Young of lesser mouse deer are called fawns or asses. The females are called does, hinds, or cows and males are called bucks, stags, or bulls. A lesser mouse deer group is called a herd. They are the smallest known hoofed mammal. These are the average mouse deer's measurements: body length is 70–75 cm, shoulder height is 30–35 cm, and tail length is 8–10 cm.

Mouse deer are shy and their fawn tend to be "hiders." They are solitary animals, and usually interact only to mate. The young are weaned at 3 months of age, and reach sexual maturity between 5 and 10 months, depending on the species. Parental care is relatively limited. Although they lack the types of scent glands found in most other ruminants, they do possess a chin gland for marking each other as mates or antagonists, and, in the case of the water mouse deer, anal and preputial glands for marking territory. Their territories are relatively small, but neighbors generally ignore each other, rather than competing aggressively.

Mouse deer are active at night. During the day, they stay in deeply shaded spots, among the dense vegetations inside original forests. Mouse deer are difficult to find in the forest during the day, but at night, they roam around the cleared areas, sometimes close to the seashore. One can often find mouse deer along the roadsides at night using flashlights. Their eyes flash very brightly once caught in the beam and they normally stare for some time before fleeing.

The cover image is from Riverside Natural History. The cover font is Adobe ITC Garamond. The text font is Linotype Birka; the heading font is Adobe Myriad Condensed; and the code font is LucasFont's TheSansMonoCondensed.

Related Titles from O'Reilly

Web Applications

Our books are available at most retail and online bookstores.

To order direct: 1-800-998-9938 • *order@oreilly.com* • *www.oreilly.com*

Online editions of most O'Reilly titles are available by subscription at *safari.oreilly.com*